Confronting Tyranny

Confronting Tyranny

Ancient Lessons for Global Politics

Edited by
Toivo Koivukoski
and
David Edward Tabachnick

ROWMAN & LITTLEFIELD PUBLISHERS, INC.
Lanham • Boulder • New York • Toronto • Oxford

ROWMAN & LITTLEFIELD PUBLISHERS, INC.

Published in the United States of America
by Rowman & Littlefield Publishers, Inc.
A wholly owned subsidiary of The Rowman & Littlefield Publishing Group, Inc.
4501 Forbes Boulevard, Suite 200, Lanham, Maryland 20706
www.rowmanlittlefield.com

PO Box 317
Oxford
OX2 9RU, UK

British Library Cataloguing in Publication Information Available

Library of Congress Cataloging-in-Publication Data

Confronting tyranny : ancient lessons for global politics / edited by Toivo
Koivukoski and David E. Tabachnick.
p. cm.
Includes index.
ISBN 0-7425-4400-1 (cloth : alk. paper) — ISBN 0-7425-4401-X (pbk. : alk. paper)
1. Despotism. I. Koivukoski, Toivo. II. Tabachnick, David.

JC381.C63 2006
321.9—dc22 2005021590

Printed in the United States of America

∞™ The paper used in this publication meets the minimum requirements of American National Standard for Information Sciences—Permanence of Paper for Printed Library Materials, ANSI/NISO Z39.48-1992.

Contents

Chapter 1

Why Talk about Tyranny Today?

Catherine Zuckert

Writing in the wake of World War II, Leo Strauss observed in the introduction to his book *On Tyranny*, "The analysis of tyranny that was made by the first political scientists was so clear, so comprehensive, and so unforgettably expressed that it was remembered and understood by generations which did not have any direct experience of actual tyranny." Nevertheless, Strauss complained of his own generation that "when we were brought face to face with tyranny—with a kind of tyranny that surpassed the boldest imaginations of the most powerful thinkers of the past—our political science failed to recognize it. It is not surprising then that many of our contemporaries . . . were relieved when they rediscovered the pages in which Plato and other classical thinkers seemed to have interpreted for them the horrors of the twentieth century" (1991 [1948], 22–23).

Twentieth-century political scientists had been reluctant to talk about "tyrannical" as opposed to "totalitarian" and "authoritarian" forms of government because the admittedly extreme and violent character of the "totalitarian" regimes had been justified, or at least rationalized by ideological claims to serve the good of an entire people, if not the human race as a whole. Neither the Soviet Union nor the Third Reich appeared, as had the tyrannies of old, to be rule for the benefit of one man, filling his coffers and magnifying his pleasures. Nor did the fear of losing their positions to domestic rivals or rebels prevent the leaders of these twentieth-century "totalitarian" regimes from engaging in active or expansive foreign policies the way ancient tyrants had been limited. On the contrary, both of these modern tyrannies were expansionist, if not explicitly imperialistic.

Subsequent revelations of the atrocities of the concentration camps and gulag, as well as of the single-minded ruthlessness and daring Adolf Hitler and

Joseph Stalin displayed in acquiring and exercising power, have made contemporary commentators much less unwilling to castigate their "totalitarian" regimes as tyrannies. Both of these regimes claimed to be based on a scientific rationale or "ideology," and they used modern technology to control their own citizens and destroy their enemies to a degree previously unimaginable. Nevertheless, they both appeared to maintain power basically by means of fear or terror the way older tyrants had. Party organization and ideology did not appear to have had as great a role in maintaining these regimes as did their secret police. Their leaders not only had personal control of an armed guard, but they also cut down potential opponents much the way ancient tyrants had. Because there had been no uprisings in the Soviet Union of the kind seen in Poland, Hungary, and Czechoslovakia, some commentators thought that communist rule there was based upon at least passive consent. By the end of the Cold War, it became clear that was not true.

Smaller, but equally vicious, governments like those of Idi Amin in Uganda and Saddam Hussein in Iraq have also been widely denounced as tyrannies. As Daniel Chirot shows in his essay on "post-colonial African and Middle Eastern tyrannies," many of the regimes currently in power in both of these areas can be described very well as tyrannies in the ancient sense. Their leaders seize power and rule by means of force; they are, indeed, little different from gangs of bandits who seize the property of peasants in order to line their own pockets and pay the troops. Middle Eastern governments have been more stable, Chirot observes, but none (except Israel) is democratic. The fact that the monarchies have been the most moderate suggests that the distinctions Aristotle drew among various kinds of "kingships" (or rule by one man) can still be fruitfully applied.

To see what have been branded as "rogue states" as tyrannies, David Tabachnick suggests, would serve to remind us that such regimes tend to be rather short-lived. Although they oppress their own citizens terribly, such regimes do not usually threaten the existence of others. Always worried about maintaining their own rule at home, tyrants rarely undertake energetic or expansive foreign adventures. The articulation of the foreign policy of a superpower like the United States in terms of opposing or overthrowing such regimes is misplaced.

Arguing that the alternatives now drawn between "totalitarian" and "democratic" regimes are both simplistic and outdated, Mark Lilla agrees that reviving the ancient conception of tyranny would enable us to describe a variety of contemporary regimes more accurately, if the term were freed from its original rather parochial Greek context. The question thus arises: To what extent does the ancient understanding of tyranny, traceable first to classic depictions of the "tyrant" in plays like Sophocles' *Oedipus Tyrannos*, but developed and filled in by later political philosophers like Plato, Xenophon, and Aristotle, apply only to "premodern" regimes in areas of the world that have not become completely modern, urbanized, or industrialized, to regimes that lack experience in self-government? Is tyranny a transitory, perhaps even transitional, if recurrent phenomenon?

Some commentators (e.g., Dahrendorf 1967) have argued that many of the horrible, violent characteristics of Nazi Germany and Soviet Communism can be explained by the fact that the parties in control had to destroy traditional communities and norms in order to establish a modern regime. Pol Pot and Mao both also came to power in nations where traditional rulers, social norms, and institutions had been seriously weakened, especially by foreign invasions, but had not yet been replaced by modern views or organizations. Such an explanation of the use of violence and terror for the sake of modernizing in the face of traditionalist resistance makes it difficult to understand the campaigns against "intellectuals" that occurred in all of these regimes. Intellectuals usually represent and favor modernization. The classical emphasis on the tyrant's need to destroy all potential sources of opposition or competition makes much more sense of the emphatically anti-intellectual policies characteristic of modern tyrannies.

If the classical conception of tyranny can help us not merely identify but explain the persistence of such deviant forms of government in the contemporary world, both in "premodern" regimes in largely agrarian areas and in newer ideological forms, it obviously becomes important to know more precisely what that classical conception is. As the essays by Mark Blitz, Leah Bradshaw, Waller R. Newell, Ronald Beiner, Toivo Koivukoski, and Nathan Tarcov show, the major sources of the classical conception have somewhat different foci, and they point, therefore, in somewhat different directions. Is tyranny to be understood, as Plato suggests in the *Republic*, as an expression and attempted realization of the unlimited desires to be found in the breast of every human being? If so, it is a possibility that will endure as long as human beings do. As Beiner argues, tyranny will be present in each and every form of government. Or is tyranny to be understood primarily as Aristotle presents it, as lawless rule for the sake of the ruler at the expense of the population as a whole? That sort of tyranny is easier to identify, observe, and avoid. It is not the preserve of a single ruler but may also be characteristic of government by a few or even a majority. Lawless rule in the self-interest of the ruling party can be countered, however, by the rule of law, checks and balances, elections, and other institutional forms of external restraint. The insatiable desires of particularly ambitious or "erotic" individuals are more difficult to perceive, much less control. If the amelioration, if not prevention, of tyranny depends upon convincing tyrants that their satisfaction in life will be markedly increased if they win the love of their people by benefiting them instead of oppressing and impoverishing them, as Xenophon suggests in the *Hiero*, the chances of actually improving the situation appear much smaller. Tyrants are and have always been selfish. As Koivukoski reminds us, Plato failed not only to moderate the tyrant Dionysus but also to convince his friend Dion of the evils that result from using force to overthrow a tyranny.

Modern tyranny is, moreover, admittedly different from ancient tyranny. It is worse. What exactly makes modern tyranny worse and why is not so clear, however. Waller R. Newell locates the source of the distinctive character of the modern tyrant, somewhat ironically, in Machiavelli's taking Xenophon's advice to heart when he urges a prince to seek to be feared rather than to be loved, but not to be hated.

> For Plato, tyranny was a misunderstanding of the true meaning of satisfaction whose cure was the sublimation of the passions in the pursuit of moral and intellectual virtues grounded in the natural order of the cosmos. The Machiavellian prince, by contrast, stands radically apart from nature construed as a field of hostile happenstance, so as the more effectively to focus his will on attacking and subduing it. (*Prince* XVII)

He does not stop merely at securing his own power by protecting the lives and property of his subjects; he seeks to mold, if not to transform, their nature. He does not recognize any higher goal or have any sense of sacred restraint. The result is a kind of cold, calculating power seeking that takes place in the name of the common good. Thomas Smith argues that the results of the modern search for unlimited power are imaginatively depicted in J. R. R. Tolkien's *Lord of the Rings*. Like Saruman, some leaders believe that they can and do seek power in order to help others, but they and everyone else who gives way to the temptation are consumed in the end by their own desire for ever more power.

As Douglas Moggach points out, however, the destruction of natural, traditional social and sacred restraints on human action can also be viewed as a source of unprecedented freedom, as well as of new dangers. Following Hegel and his left followers like Bruno Bauer, Moggach points out that human beings aware of their own autonomy have to be reorganized if their isolation and alienation are not to constitute the conditions under which a new, larger, and more powerful form of tyranny arise. Tyranny on this understanding is not an inevitable offshoot but an accompanying pathological possibility of the liberation impulse of modernity.

Hegel observed that not merely the French Revolution, but the Terror more specifically, was necessary to destroy the last vestiges of "objective," natural or traditional, restraints on the freedom of individual subjects. This observation could be used, of course, to justify mass murders of the kind the Khmer Rouge inflicted upon Cambodia. The most fundamental question raised about the distinctive character of modern tyranny arises, indeed, with regard to the prevalence of genocide. Are the systematic killings of whole segments of the population, which are made possible by modern technology, racially or biologically based ideologies, and the efficiencies of "scientific" bureaucratic social organization, merely a tactic that ruthless, unscrupulous leaders like Hitler and Stalin use to accumulate and secure their own power, as Leo Strauss ([1962] 1997, 216–17; [1965] 1968, 225) has suggested? Or are these genocidal policies a reflection of, if not simply a result of, distinctively modern factors and conditions?

In his classic study of *Democracy in America*, Alexis de Tocqueville observed that the more equal human beings became in their condition—intellectually, politically, and spiritually, as well as economically—the less able they were to act as individuals on their own. Modern people and conditions were thus characterized more fundamentally by their equality than by their freedom. Indeed, if steps were not taken to teach such people how to organize, by intentionally establishing decentralized political institutions, the people would find themselves increasingly in need of a centralized government to which they would also, of necessity, increasingly become subject. The use of overwhelming force or "terror" would not be necessary to establish the "tyranny of the majority" or a new form of "soft despotism." But, as Roger Boesche points out, the informal pressure of popular opinion on individuals to conform, along with their economic self-interest, could and would be joined to the power of modern technology and of rational, bureaucratic organization to produce the genocidal policies characteristic of very unsoft forms of modern tyranny across the globe. These tyrannies are different from their ancient predecessors, Boesche argues, primarily because they do not act through or on behalf of a single leader. Classical tyrants understood why they should prevent their subjects from gathering together in public. It is not their isolation or the essentially private lives and concerns of modern individuals that make them subject to an exacerbated form of tyranny. It is the capacity of modern governments, *in response to rather than in opposition to the opinions and interests of the greater part of the population*, to use technology and organization to destroy whole peoples, if not races, that distinguishes modern tyranny from ancient. Reverting to ancient examples, Barry Strauss thus suggests that the roots of tyranny are to be found in wealth seeking, on the part of the population as well as the tyrant. Modern observers make a mistake when they identify freedom primarily with freedom of thought and artistic expression. They should be looking to Sparta rather than to Athens as a model of political liberty. Ancient tyrants often employed artists, Strauss points out; so did the Nazis. Classical republican politics and polities represent the only way to preserve liberty, both individual and communal.

Modern tyranny appears to differ from ancient tyranny not merely in the level and destructiveness of the violence it can muster. It also threatens to invade and control the thoughts and feelings of its subjects in ways earlier thinkers could not have imagined. Tocqueville's *Democracy in America*, once again, represents a classic statement of this distinctively modern trend. People living under equal conditions are not willing to take much, if anything, on authority, Tocqueville observed, because they believe that they are basically equal to all others. Because no one is able to think all things out for him- or herself, however, most people are forced to take some things, especially the most important things, on trust. Believing that everyone is equal, democratic people tend, therefore, to follow the opinion of the greatest number. Later political leaders saw that the tyranny that majority opinion tended to exercise on individual beliefs could be fostered or strengthened, however, by various kinds and techniques of "thought control." In his seminal work, *On Tyranny*, Strauss argued that the greatest threat to the preservation of freedom of thought was the possible institution of a world-state. Tyrants—whether individual or majoritarian—had forced freethinkers and dissenters to go underground before. When the oppression became intolerable, those who opposed the regime could flee. Modern technology had made the institution of an effective world-state a real possibility, and if such a state were established, all hope of escape would be destroyed. According to Strauss, both tyranny and the means of avoiding it are fundamentally political phenomena.

Simon Tormey, on the other hand, challenges the adequacy of the terms of discourse employed by most of the other studies of tyranny—classical and modern—included in this volume. As Vaclav Havel shows at the beginning of *The Power of the Powerless* in his famous interpretation of the significance of the greengrocer's placing a sign urging "workers of the world [to] unite" in his window, the exercise of power in the contemporary world is much more insidious, invisible, and indirect, but nevertheless more all pervasive, than even Tocqueville saw. The irresponsible and invidious use of power can no longer be accurately described as "tyrannical," therefore, either in the "classical" sense of the use of force, unrestrained by law, in the interest of the ruler rather than of the ruled, or in the modern "liberal" sense of rule without basis in popular consent. The difference or line between the "sovereign" ruler and the "sovereign" people who consent to be ruled is no longer clear.

Tracy Strong goes even further in challenging the near universally expressed antipathy to tyranny—in this book and elsewhere—by suggesting that a certain kind of internal tyranny may constitute the only possible remedy for the effects of the diffused exercise of power that both Tocqueville and Foucault analyzed. Confronted with the fragmentation and apparent multiplicity, but factual sameness, of modern life, Strong reminds us that Friedrich

Nietzsche argued that individuals would emerge and disagree with each other only if they acquired and exercised a kind of internal, spiritual discipline he called "tyrannical." Such tyrannical discipline was required particularly on the part of artists and philosophers if they were to be able to oppose the reductive standardization and consequent homogenization that results from the development and spread of rationalism or science. The only way to avoid the "tyranny of the majority" was, in other words, to exercise a kind of tyrannical power over oneself and one's own thought. According to Nietzsche and Strong, both tyranny and the means of avoiding it, in ancient times as well as modern, were essentially intellectual.

As the essays in this collection make clear, tyranny is a persistent but complex human phenomenon. It is emphatically a part of the contemporary world, not just of our history. We need to try to understand it in all its manifold forms, lest we, like the dreamers of the last century, fail to recognize the tyrant when he comes in the "sheep's clothing" of a popular benefactor.

SOURCES

Dahrendorf, Ralf. 1967. *Gesellschaft und Democratie in Deutschland.* English. Garden City, NY: Doubleday.

Strauss, Leo. [1948] 1991. *On Tyranny.* Ed. Victor Gourevitch and Michael S. Roth. New York: The Free Press.

———. [1965] 1968. "Preface to Spinoza's Critique of Religion." Reprinted in Leo Strauss, *Liberalism: Ancient and Modern.* New York: Basic Books.

———. [1962] 1997. "Why We Remain Jews." Reprinted in Kenneth Hart Green, ed., *Jewish Philosophy and the Crisis of Modernity.* Albany, NY: SUNY Press.

Chapter 2

Tyranny, Ancient and Modern

Mark Blitz

The urgent issue with tyranny is to recognize it, and then to prevent, resist, or overthrow it. At first glance it seems enough to say that a regime that slaughters its citizens, enslaves them, vulgarizes their characters, and impoverishes or prevents free thought is tyrannical. Such actions should be easy to notice. Even if we are unsure that a ruler's harmful acts are so frequent and great that we should deem him a tyrant, being close is reason enough to decry his government and to change it.

Why, then, should we discuss a topic as academic as ancient and modern tyranny? What could we learn that common sense does not teach us already or clearly enough? Is the subject not merely an invitation to wheel spinning and wool gathering, the kind of thing scholars do merely because it is the kind of thing they do? Worse, does it not detract from the simplicity and immediacy of noticing tyranny and responding to it by making needlessly subtle and complicated a matter that is cold, hard, and direct? One might even say that academic chatter about life-and-death matters that call for action is perverse.

Yet, the characteristics that define tyranny and that should strike us clearly in their evil are apparently not so obvious. How else can we explain the tepid and often welcoming response of Europe to the Nazis, the acquiescence to or enthusiastic engagement with them by so many Germans, and the routine blindness to and excuses for the Soviet Union by the West? Of course, we are less likely to be mistaken today than we were in the past, having recently been so foolish. Yet, generations quickly come and go, and with them intelligent memory. The clear paths of political judgment blazed by a few become overgrown with neglect. The bloody soil from which intellectual understanding rises is worked so often that it soon supports only weak and colorless natures.

So, we are in danger of forgetting, even today. Indeed, we now are subject to the political irresponsibility, the wishful daydreaming, of vast numbers of citizens and politicians who deal with Islamic extremists. Moreover, as tyranny pulls back from its most visible measures and extreme goals, from outright slaughter to subtle infantilizing, it is more difficult to notice or challenge. One recoils from the jackboot on one's neck, but the subtle caress of Tocqueville's soft despotism is gentle and enticing.

We therefore, perhaps surprisingly, need to be reminded about the elements that make tyranny bad, and their unity. Why, however, can this recollecting not occur sufficiently in the ordinary course of political affairs? Perhaps the fog of wishful thinking, foolish inattention, and venality that leads us to ignore, or even welcome, tyranny can be dissolved politically, as we deal with immediate concerns. Surely, the clear terms of description and evaluation of tyranny—slaughter, vice, and thought control—need only to be brought to the fore in practical discussion and debate. This task does not need, indeed will only be harmed, by obfuscating academic help.

This point is obviously correct in some respects. Otherwise, we would be claiming that citizens and politicians have few resources of their own for noticing and (perhaps) combating tyranny. Nonetheless, their resources are insufficient, which is why an academic approach properly understood can usefully supplement them.

One problem that practical intelligence cannot deal with by itself is the link between contemporary tyranny and the intellect, visible in Marxism and in the support that Hitler's racial theories gave to his opinions and practices. We also can notice this link in today's connection between tyranny and some strains of Islam. Unless one considers and counters, through reason, arguments that claim to be validated by reason, and unless the truly reasonable elements in religion can be defended and made evident, the mind may well be mastered by devilish or alluring sophistry. Healthy politics needs intellectual help even beyond what it receives from the better biographers and historians.

Not only does tyranny today have intellectual roots that we must uncover and combat intellectually, but there also exist natural tendencies to tyranny that good regimes hide but that we must consider so we can handle them properly. In fact, within each area whose ill use is a mark of tyranny, a tendency exists to exercise one's own tyranny, or at least to blink at tyrannical action. Tyranny violates personal security, but wishing full security or the complete control of fear for oneself is only a step away from seeking security at all costs, hence murdering or enslaving others or diminishing the virtue, risk, freedom, and challenging thought that make life uncertain. "Freedom" is violated by tyrants, but full freedom is easy to misunderstand as unbridled license, the satisfaction of all one's desires, and hence the misuse of others as one wishes, the destruction of moral restraint, and the inability to take the time to think.[1] Even virtue, the excellence of character that tyrants seek to diminish or corrupt, tends to seek honor, fame, and the (political) position it deserves in order to display its talents or the purity of its justice. Consequently, men of excellence can dismiss the just claims of others in ways that to these others might appear little different from tyranny. Needless to say, it also is difficult (for oneself or others) to distinguish one's supposed virtue from vice, pride from arrogance, or glory from vainglory. Even unchecked thought may move in a tyrannical direction, clearly when it is knowing or unknowing sophistry and claims a perfection or station it does not have, but even when it is less false. For, what room remains for the rest of us to rule ourselves when priests, physicians, scientists, or philosophers who claim to know better, who may in fact know better, exercise the complete authority that knowing better seems to deserve?

These natural tendencies to excess belong to or have at various times fostered the very brutality, rigidity, arbitrariness, vice, and intellectual enslavement that make up tyranny. Unless we understand such matters, we will be at our own and others' mercy. So, although sound politics or sound common sense goes far in protecting us from tyranny, it does not always go far enough.

I suggest that we arm ourselves intellectually by beginning with Aristotle. But why start with Aristotle rather than with someone else, or why not start more directly? Aristotle's political science is among the first, so by grasping it we will find it easier to understand what is new about contemporary tyranny and what tyranny is in general. It also is very intelligent and is more likely to illuminate than "original" efforts that are unwittingly derivative and inferior. Aristotle's discussion, moreover, is visibly closer to the concerns and terms of political life than are Xenophon's or Plato's, other classic analyses with which we might begin.[2] It therefore helps support the healthy perspective of citizens and statesmen, a perspective that is necessary although, as we are claiming, not quite sufficient to prevent, resist, or overthrow tyranny. I therefore begin with Aristotle and then turn to the modern world, discussing some but not all of the questions I have raised.

ARISTOTLE I

How does Aristotle understand tyranny? Tyranny is monarchy, the rule of one for his own advantage or aggrandizement rather than for the common good. The extreme tyrant rules according to his choice, that is, not by law, and has full, forceful, and ultimately imperial power over as many people as possible. Tyranny is completely dominant lawless rule over an empire of the unwilling for the ruler's advantage or aggrandizement alone. Hence, it is unjust (Aristotle 1984, II 6; III 7, 8, 13, 14; IV 2, 4, 10; VII 3, 4, 7).[3]

Extreme versions of the dynastic rule of a few or of the rule of the many solely for their own advantage are comparable to tyranny and often become it (Aristotle 1984, V 10). Tyranny is never justified, although full kingship, which is rule of one for the common good, is just when the gap in virtue between the king and all others is sufficiently great. A complete kingship would mean that the king's choice would substitute for law, for law follows reason and reaches justice only when it is properly made and applied without passion. Law's worth is measured by justice and the reasonable common good, and law may not always live up to this standard. Active politics must deal with circumstances that no general law can cover adequately.

Such a chasm between kings and others might exist between the political founder who initiates arts and other goods and his unformed people. It also exists between gods or heroes and men (Aristotle 1984, I 12; III 10, 11, 13, 14, 15; VII 14). It is, however, hard to think of ordinary circumstances in which the gap in virtue would be great enough to justify such a kingship. Aristotle suggests that the soul's rule over the body and reason's over the rest of the soul is of this sort (Aristotle 1984, I 5, 10; V 10). Perhaps the philosopher or political scientist might deserve (although he would not desire) such rule, which, if just, places the ruler at least partially beyond his community (Aristotle 1984, VII 2, 3, 13, 15). In any event, most kingships are not complete but are limited to particular purposes, such as leading foreign expeditions (Aristotle 1984, III 13, 14, 15).

If tyranny is rule of one for his advantage alone, the tyrant is dealing with other citizens as slaves. Tyranny is unjust mastery, treating others as if they are not or could not be free. Proper mastery, however, is to the slave's advantage as well as the master's or, at any rate, is justified only over the naturally slavish. Who is deservedly treated as a slave depends on what qualifies as natural slavery. Someone who lacks the reason to guide himself would be a natural slave, but this hardly allows the enslaving of most of those actually held as slaves (Aristotle 1984, II, 5). If people are so lacking in spirit as to be easy prey in war, there also is a natural element in their slavery. Slaves do have virtues, but their virtues of servitude meet human necessities and serve what is noble without deserving to rule (Aristotle 1984, I 5, 6, 7; II 5; VII 7).

In Aristotle's account, as in fact, there is clearly something irredeemably conventional and unfair about slavery: many (if not almost all) conventional slaves have too much intellect to be naturally slavish, many have virtues that would be useful in ruling even if they lack sufficient spirit to defend their freedom successfully, and many (if not almost all) have possibilities that they cannot actualize because of their poor education.[4] Nonetheless, without slavery there would be no leisure in Greek cities, and hence no ethical nobility or philosophy, because each would need to attend at length to his own necessities.

This tension between the unfairness of slavery and what Aristotle sees as its necessity is one of the facts that gives his *Politics* an anti-utopian or unmessianic tone. Contributing to this tone are other problems: uncertainty about whether the rule of law or of the single virtuous individual is best, and lack of clarity about whether it is more fair to distribute offices to several who are somewhat virtuous or, rather, to give them all to the one who is most outstanding. These issues cannot receive an unambiguously just answer politically. Moreover, Aristotle's observation that the best regime is so exceptional and rare, in conjunction with the reduced political role of priests in his discussion, also gives his *Politics* an anti-utopian and unmessianic air. This prudent standpoint is a useful antidote to the infectious utopianism of intellectuals, and modern tyrants.

Tyranny treats the free as if they are slaves. It is not their mere independence, however, but their nobility or virtue, their full liberality, that is the true political issue. Having and prudently acting on virtuous habits such as courage and moderation is the heart of happiness as Aristotle sees it, and ethical virtue requires a share in political deliberation and offices. Politics also must meet necessities, of course, but even just punishment is fully excellent only when it serves a noble end. Even courage in war ultimately serves the truly liberal activities of virtuous men at peace, namely, politics and philosophy. The effect of tyranny is to destroy happiness by destroying virtue.

The tyrant ultimately desires to dominate as many as possible, or to achieve empire. He therefore finds constant war and the spirit to prosecute it to be necessary. But engaging his spirit or attaining victory do not seem to be his final goals. What, indeed, is his ultimate purpose? The many who foolishly admire tyrants apparently believe that empire is a means to unbridled physical satisfaction, and Aristotle himself suggests that tyrants commit their injustices from excess, not necessity. The tyrant is indeed immoderate, although desire as such seems to be limitless simply (II 7). Perhaps, however, this emphasis on satisfaction is primarily the view of the vulgar, and the tyrant himself, or some tyrants, love or also love other things, or dominion itself. To understand the tyrant's purposes and practices further, we turn next to Aristotle's discussion of tyranny in his analysis of revolution in Book V of the *Politics*.

ARISTOTLE II

Aristotle's discussion in Book V first characterizes tyranny and what causes people to revolt against it and then largely assumes the tyrant's standpoint to discuss how to preserve it. Here, Aristotle develops two main answers: become more of a tyrant, or less (by acting more like a king).[5]

Tyrannies compound the errors of both oligarchies and democracies, but tyrants usually arise from the people, to counter the few. Having so arisen, they then convert into tyranny the position that their popular support first brought about. So, whereas the king's goal is nobly to protect the people and the wealthier few from each other, the tyrant's goal is his private pleasure. He aggrandizes himself through goods, while the king seeks honor.

To say that tyrannies are the worst of both oligarchies and democracies is to say that they mistreat both rich and poor. The tyrant needs wealth for defense and luxuries, and he resettles and otherwise ill-treats the many as his needs require. He also exiles and kills the few, especially the preeminent, who are rivals.

Revolution against tyrants begins because others seek monarchs' great wealth and honor, especially when tyrants breed contempt by living softly or because people seek revenge against a tyrant who treats them arrogantly. Other cities, including those formed by regimes that oppose tyrannies simply, also may threaten a tyranny, and tyrannies also fall because of internal faction.

Of these reasons for revolution, many of which threaten kingships and other regimes too, Aristotle singles out contempt and anger or hatred. A tyrant's life of gratification leads others to hold him or his immediate successors in contempt and to overthrow him. Anger, following one's spiritedness because of, say, arrogant treatment, is hatred accompanied by pain and is therefore even more conducive to revolt than is calculating hatred per se.

Aristotle then tells us how to preserve tyrannies, a discussion that illuminates their methods and therefore, if often silently, indicates how to attack them. Tyrannies are preserved through methods attributed to Periander of Corinth, which are visible among the Persians and the barbarians. The preeminent are lopped off, those with high thoughts are eliminated, and common meals and clubs are not allowed. The tyrant's goal is to prevent whatever might facilitate conspiracy and challenge.

The tyrant must go beyond preventing meetings and eliminating those with high thoughts, for he would like high thoughts and trust never to emerge or be contemplated in the first place. He therefore prevents any leisured activity or discussion with others, "since knowledge tends to create trust of one another"; he forces citizens always to be publicly visible; he uses spies and eavesdroppers so citizens fear to speak freely; he sets friend against friend and rich against poor; he impoverishes citizens generally; he forces them to work on huge projects such as Egypt's pyramids or the Pisistratids' "temple of Olympian Zeus"; he taxes them steeply; and he keeps them constantly at war. He seeks, in a word, to form people who are habituated to being small-minded and slavish, primarily by immiserating them and eliminating their leisure.

These methods and this goal of tyranny are supplemented by characteristics that we also see in extreme democracies—methods that eliminate natural or conventional hierarchies. Women dominate in the house and report on husbands, and slaves are treated mildly, as are obsequious flatterers and the base. None of these threaten or conspire against tyrants, who enjoy being flattered. The respectable, however, those with freer thoughts, do not flatter. Indeed, tyrants hate those with "a rival dignity and a spirit of freedom," for these detract from the mastery and preeminence that the tyrant believes should be his alone.

Aristotle sums up these practices that help preserve tyrannies, even depraved ones, as follows: keep the ruled small souled; with modest thoughts (and therefore incapable of conspiracy); distrustful, because respectable men do not denounce each other; and incapable of acting.

The other way to preserve tyranny is to be less tyrannical and more kingly as long as one's power is preserved, that is, as long as the tyrant continues to rule the unwilling as well as the willing. The more kingly tyrant accounts for expenditures and does not "give lavishly to prostitutes, foreigners, and artisans." He seeks a military reputation so others feel awe, not fear or contempt. He refrains from the arrogance and excessive bodily gratification in which other tyrants indulge and for which they want to be noticed so others will think them happy and blessed. He appears to be moderate. He shows himself to be "seriously [not foolishly] attentive to the things pertaining to the gods," for others are less afraid that a god-fearing man will treat them contrary to law and more afraid to conspire against those with gods as allies. He specially honors the good but lets others punish the bad, and he allows no single person to become great, while removing people from power "gradually." He does not dishonor the ambitious and refrains from arrogance, especially involving physical abuse and sex; his punishments seem paternal and deserved, and his loves erotic rather than the flaunting of abusive license. He compensates perceived dishonor and is especially aware of those whose spiritedness might lead them to give up their own lives to assassinate him. He tries to be perceived as treating both rich and poor justly and attaches himself to the more powerful class in his city.

Aristotle suggests that rule as a moderate kingly manager brings the tyrant several rewards: virtue or at least half virtue, longer-lasting control than other tyrants, domination that the noble do not hate or fear, and rule that is enviable because it is over the better, who have not been humbled. Although almost all tyrannies are short-lived, the longest lasting is indeed a modest one, the hundred-year tyranny of Orthagoras and his sons. We are chagrined to learn, however, that the warlike Periander, said to have established the unsavory ways of tyranny we noted, remained in power for over forty years.

What can we glean from this discussion? First, the goal of tyranny seems to be unbridled gratification, and it is gratification that takes pleasure in arrogance, not only in physical satisfaction. More, the tyrant wants his gratification to be visible because he also wishes to appear to be preeminently happy and blessed. Indeed, although Aristotle seeks to lead tyrants to being concerned with reputation among the notables, flattery by the base seems sufficient for them. From tyrants' taste for visible gratification, their wish to be flattered, their usual impiety, their projects of ostentatious worship, their similarities to Persian and Egyptian kings, their warlike imperialism, and their desire to be the only ones who are free and dominant, we might also conclude that eminence itself, even godlike eminence, is the tyrant's goal. Aristotle does not suggest this, however, at least directly, and he treats the tyrant's warlike imperialism and his making everyone else small-minded more as means against conspiracy than as ends in themselves. Perhaps we may say that tyrants do indeed wish to be, and be recognized as, gods or godlike in their happiness and eminence, but that, along with the vulgar, they mistakenly equate happiness with a life of unbridled satisfaction and arrogance. Aristotle tries to moderate tyrants by opening their desire for lengthy rule to the practices of better rule, and their wish for eminence to looking enviable in the eyes of the notable, not the flatterers. He does not, however, seek to persuade them to a life of thought or try to restrict them to rule over the willing only. If slavery is necessary, so is mastery over some.

The second thing we glean from this discussion is a more substantive sense than earlier of the meaning of tyranny's lawlessness, force, rule over the unwilling, and orientation to private advantage. This substance is evident in the methods and practices Aristotle discusses here: use of spies and informants, high taxes, forced labor, massive projects, abrogation of free meetings and discussion, and ostentatious satisfaction. Indeed, tyranny's harm would be visible in the effects of such actions even were they lawful: the harm is the forming of small-souled, distrustful men, incapable of virtue and of free discussion.

Third, we take from this discussion the characteristics and methods that resist tyranny and overcome it: men of virtue; freedom of thought and discussion (e.g., works such as Aristotle's); trust; unity in a well-ordered family; outside (foreign) help; and the conversion of tyrants or would-be tyrants to men who have or simulate genuine if limited virtue or piety.

MODERN TYRANNY AND THE INTELLECT

When we turn to modern tyranny, we see first that many tyrants—Idi Amin, for example—apparently display nothing that Aristotle has not uncovered already. It does seem, however, that even such tyrants engage in a level of random or intended violence beyond anything that Aristotle discusses. Moreover, some tyrannies (in the Balkans or Africa, for example) have an ethnic focus, with violence and impoverishment directed especially to particular ethnic or tribal groups.[6]

The characteristic modern tyrannies of the Nazis and the Communists in the USSR and China seem at first to differ from ancient tyrannies because they, too, intensify violence and orient violence to particular groups.[7] Stalin killed many of his comrades, he and his cohorts killed massive numbers of independent or relatively wealthy peasants, and after his death the Kremlin's leaders continued to imprison large numbers of intellectual, political, and artistic "dissidents." Hitler murdered millions of Jews in Germany and the rest of Europe, hundreds of thousands of the mentally ill and infirm in Germany and elsewhere, and (similarly to Stalin, through ill treatment and direct killing) massive numbers of prisoners of war.

Do these devastations differ from ancient tyranny only in degree, or is there something different enough about them to change our understanding of tyranny qualitatively? One apparently new factor involves the cause, reason, or justification for the destruction. For, in addition to the tyrant's wish to attain empire and dominion in order to indulge in unchecked or unbridled gratification, at least some Nazis and Communists were motivated by, and almost all justified themselves in terms of, a set of intellectual explanations.

The Communists argued that history led inevitably to a classless society. Common ownership of the means of production, the end of social distinctions, the withering away of the state, the disappearance of bourgeois rights, and a life largely of ease and abundance were not mere wishes, dreams, hopes, or prayers, they believed, but were necessary and knowable results of the way things were. They distinguished their "scientific" socialism from other socialism, and the occasional outcropping of small and short-lived utopian communities from the worldwide permanent spread of Communism. Communism is "Marxism" because Marx's thought, or the truth of matters as Marx saw it, supposedly distinguished it from its competitors.

Hitler and the Nazis believed they knew beyond doubt that a racial hierarchy existed; that the Aryans were at the top; and that the Jews, although unaccountably dangerous, were at the bottom, with Poles, Russians, and other Slavs only one step up and suited for helotry at best. Among other qualities, this hierarchy was thought to distinguish the more noble and brave from other races. Jewish capitalists and Marxists, moreover, were said to be common enemies of the German people, whose national socialism, when properly led, would create an empire to last one thousand years.

These beliefs were based on a mélange that combined Nietzsche's thought and various views of racism and eugenics, with nihilistic destruction of supposed enemies always a more evident result of Nazism than the positive meaning of racial superiority itself. Nonetheless, these views were thought to be true; were discussed as science, not myth; and attracted or were supplemented by various intellectuals.

The tactics that Lenin, Stalin, Mao, and Hitler used to bring about and spread their control varied, and one may doubt how many Communists and Nazis were, as time went on, motivated by the desire to institutionalize the regime they claimed to prefer rather by the desire simply to hold and expand their power. Nonetheless, at a minimum, the intellectual justification helped them select classes of enemies beyond their ordinary political foes; it set the public rhetoric and justification of the regimes; it oriented the Soviet Union (and when the Nazis thought it necessary, Germany) to state control of modern economies; and, especially with the Marxists, it formed the basis of alliances and allegiances across the world.

Let us examine these areas more carefully to see whether the intellectual or scientific element justifying these regimes is as novel as it seems. The USSR was aided and supported by large numbers of Communists and fellow travelers in other countries. Vicious debates about the status and interests of the Soviet Union in particular versus world communism in general were largely resolved in favor of support of the USSR by other communists before, during, and after World War II. Many, of course, ended their support once the truths about Stalin's purges and murders in the 1920s and 1930s emerged; once the meaning of his pact with his supposed arch enemy, the Nazis, was absorbed; and once his control of East Europe after World War II was grasped. What had attracted these supporters and others was less (or not only) communism's scientific inevitability but the supposed justice of its way of life and its falsely advertised economic success. Its justice was thought to be the justice of equality, peaceful cooperation, and unbridled freedom. Marx and Engels famously described the communist society of the future as one in which "nobody has one exclusive sphere of activity, but each can become accomplished in any branch he wishes, [and] society regulates the general production and thus makes it possible for me to do one thing today and another tomorrow, to hunt in the morning, fish in the afternoon, rear cattle in the evening, criticize after dinner, just as I have a mind, without ever becoming a hunter, fisherman, shepherd or critic." "From each according to his abilities, to each according to his needs" was the dominant slogan.[8] The conflicts between free individual choice in using one's abilities and social demands upon them; the questionable dominance of self or even publicly defined need rather than of excellence; and the natural and conventional limits to human pleasure (not all can fish in the best ponds exactly when they want, hunt where animal lovers have taken a stand, or be intelligently "critical" on a casual schedule) were ignored, wished away, or never seen.

Some element of dragging down the unequal was surely also at work in this understanding of justice, even if for many it was well disguised. Moreover, the attack on inequality per se, without benefit of its intellectual justification, structured much internal and external rhetoric by the Marxists about fascists, capitalists, and industrialists, and it directed or helped direct the Soviet tyrants to the groups whom they dispossessed or killed.

From this discussion, we conclude that Marxism's scientific or intellectual justification brought out and exacerbated the egalitarian extremism that can inherently distort the democratic justice of equal to equals. Such extremism is, as Aristotle discussed, one path to or version of tyranny simply. The Marxist intellectual argument, with its scientific claims, covered over the harmful leveling nature of its goals and the destruction that even a "sincere" effort to bring about what is utopian or impossible must cause. It therefore clouded the understanding even of those who would have recoiled at being thought tyrants, and it justified extreme injustice as proper and inevitable, thereby aiding the tyranny of people who eventually (and in some cases from the start) needed little such justification. The novel element in tyranny that Communism's intellectual justification displayed was not some new discovery about justice, the common good, or political excellence, but rather it was the way the theoretical or scientific intellect abetted a tyranny that was based on or employed extreme egalitarianism and leveling, which Aristotle already had discussed, by appearing to justify it and by rallying support for it.[9]

We see something similar with the Nazis. Their attack on Jews went beyond even today's tyrannical attempts to "cleanse" ethnic rivals from one's own territory, because it sought ultimately to eliminate Jews everywhere, not merely to dispossess or control them. Such brutality is an extreme of inequality or oligarchic tyranny, fueled by racial and *volkisch* theories and fears that distort the natural understanding of human differences by identifying the supposedly noble and base with ethnic splits. Those views so corrupted a proper understanding of the moral virtues that naturally distinguish the better among us from the worse that the Nazis mistook courage for reckless, unmeasured violence, and the supposedly ignoble were seen as so inhuman that any treatment of them became acceptable, with no limits of justice or necessity applying. This ungodly racial excess shaped whatever other factors formed Nazi leaders and directed the legal, political, and military content of their actions. Here, too, therefore, intellectual or theoretical distortion and excess abetted, indeed helped to bring about, tyranny and made it completely immoderate.

The intellectual justification of tyranny, that is, the claim to scientific or philosophic truth and not only to political justice, also has the effect of stultifying or controlling the intellect itself. What room can exist for free thought if a regime claims to be based on unchallengeable scientific truth that covers every area of importance?

To examine further the degree to which this theoretical element or other factors make modern tyranny qualitatively different from ancient tyranny, we will turn next to Communism's and Nazism's so-called totalitarianism.

MODERN TYRANNY AND TOTALITARIANISM

Nazism and Communism often are called "totalitarian" to differentiate them from other tyrannies. One element of totalitarianism is what we have just discussed, its theoretical or (as we sometimes say, following the Marxists) its ideological basis. Its second major element is totality itself, the total control by the regime of all elements of human life.

This totality is visible in the Nazis' coordination of all spheres of activity so that youth activities and education, the private economy and professions, and religion and intellectual life were controlled to the degree the regime required. Academic administrators became party members. Youth groups were Nazi youth groups. Churches had or sought only limited independence. Lawyers and physicians were severely restricted in their judgments; judges were selected who desired little freedom to begin with. Law was abrogated as deemed necessary, or changed at will. Various security and police forces acted more as threats than as protectors, jailing, sending to concentration camps, and killing unimpeded by restraint. Communication was controlled. Transportation and industry were commandeered for the war. Private property of Jews and others was stolen and given to favorites.

Similar coordination existed in the Soviet Union. One can in both cases overstate or over-imagine this coordination, of course, and believe one will see complete cooperation among officials and with citizens, all marching to tunes precisely played from on high. To notice conflicts in ambitions and judgments can then mislead one into thinking that there was something like genuine independence or even pluralism in Nazi Germany or the USSR.

This academic reaction to the overstatement of monolithic direction, however, is more mistaken than the overstatement itself. For, the essential nature and horror of tyranny is much better grasped by remembering the always threatened and usually exercised control of privacy, the professions, law, religion, and education than by emphasizing geographic or bureaucratic differences among the controllers.

In what way, however, does this total control differ from ancient tyranny? Aristotle's discussion of Periander's methods seems to presage this degree of domination. Not all ancient tyrannies, but precisely the worst, imitate in advance the totality of totalitarianism.

Differences appear when we concentrate on the kind and degree of cooperation modern tyrannies enjoy from their citizens. Modern tyranny is not merely the dominance by a handful but their dominance with the cooperation, perhaps the willing cooperation, of millions of others. The Nazis in particular were actively or passively supported by huge numbers of Germans for many years. This cooperation is perhaps similar to ancient tyrants' support from flatterers and slaves, from the obsequious and those with the least to lose. Nonetheless, modern tyranny appears to require the active engagement of many, not merely acquiescence from a limited number. Moreover, modern tyranny requires cooperation from the educated and able, not only from the run of the mill.

Do fear, benefit, and some belief in the special place of the German people (or socialist egalitarianism) explain sufficiently the cooperation and acquiescence of many of the gifted and so many others in tyrannical brutality and control? Or must we add other, novel causes?

One explanation for the novel degree of ongoing, active engagement by large numbers of citizens in modern tyrannies concerns the emergence of isolated individuals, sundered from ordinary connections to church, neighborhood, family, and professions. Such individuals, whom one finds, say, in the original groups around Hitler (who can himself be described in this manner), are visible versions of a way of life or attitude that some think defines contemporary man generally. Each of us is an interchangeable member of a mass, or a cog in a machine, who experiences himself as rootless at the core even if his own life is richer and more complex than the everyday life of the actual urban mass. Totalitarianism wins the cooperation of such people, it is said, because its justification gives them meaning as members of a superior people or as the cutting edge of the socialist revolution, and it reinforces this meaning with quasi-religious rituals and spectacles bathed in sentimentality and frenzy. At the same time, such individuals' rootlessness suits them well for organizational arrangement and rearrangement in the regime's enterprises.[10]

One feature (and danger) of this explanation is to lose or downplay the difference between modern liberal democracy and modern totalitarianism.[11] Totalitarianism is seen to be the evil twin of liberal democracy, or hardly worse than its twin. It is said that without liberal democracy's grounding in individual natural rights, its limitation of government to representing interests rather than forming character, its separation of powers and therefore its ineffective government, its preference for satisfaction over "nobility," its liberation of technology to enhance satisfaction, its toleration and therefore its privatization and desacralization of religion, and its entry into professions and contracts so freely and voluntarily that occupations and ownership are freed from all but market obligations—it is said that without all this, we would not have created the isolated individual, easy to organize and ripe or even desperate for meaning and totality. Modern totalitarianism, it follows, would therefore not exist.

From a practical standpoint, however, there is all the difference in the world between liberal democracy and totalitarianism. Indeed, it is precisely the Nazis' and Communists' murderous attack on individual security; their abrogation of freedoms of speech, press, religion, occupation, and economy;

and their destruction of the legal independence protected by separation of powers that compel us to understand them as tyrants. Modern freedom taken to an alienated extreme may indeed make us vulnerable to tyranny, soft as well as hard. Although totalitarianism may use this vulnerability, however, it is not in the end formed or enabled by a particular kind of freedom liberated by the modern liberalism of, say, John Locke and the American founders. Rather, we should say that despite totalitarianism's talk of nobility or active happiness, it employs and develops in many of its citizens the smallness of soul that Aristotle discusses, especially in the guise of an extreme concern with security and a certainty that masquerades as equal freedom.[12]

The antidote or preventive for this smallness of soul, this cowardly ignobility, is not to eliminate modern freedom but, rather, to ennoble or educate it, and to develop its own resources for excellence. (After all, Soviet and Nazi tyranny were in the end overcome by responsible liberal democrats.) During his dissident years in Czechoslovakia, Vaclav Havel wrote that if each citizen held himself responsible for exercising his own freedom honestly in his own sphere, totalitarian lies would be exposed, the chains of totalitarian collaboration would be loosened, and the totalitarian regime would topple.[13]

A responsible exercise of freedom that looks to freedom's excellent, elevated, or virtuous use and that roots itself in equal natural rights whose ground is correctly understood is, together with the other elements we mentioned when discussing Aristotle, the best measure against tyranny. This is true, too, for controlling priestly tyrannies, old and new. Central here (as, also, in combating totalitarianism and the possibly permanent harm of untrammeled modern technology) is for reason to keep itself responsibly independent from political and religious control.[14] For, tyranny justified on "reasonable" or "higher" grounds, that is, tyrants hiding behind an intellectual mission taught to or spread among many followers, is its most threatening and perhaps its only significantly new element.[15] As a group, the measures I have mentioned will, through a political common sense that is aided by the intellect so we do not fall prey to the seductive extremes or false images of security, freedom, virtue, and thought, enable us to recognize and resist tyrannical action.

NOTES

1. Our most common or obvious example here is our loosely calling any law or parent tyrannical that does not allow us to do exactly what we want when, where, and with whom we desire. "Liberty" is in these cases being understood in an extreme, unlimited manner that, on reflection, requires complete control over others, whenever one chooses to exercise it—that is, one's own tyranny.

2. One would consider especially Plato's *Republic* and Xenophon's *Hiero.*

3. References are to book and chapter from Aristotle's *Politics.* I have used the translation by Carnes Lord (Chicago: University of Chicago Press, 1984). See also the chapters on Aristotle in Harvey Mansfield Jr., *Taming the Prince* (New York: The Free Press, 1987), and Nathan Tarcov, "Tyranny from Plato to Locke," in this volume.

4. Aristotle mentions that helots and slaves are capable of high-minded thoughts, although they perhaps lack the daring to act on them.

5. All quotations in this section will be from the 10th and 11th chapters of Book V of the *Politics.*

6. Such ethnic and tribal divisions are also often religious divisions. Cf. Roger Boesche, "An Omission from Ancient and Early Modern Theories of Tyranny: Genocidal Tyrannies" in this volume.

7. I have drawn in the remarks below from many books, including, on the Nazis, Michael Burleigh, *The Third Reich* (Hill and Wang, 2000), and Ian Kershaw, *Hitler*, 2 vols. (W. W. Norton, 2000); on the Soviets, Robert Conquest, *The Great Terror* (Macmillan, 1968), Merle Fainsod, *How Russia Is Ruled* (Harvard University Press, 1953), and Alexander Solzhenitsyn, *The Gulag Archipelago* (Harper & Row, 1974ff); and on totalitarianism generally, Carl Friedrich and Zbigniew Brzezinski, *Totalitarian Dictatorship and Autocracy* (Praeger, 1956). One also should consider Winston Churchill's writings on the Nazis and Communists, in particular *The Gathering Storm* (Houghton Mifflin, 1948).

8. The first quotation is from Marx and Engels, *The German Ideology* (1846). The second is from Marx, *Critique of the Gotha Program* (1875).

9. This aid is perhaps already visible in justifications of the French Revolution. Consider Hegel's *Philosophy of Right.*

10. This view is expressed in various forms. It underlies work on "mass" men or "crowds" as well as some views of totalitarianism. In addition to some of the works footnoted earlier, see, for example, Jose Ortega y Gasset, *The Revolt of the Masses* (W. W. Norton, 1957, first published in 1930); Hannah Arendt, *The Origin of Totalitarianism* (Harcourt Brace Jovanovich, 1951); Martin Heidegger, *Being and Time*, trans. John Macquarrie and John Robinson from *Sein Und Zeit* (Harper & Row, 1962, first published in 1927); and Martin Heidegger, *Introduction to Metaphysics*, trans. Gregory Fried and Richard Polt from *Einfuhrung in die Metaphysik*, based on lectures delivered in 1935 (Yale University Press, 2000, first published in 1953). Consider also Waller Newell, "Is There an Ontology of Tyranny?" in this volume.

11. Heidegger's works display a version of this difficulty.

12. One might argue that one sees this fear especially during the onset or decay of liberalism.

13. See Vaclav Havel, *Open Letters*, ed. Paul Wilson (New York: Vintage, 1992).

14. The place of technology in contemporary tyranny is an important issue. The burden of my discussion here is that while technology may abet and expand contemporary tyranny, the essence of modern technology is not technological per se. Rather, its heart is the question of justice. Nor is the essence of modern technology tyrannical, for liberal democracy is a proper home of technology, and liberal democracy is not tyranny.

15. For the question of the ancient understanding of the connection between philosophy and tyranny, consider, in addition to the references and discussions in the papers by Nathan Tarcov and Ronald Beiner in this volume, Plato, *Hipparchus*, 228b1–229d7.

SOURCES

Arendt, Hannah. 1951. *The Origin of Totalitarianism*. New York: Harcourt Brace Jovanovich.

Aristotle. 1984. *Politics*. Translated by Carnes Lord. Chicago: University of Chicago Press.

Brezezinski, Zbigniew, and Carl Friedrich. 1956. *Totalitarian Dictatorship and Autocracy*. New York: Praeger.

Burleigh, Michael. 2000. *The Third Reich*. New York: Hill and Wang.

Churchill, Winston. 1948. *The Gathering Storm*. New York: Houghton Mifflin.

Conquest, Robert. 1968. *The Great Terror*. New York: Macmillan.

Fainsod, Merle. 1953. *How Russia Is Ruled*. Cambridge, MA: Harvard University Press.

Havel, Vaclav. 1992. *Open Letters*. Ed. Paul Wilson. New York: Vintage.

Heidegger, Martin. 1962. *Being and Time*. Trans. John Macquarrie and John Robinson. New York: Harper & Row.

———. 2000. *Introduction to Metaphysics*. Trans. Gregory Fried and Richard Polt. New Haven, CT: Yale University Press.

Hegel, G. W. F. 1991. *Philosophy of Right*. Trans. H. W. Nisbet., ed. Allan W. Wood. Cambridge: Cambridge University Press.

Kershaw, Ian. 2000. *Hitler*. 2 vols. New York: W. W. Norton.

Mansfield, Harvey, Jr. 1989. *Taming the Prince*. New York: The Free Press.

Marx, Karl. 1846. *The German Ideology*.

———. 1875. *Critique of the Gotha Program*.

Ortega y Gasset, Jose. 1957. *The Revolt of the Masses*. New York: W. W. Norton.

Plato. 1968. *The Republic*. Trans. Allan Bloom. New York: Basic Books.

Solzhenitsyn, Alexander. 1974ff. *The Gulag Archipelago*. New York: Harper and Row.

Xenophon. 1991. *Hiero*. In Leo Strauss, *On Tyranny*, ed. Victor Gourevitch and Michael S. Roth. New York: The Free Press.

Chapter 3

Tyranny Bound

David Edward Tabachnick

In his chapter, Mark Lilla argues that the Bush Doctrine conceals the true nature of modern tyranny. I continue this line of criticism by questioning the link between domestic tyranny and global turmoil. According to President George W. Bush, the states identified as the "Axis of Evil" are not merely a danger to their own people but also threaten "the peace of the world." In the 2002 State of the Union Address, Bush warned:

> States like these, and their terrorist allies, constitute an axis of evil, arming to threaten the peace of the world. By seeking weapons of mass destruction, these regimes pose a grave and growing danger. They could provide these arms to terrorists, giving them the means to match their hatred. They could attack our allies or attempt to blackmail the United States. In any of these cases, the price of indifference would be catastrophic. . . . The United States of America will not permit the world's most dangerous regimes to threaten us with the world's most destructive weapons (January 29, 2002).

Certainly, "weapons of mass destruction" in the hands of an evil, rogue regime are a legitimate reason for alarm. Even more disturbing is the possibility that these weapons will be handed over to international terrorists. But, as we now know from the case of Iraq, the existence of these weapons and linkages to terrorism are not mandatory requirements for membership in the Axis of Evil.[1] Rather, it is the nature of these states as tyrannies, domestically undemocratic and unfree, that makes them an international threat. The American-led overthrow of Saddam Hussein was not merely to liberate the Iraqi people from an "outlaw dictator" but to save the world from a "grave and gathering threat." As Bush says in a later speech, "Today, because America has acted, and because America has led, the forces of terror and tyranny have suffered defeat after defeat, and America and the world are safer" (July 12, 2004).

Yet, it is not entirely obvious or clear why tyranny *now* represents a threat to the peace of the world. Historically, tyrannies have threatened local or regional stability, but not disproportionately when compared to other kinds of regimes. The Peloponnesian War, for example, was fought between a timocratic Sparta and a democratic Athens; the Roman Republic defeated the Carthaginian Empire in the Punic Wars; and World War I was fought among monarchs, czars, hereditary emperors, and democracies. And, while World War II is often described as a war against tyranny, Germany and Italy are better described as totalitarian states and Japan as a historical empire. So, while the Gulf War of 1991 and the stalemate on the Korean Peninsula do illustrate the expansionist tendencies of at least two of the members of the Axis of Evil, they do not prove that these states are inherently more dangerous than any other. In fact, a tyranny is more likely to be tolerated, contained, ignored, or even supported than to be treated as a danger to global stability. The United States, for example, has had relatively recent and friendly dealings with a whole host of tyrants: Batista in Cuba; Duvalier in Haiti; Marcos in the Philippines; Pinochet in Chile; and, most recently, Musharraf in Pakistan.[2] All of this suggests that tyrannies do not represent a special or exceptional threat to international peace.

There are of course examples we could point to. Although not quite a tyrant by classical definition, the Roman emperor Caligula extended his paranoid and volatile domestic leadership to disastrous military campaigns. General Suharto of Indonesia replicated a similar brutality in both a civilian crackdown and in the invasion of East Timor in the mid-1970s. But, it is hard to attribute this international behavior to a particular form of domestic order. We could as easily mine the colonial history of the British, the Dutch, or the Spanish and find comparable acts and events. The ancient world is equally filled with examples of aggressive expansion, imperialism, and genocide. In any case, international ruthlessness is not exclusive to tyrants or tyrannies.

As many of the contributors to this volume point out, political philosophy does single out tyranny as a particularly awful form of *domestic* political order. Plato, Aristotle, and Xenophon correlate the vicious character of the tyrant and the character of the tyrannical regime—the unhappy tyrant brings forth an unhappy city. However, the same connection is not made between the character of the domestic regime and its behavior in the international sphere. We cannot, it seems, predict the behavior of states on the global stage in the same way Plato and Aristotle predict the internal cycle of domestic regimes. Nor can we categorize the international character of a state in the same way that Plato and Aristotle classify its internal character. Whereas there is a recognized connection between the virtue and viciousness of the policies and practices of the political leadership of the polis and the character of the citizenry (i.e., the city and man), the connection between the domestic and international affairs of a state (i.e., the city and the world) is not as obvious.

Traditionally, the field of international relations tells us it is impossible to make this sort of connection because every state is thought to act in the exact same way internationally, whether democracies, kingdoms, or tyrannies.[3] All states, regardless of how they handle their internal affairs, act and are treated as equals on the international stage. While a state may be a democracy at home, it may act as a tyrant abroad. While brutal, immoral, and erratic to his own people, a tyrant may still be an accepted member of the international community. The anarchical state system requires that we disconnect the domestic from the international.[4] In turn, it is not easy to predict how a domestic regime will act globally.

Therefore, it seems that neither political philosophy nor international relations can help us understand the connection between domestic and international tyranny. Yet, obviously, tyrannies are more than just a domestic or psychological phenomenon—they affect other states. It is just not clear why a state functioning domestically on avarice, fear, and the indiscriminate impulses of its leader(s) will not predictably act in a similar way internationally.

The one thinker embraced by both political philosophers and international theorists may provide some insight.[5] While adopted by the "realists," Thucydides nowhere treats "international relations" as a separate area of study, fundamentally distinct from domestic politics. Instead, he describes a dynamic relationship between the foreign affairs and the internal order of a state.[6] For example, in his account of the civil war at Corcyra in Book III of *The History of the Peloponnesian War*, Thucydides observes that the disruption of international war had brought every state in the Hellenic world to the brink of revolution: "It became a natural thing for anyone who wanted a change of government to call in help from the outside" (5.82). The ancient city-states of the Hellenes were not at all bound to the modern logic of sovereignty that suggests that states are like billiard balls, impervious to international events. In a similar reference to the dynamic relationship between the international and the domestic, Thucydides suggests that war had caused Athens to move away from democracy toward tyranny. In Book II, we learn that the domestic chaos created by the plague and the war required that the respected General Pericles be given emergency powers: "It was he [Pericles] who led them, rather than they [the people] who led him. . . . So, in what was nominally a democracy, power was really in the hands of the first citizen" (2.65). Here, rather than reflecting a natural and internal cycle of regimes, domestic order in Athens moves from democracy toward tyranny due to both domestic *and* international events.

Thucydides further suggests that things also move in the other direction: the domestic influencing the international. In Book I, Thucydides describes tyranny as unable to achieve anything great internationally because of the nature of the regime. Where a monarch or emperor should be able conquer other civilizations and territories and build large empires, the tyrant is limited to a small sphere of control. Thucydides writes,

> And in the Hellenic states that were governed by tyrants, the tyrant's first thought was always for himself, for his own personal safety, and for the greatness of his own family. Consequently security was the chief political principle in these governments, and no great action ever came out of them—nothing, in fact, that went beyond their immediate local interests, except for the tyrants in Sicily, who rose to great power. So for a long time the state of affairs everywhere in Hellas was such that nothing very remarkable could be done by any combination of powers and that even the individual cities were lacking in enterprise. (1.17)

If this can be taken as a general theory of the international behavior of tyranny, we might conclude that Thucydides' tyrant, like Plato's and Aristotle's, is limited by his appetites, unable to think beyond his own stomach toward national interests, higher purposes, or greater power. Rather than focusing on new acquisitions, the tyrant seeks to keep safe his existing wealth and territory. As described here, the tyrant is merely a "local" actor. While able to achieve small military successes, Thucydides notes that for the tyrants, "There was no warfare on land that resulted in the acquisition of an empire. What wars there were were simply frontier skirmishes. . . . Wars were simply local affairs between neighbours" (1.15). The power of the tyrant is limited to raising revenue: they pillage and tax the surrounding islands but are unable to either consolidate this power into any higher form or create alliances to increase their sphere beyond the local. Bereft of any inspiration for large-scale domination or an ideological vision of global transformation, the tyrant is obliged to focus all of his attentions on maintaining what he already has. Arguably, any effort at expansion will lead not only to failure abroad but also to domestic collapse.

Thucydides' account may remind us of the long line of "petty dictators" that have risen quickly to power, have instituted vicious domestic oppression, have built grand palaces for their families, and have led unsuccessful military campaigns only to be toppled, assassinated, chased away, or arrested: they are local but not global threats. Slobodan Milošević ruled for eleven years, Idi Amin ruled for only eight years, and Pol Pot ruled a mere four years. Even Kim Il Sung and Hafez Assad, who were able to pass the reins of power to their sons, cannot expect to match the power and longevity of the dynasties of the Far East and the centuries-old democracies of the West. But, regardless of their time in power, none of these petty dictators compromised or compromise the safety of the world. What is more, Thucydides is not simply saying that tyrants were unable to achieve anything great but also that the citizens and cities under the tyrannies were held down or bound (*katechô*). Not only were individuals and cities bound by tyranny, but also the whole of Greece.

Put this way, tyranny served as a barrier to the later expansion, imperialism, and "world" war that would come to characterize the Hellenes a century later.

Still, there are problems with drawing a general theory of international tyranny from the above passage. In general, the pre-Platonic view of tyranny is ambivalent, implying neither reproach nor praise but simply describing the method of attainment and form of a certain kind of political leadership,[7] and, upon closer inspection, Thucydides' account of the tyrant more or less mirrors this ambivalence, describing some tyrants as cruel and repressive and commending others for their evenhandedness and honesty.[8] More problematic is his reference to the "great power" of Sicily that clearly indicates that not all tyrants are bound to local interests. Then again, the point is that Sicily is the exception. While it was able to achieve some international success, by and large, tyrants are bound to the local. The reason for this does not so much lie in the psychology, personality, or character of the tyrant but in his subjects. Because they lack a desire for glory and honor, they are not compelled to fight for the regime.[9]

Herodotus makes the same point. He argues that once the yoke of tyranny is thrown off, the emancipated citizenry can achieve greatness. In Book V of his *Histories*, Herodotus writes,

> And it is plain enough, not from this instance only, but from many everywhere, that freedom is an excellent thing since even the Athenians, who, while they continued under the rule of tyrants, were not a whit more valiant than any of their neighbours, no sooner shook off the yoke than they became decidedly the first of all. These things show that, while undergoing oppression, they let themselves be beaten, since then they worked for a master; but so soon as they got their freedom, each man was eager to do the best he could for himself. So fared it now with the Athenians. (5.78)

Again, Herodotus argues that the tyrants held down or bound (*katechô*) the Athenians from greatness—the tyrant actually limits the ability of a state to expand. The citizenry under the tyrants, he says, are cowardly, lacking any sense of loyalty to the state or desire for honor or glory in battle. Even if the tyrant had aspirations for international conquest, he will never have a galvanized population, army, or culture to back his efforts. Arguably, a soldier motivated to fight out of fear of domestic oppression will abandon his post when faced with death from his enemy. Clearly, the Athenians under these tyrants are a far cry from the unified, heroic soldiers that helped build the great empire described by Pericles in his famous funeral oration.

At this point, we can also understand Aristotle's account of the domestic character of tyranny in the larger context of international tyranny. According to Aristotle, tyranny aims to keep its subjects small (*mikra*), to have them always distrust one another, and to discourage friendship, public gatherings, and all political action (Aristotle 1995, 1314a). The tyrant also makes his subjects poor so that they are kept busy with their daily affairs, not having leisure to plot against him (Aristotle 1995, 1313b). Tyranny favors fear rather than loyalty, private subsistence rather than public glory, and insular suspicion rather than international conquest. Aristotle thinks tyranny is deviant, but not because the people under it are necessarily oppressed. He even has praise for specific tyrants, describing the tyranny at Sicyon as treating its subjects moderately and the tyrant Cleisthenes as looking after the interests of the people (Aristotle 1995, 1315b; see also 1285a–b, 1295a). For Aristotle, tyranny is deviant because it does not allow for a sense of civic responsibility, open expression, plurality of opinion, and public action. Not only does this keep the individual from achieving greatness, but so too does it limit the greatness of the regime. This same suppression of the public realm was in clear display in Saddam Hussein's Iraq and still persists in Kim Jong-Il's North Korea.

Even warfare under tyranny is of a deviant sort. Aristotle explains that "the tyrant is a stirrer-up of war, with the deliberate purpose of keeping the people busy and also of making them constantly in need of a leader" (1313b). War is engaged to fulfill a private agenda—to maintain what the tyrant already has—rather than to satisfy aspiration for conquest. Again, the tyrant is far more concerned with maintaining his control over the domestic population than with expanding his power to new peoples and territories. In fact, not only is the tyrant less than concerned with expansion, but, according to Aristotle, even if he was so concerned, the citizens of a tyranny lack spirit and are ill equipped for international conquest.

Taking our cue from these ancient thinkers, we can conclude that Bush is wrong: tyrants and tyrannies may be a local threat to domestic populations and a regional threat to neighboring states, but they are not global threats and do not compromise the safety of the world. The unpredictability or rogue character of international tyranny is really due to the skewed intentions of the tyrant to maintain his grip on his population rather than a real or concerted effort to rule the world. And, until recently, this has been reflected in American foreign policy: tolerating, containing, and even working with and supporting tyrants including Saddam Hussein.

NOTES

1. The member states of the Axis of Evil are Iraq, Iran, and North Korea. Many other oppressive, rogue, locally aggressive states are left out of this Axis of Evil: Syria, Zimbabwe, Burma, Egypt, Pakistan, India, China, and Israel, the last four having nuclear capability.

2. See Daniel Pipes, *Friendly Tyrants: An American Dilemma*, ed. Adam Garfinkle (New York: St. Martin's Press, 1991).

3. Because there is no overarching global government, legislator, or judge, sovereign states recognize no superior political authority and are the sole arbitrators of the rightness, justness, and legality of their own actions. See, for example, Martin Wight, *Power Politics* (Leicester: Leicester University Press, 1978), especially p. 105.

4. According to Michael T. Clark, "IR presupposes for its justification as a distinct subdiscipline of political science a discrete domain of social phenomena (most strenuously, Waltz 1979). The aim of IR is to identify, assess, and explain the relatively independent causal forces emanating from the international system itself" (493).

5. Thucydides is common ground for both international relations theorists and political philosophers. He is often cited as the first "realist" thinker. See Laurie M. Johnson Bagby "The Use and Abuse of Thucydides in International Relations," *International Organization* 48, no. 1 (Winter, 1994): 131–53, as well as Nancy Kokaz "Between Anarchy and Tyranny: Excellence and the Pursuit of Power and Peace in Ancient Greece," *Review of International Studies* 27 (2001): 91–118.

Political philosophy has also adopted Thucydides to help explain the nature of imperialism, war, and aggression. For example, *The Necessities of War* by Peter R. Pouncey, *The Ambition to Rule* by Steven Forde, *Greek Imperialism* by William Ferguson, *Thucydides and Athenian Imperialism* by Jâcqueline de Romilly.

6. For an excellent account of this relationship, see W. Daniel Garst "Thucydides and the Domestic Sources of International Politics" in Thucydides *Theory of International Relations*.

7. Where monarchs gained power through inheritance, the tyrant gained power through some kind of violent movement. The general characteristics of the tyrant were that he was bound by no external law, authority, or ethics.

8. For example, the "digression" on the Pisistratid tyranny, which ruled Athens a century before the start of the Peloponnesian War, challenges contemporary conceptions of tyranny. Thucydides writes of these tyrants:

> Indeed, generally their government was not grievous to the multitude, or in any way odious in practice; and these tyrants cultivated wisdom and virtue as much as any, and without exacting from the Athenians more than a twentieth of their income, splendidly adorned their city, and carried on their wars, and provided sacrifices for the temples. For the rest, the city was left in full enjoyment of its existing laws, except that care was always taken to have the offices in the hands of some one of the family. (6.54)

As Michael Palmer points out, Thucydides goes out of his way to correct the common misperception among the Athenians that this hereditary tyranny descended into a very bad regime. Rather than the result of some necessary and natural cycle of decline, the Pisistratid tyranny collapsed due to the private jealousy of a scorned lover (Palmer 1982, 106–109). Palmer goes on to detail the link between tyranny and piety in Thucydides citing the stories of Polycrates (1.13), Cyclon (1.126), Themistocles (1.135–1.138), and Alcibiades. For another account of Thucydides' correction, see Leo Strauss, "Thucydides' Peloponnesian War," in *The City and Man*, 195–97.

Finally, as mentioned earlier, Pericles is given the opportunity to exercise absolute power over Athens. Nonetheless, he is still described as intelligent and known for integrity, ruling with foresight and respect for the liberty of the people.

9. See 8.66.

SOURCES

Aristotle. 1995. *The Politics of Aristotle*. Trans. Ernest Barker. Oxford: Oxford University Press.

Bagby, Laurie M. Johnson. 1994. "The Use and Abuse of Thucydides in International Relations." *International Organization* 48 (Winter): 131–53.

Bruell, Christopher. 1974. "Thucydides' View of Athenian Imperialism." *American Political Science Review* 68: 255–80.

Bush, George W. 2002. "The President's State of the Union Address." The United States Capitol, Washington, DC, January 29.

———. 2004. "President Bush Discusses Progress in the War on Terror." Remarks by the president on the War on Terror, Oak Ridge National Laboratory, Oak Ridge, Tennessee, July 12.

Clark, Michael T. 1993. "Realism Ancient and Modern: Thucydides and International Relations." *Political Science and Politics* 26 (September): 491–94.

Ferguson, William Scott. 1913. *Greek Imperialism*. Boston: Houghton Mifflin.

Forde, Steven. 1989. *The Ambition to Rule: Alcibiades and the Politics of Imperialism in Thucydides*. Ithaca, NY: Cornell University Press.

Garst, W. Daniel. 2000. "Thucydides and the Domestic Sources of International Politics." In *Thucydides' Theory of International Relations*, ed. Lowell Gustafson. Baton Rouge: Louisiana State University Press.

Herodotus. 1920. *Histories*. Trans. A. D. Godley. Cambridge, MA: Harvard University Press.

Kokaz, Nancy. 2001. "Between Anarchy and Tyranny: Excellence and the Pursuit of Power and Peace in Ancient Greece." *Review of International Studies* 27: 91–118.

Palmer, Michael. 1982. "Alcibiades and the Question of Tyranny in Thucydides." *Canadian Journal of Political Science* 15 (March): 103–24.

Pipes, Daniel. 1991. *Friendly Tyrants: An American Dilemma*. Ed. Adam Garfinkle. New York: St. Martin's Press.

Pouncey, Peter R. 1980. *The Necessities of War: A Study of Thucydides' Pessimism*. New York: Columbia University Press.

Romilly, Jâcqueline de. 1963. *Thucydides and Athenian Imperialism*. Trans. Philip Thody. Oxford: Basil Blackwell.

Strauss, Leo. 1964. *The City and Man*. Chicago: Rand McNally.

Thucydides. 1972. *History of the Peloponnesian War*. Trans. Rex Warner. London: Penguin Classics.

Waltz, Kenneth. 1979. *Theory of International Politics*. Reading, MA: Addison-Wesley.

Wight, Martin. 1978. *Power Politics*. Leicester, UK: Leicester University Press.

Chapter 4

An Omission from Ancient and Early Modern Theories of Tyranny: Genocidal Tyrannies

Roger Boesche

From the ancient Greeks to just past the edge of the modern world or, roughly, from Plato to Marx, a significant number of political theorists sought to analyze the tyrannies of their own times: Plato and Aristotle the various Greek tyrants, Tacitus the Roman emperors, Machiavelli the Italian princes, Montesquieu *les despotismes* of European and especially French monarchs, Tocqueville a possible suffocating democratic despotism, and Marx the despotism of capital and the workplace. Of course, these thinkers did not always agree in their analyses of tyrannies, but there was, I will argue, a more-or-less coherent consensus about what characteristics one would expect to find in the regime of a tyrant. And these characteristics still describe and help us to understand tyrannies of the twentieth and the twenty-first centuries, so that, for the most part, Aristotle and Machiavelli reborn would not be surprised by how Mussolini, Ceaușescu, Marcos, Saddam Hussein, Idi Amin, or Pinochet dominated their subjects. Without question, these earlier thinkers can help us analyze and understand modern forms of tyranny. Nevertheless, a small number of new features emerged in some tyrannies of the twentieth century, features that allowed a new species of tyranny to emerge, what I call genocidal tyranny. All tyrannies are violent, but not all set out in a systematic way to kill a substantial portion of their population. This was something new in the twentieth century, and it was omitted from the earlier brilliant, but now crucially limited, accounts of tyranny.[1] After I first sketch the key characteristics found in ancient and early modern political theorists, I will show how new developments brought a new and more murderous kind of tyranny, by looking at the case studies of the Armenian genocide and the genocides committed by the Khmer Rouge.

CHARACTERISTICS OF ANCIENT AND EARLY MODERN TYRANNIES

One Tyranny, One Tyrant

Aristotle offered the classical Greek definition of a tyranny, that is, rule by one person who thinks not of the general good but of his or her self-interest. "This tyranny is just that arbitrary power of an individual which is responsible to no one, and governs all alike, whether equals or better, with a view to its own advantage, not to that of its subjects, and therefore against their will" (Aristotle 1941b, 1295a19–1295a22). Despite obvious exceptions to this depiction, for example the period of Thirty Tyrants in Athens, Plato also would have agreed with Aristotle's definition of tyranny as rule by a single and self-interested tyrant. In describing the absolute rule (*dominatio*) of Tiberius, Nero, and other emperors, Tacitus also described such tyranny as rule by one person, even though we can now see clearly a structure of power, including both a dominant class and a central role for the military. Montesquieu feared the power of Louis XIV and XV and sought to check monarchical power threatening to become absolute. Despite the fact that he most famously focused on rule by a prince, Machiavelli came closest to breaking from the Greek definition of tyranny, because, especially in his *History of Florence*, he analyzed the roles of classes, parties that generally represented class interests, and factions that fought for the narrow interests of one man or one family. In arguing that "a prince alone, lacking a nobility, cannot support the weight of a princedom" (Machiavelli 1965a, 107), Machiavelli initiated but did not follow through with a more complete class analysis. Thus, with some merely minor exceptions, the ancient and early modern view assumed that for each tyranny there was one ruling tyrant, a view not challenged seriously until Tocqueville, who depicted a faceless despotism with no identifiable despot, and Marx, who focused on classes.

Isolated in Private, or the Disappearance of Public Space

Aristotle articulated originally and most forcefully that tyrants must prohibit subjects from gathering in public space where they might deliberate and organize, and instead confine them to private space. Tyrants should "sow quarrels among the citizens," separating citizens and breaking apart friendships, and they "must not allow common meals, clubs, education," or any other public "meetings" during which people might communicate, trust one another, and organize (Aristotle 1941b, 1313b17–18, 1313b1–3). Force and violence were the means to eliminate public space. Similarly, Tacitus wrote that fear of the army forced people out of public space and into their private homes. Rome resembled a captured city on the next day. The great houses were shuttered, the streets almost empty, and the populace in mourning" (Tacitus 1975, 1.36). Recognizing that republics require public political deliberation and even public "quarrels," "agitations," and "disturbances occasioned in the public places," (Machiavelli 1950, 119–20), Machiavelli understood that a tyrant must keep people "dispersed" and "the state disunited" (Machiavelli 1950, 105, 283).

The most obvious way to close down public space is by prohibiting meetings with threats of violence that obviously induce fear. For Montesquieu, fear was the principle or motivating force of despotism (Montesquieu 1949, 3.9). By describing the frightful role played by spies and informers—the hated *delatores*—Tacitus noted that fear of violence confined people to private space but also destroyed any genuine conversation, because no one knew if he or she could trust either friend or family. Romans "have indeed set up a record of subservience . . . robbed as we are by informers even of the right to exchange ideas in conversation" (Tacitus 1970, chap. 2). Fear and mutual suspicion created a psychological isolation, a fearful loneliness.

When subjects know that they are being—or even might be—watched by spies, they avoid sincere conversations, they say what they believe tyrannical power wants to hear, and they even must carefully arrange their facial expressions. While Nero pranced on stage, spies watched the audience. "There were many spies unconcealedly (and more still secretly)," observed Tacitus, "noting who was there—and noting whether their expressions were pleased or dissatisfied" (Tacitus 1977, 16.5). Under tyranny, each plays a role, dissimulates, and pretends in order to survive. This helps us understand both how people in Mao's China confessed to some error that they thought the authorities wanted to hear, and also the exaggerated grieving in North Korea after Kim Il Sung's death. Said Tacitus of imperial Rome, "Men had constantly to attune their attitudes and expressions to the latest rumor" (Tacitus 1975, 1.85). To survive tyranny, one must often become a role-playing hypocrite.

To return to the phenomenon under tyranny of being confined to private life, Tocqueville somewhat later noted the rich and rewarding life of public participation in American democracy, but he deduced that the acquisitive ethic of the new commercial classes might well undermine the public world as individuals shirked their public and political obligations to pursue their private and economic affairs. "A man absorbed by the cares of making money has always been a timid or indifferent citizen" (Drescher 1968, 195). Tocqueville observed a tension between democracy and commerce, between democracy that encourages one to be a citizen acting for the general good, and commerce that urges one to look after one's private self-interest by accumulating wealth and property. "The time will come when men are carried away and lose all self-restraint at the sight of the new possessions they are about to obtain. . . . It is not necessary to do violence to such a people in order to strip them of the rights they enjoy; they themselves willingly loosen their hold" (Tocqueville 1945, 2.149). A modern tyranny would not need violence and fear to force people out of public space because, over time, the commercial ethic would undermine public and democratic deliberations, which would quietly and logically decline and disappear.

Monopoly on the Means of Violence

Violence was seen as the cornerstone of ancient and early modern theories of tyranny because violence could eliminate or intimidate any possible opposition. Said Aristotle of any men capable of leading an opposition, "The tyrant should lop off those who are too high; he must put to death men of spirit" (Aristotle 1941b, 1313a40–1313b1). Whereas control of the army is of paramount importance, tyrants must be able to wield extralegal violence with their own private paramilitary forces. The tyrant Pisistratus tricked Athenian citizens into disarming, formed his own private bodyguard, and with this bodyguard "rose against the people and seized the Acropolis" (Aristotle 1984, chap. 2). Even before Augustus died, Tiberius was supreme commander of the army and had a private army loyal only to him escorting him through the streets of Rome (Tacitus 1977, 1.7). Machiavelli noted that Lorenzo the Magnificent was always "accompanied by many armed men (Machiavelli 1965b, 8.9.1393), and Machiavelli urged princes who wished to stay in power to study military affairs. "A prince therefore should have no other aim or thought, nor take up any other thing for his study, but war and its organization and discipline" (Machiavelli, 14.53). The twin foundations of any successful state are "good laws and good armies" (Machiavelli 1950, 12.44). Nevertheless, if any tyrant continues to use violence, killing, and cruelty, then that tyrant is mismanaging the state, because Aristotle, Tacitus, and Machiavelli all thought that one should need some minimal number of examples of cruelty to provide order, some sort of economy of violence. Endless killing is a symptom warning that the tyranny is unstable. Said Machiavelli, "Well-committed [cruelties] may be called those . . . which are perpetuated once for the need of securing one's self, and which afterwards are not persisted in, but are exchanged for measures as useful to the subjects as possible" (Machiavelli *Prince*, 8.34). Moreover, "the more cruelty [a man] employs the feebler will his authority become" (Machiavelli 1950, 162).

The Appearance of a Republic, the Reality of Tyranny

Many ancient and early modern political thinkers recognized that those who practice tyranny find it useful to keep up appearances of some sort of popular government. In his *Discourses*, Machiavelli argued that the people are all too willing to be deceived by appearances. "He who desires or attempts to reform the government of a state . . . must at least retain the semblance of the old forms; so that it may seem to the people that there has been no change in the institutions, even though in fact they are entirely different from the old ones. For the great majority of mankind are satisfied with appearances, as though they were realities" (Machiavelli 1950, 182). Although this advice will work only if one is willing to bring about a tyranny gradually, all tyrannies rely on some deception, which is why Machiavelli advised princes that they cannot always be merciful, humane, and religious, but they must appear to be so (Machiavelli 1950, 18.65).

Tacitus described this well in his analysis of Tiberius. Emerging from years of civil war, the Roman populace no longer seemed to want genuine republican government, and Augustus obligingly brought them peace, authoritarian rule, and the appearances of republican freedom. "Then [Augustus] gradually pushed ahead and absorbed the functions of the senate, the officials, and even the law. Opposition did not exist. War or judicial murder had disposed of all men of spirit" (Tacitus 1977, 1.2). His successor Tiberius similarly left the senate only "the pretenses of freedom" and therefore but "a shadow of its ancient power" (Tacitus 1977, 1.77, 3.60). In appearance, Rome was a republic; in reality, a tyranny. While the senate deliberated, but only about trivial matters such as festival dates on the calendar, and while the law courts carried on but not if a judicial decision went against the emperor, Rome maintained the illusion of popular government. "The impressiveness of the Republican facade only meant that the slave-state . . . would be all the more loathsome" (Tacitus 1977, 1.81).

Actually, Augustus himself eliminated most popular deliberations, but he left the judiciary and the law courts somewhat independent so that while Augustus was alive, Rome's impressive legal codes could protect individuals. By contrast, Tiberius captured the courts. Virtually every analyst of tyranny after Tacitus—especially, for examples, Montesquieu and Tocqueville—understood that no tyranny can be complete if one allows judicial independence. Tiberius sat in on important legal cases to intimidate judges, and he extended the Roman law against treason to the words an individual wrote or spoke, no longer confining it, as before, only to actions. Personally disgusted that great Roman citizens and senators seemed too eager to deliver their freedom to him, Tiberius allegedly said after leaving an obsequious senate, "Men fit to be slaves!" (Tacitus 1977, 3.65). Citing Tacitus and admiring the legal tradition with some of its roots in Rome, Montesquieu argued that the executive, legislative, and judicial branches must all be separate, and that if one power controlled them all, that would be a certain sign of despotism. In particular, he loved the judiciary. "It is not enough to have intermediate powers in a monarchy; there must be a depositary of the laws. This depositary can only be the judges of the supreme courts of justice" (Montesquieu 1949, 2.4).

Fears of Centralization

Like his predecessor Bodin, Montesquieu feared a centralized government with no check on its powers by intermediate bodies, groups, and associations. Dearest to Montesquieu's heart, of course, was an independent judiciary that could protect individual rights from government arbitrariness. Nearly as important, Montesquieu defended the rights of classes, extended families, provinces, guilds, parishes, and localities against the all-too-frequent extensions of monarchical power. "Abolish the privileges of the lords, the clergy and the cities in a monarchy, and you will soon have a popular state, or else a despotic government" (Montesquieu 1994, 2.4). Tocqueville merely extended the argument. Because the acquisitive ethic of the new commercial democracies acts as a centripetal force fastening people to their private lives, intermediate bodies—especially classes and provinces and extended families—tend to disappear. In their place steps a centralized administration. "After the destruction of classes, corporations, and castes, [the state] appeared as the necessary and natural heir to all the secondary powers. The idea of centralization and that of the sovereignty of the people were born on the same day" (Boesche 1996, 222). Why did Tocqueville think that democratic states would inevitably centralize? First, after public life begins to disappear and citizens retire to their private homes, and after local groups and intermediate institutions start to dissolve, individuals seeking help will turn to the central government, which can only become more powerful as groups and institutions decline. Second, every time a new war comes along, more power extends to the central government and powerful wartime corporations. And finally, in mediating between labor and industry and in attempting to lessen the deprivation occurring during the business cycle, the central government will need more power. "Thus, the manufacturing classes require more regulation, superintendence, and restraint than the other classes of society, and it is natural that the powers of government should increase in the same proportion as those classes" (Tocqueville 1945, 2.327). Against all these powerful trends, all tending toward increasing the powers of the central government, Tocqueville suggested that associations might offer a new sort of intermediate body between the individual and the state, new intermediate powers so much beloved by his mentor Montesquieu, that might restrain a nearly all-powerful centralized government. Against this ever-encroaching and eventually despotic state, Tocqueville put his hopes in associations that in the end seem rather weak when juxtaposed to big business and the powerful state. "It would seem as if despotism lurked within [the manufacturing classes] and naturally grew with their growth" (Tocqueville 1945, 2:328–29).

Distortion of Language, Control of Discourse

Tacitus repeatedly observed, often on the very first page of his works, that emperors in part controlled the populace by the distortion of language. In the beginning of his *Annals*, he noted that some spoke freely under Augustus, "but then the rising tide of flattery [*adulatio*] exercised a deterrent effect. The reigns of Tiberius, [Caligula], Claudius, and Nero were described during their lifetimes in fictitious terms, for fear of the consequences" (Tacitus 1977, 1.1). Some distortion of language came from fear; one said what the authorities wanted to hear. But long before Orwell's brilliant essay "Politics and the English Language," Tacitus noted that the emperors and their spokesmen concealed their evil deeds behind fine-sounding words. His most famous sentence, one about the Roman imperial conquest of the Britons, alerts us to the falsity of language. "To robbery, butchery, and rapine, they give the lying name of 'government'; they create a desolation and call it peace" (Tacitus *Agricola*, 30). In describing the civil war of 69 C.E., Otho accused Galba of distorting language. "By a misuse of language, he describes cruelty as severity, greed as economy, and the execution and insults you have suffered as a lesson in discipline" (Tacitus 1975, 1.37). Noting that the Germans had frequently invaded the Gauls because of greed and lust, Tacitus also observed that nations always justify their invasions with brave words of liberty and independence. "But 'liberty' and other fine phrases serve as pretexts. Indeed, no one has ever aimed at enslaving others and making himself their master without using this very same language" (Tacitus 1976, 4.73). Although Marx recognized it much later, he also recognized that words such as *freedom, equality,* and *justice* were defined to defend class interests, and one could oppress a people with force less easily than with "intellectual bondage" (Engels and Marx 1969, 70). Both Tacitus and Marx wondered if language was ever neutral.

Aristotle had made a point more subtle but equally important about political discourse. He began by arguing that a citizen who had practical wisdom was one who knew the proper ends or goals of life, indeed, knew the good life, that is, "what is good for men in general" (Aristotle 1941a, 1140b7–11). Such knowledge came from deliberation among citizens in public space. However, tyrants close down public life and thus the deliberation needed for practical wisdom, and so in a sense, practical questions cannot be asked under a tyranny. One might ask technical questions about how to make money, increase pleasure, or build a road, but practical discourse, or that discourse or language that debates what constitutes a good life, disappears. Cicero recorded a fragment of Aristotle that we no longer have, a statement to the effect that it was only when the tyrants of Sicily had been removed that citizens could develop the art of eloquence (Boesche 1996, 70).

Classes

Of course ancient and early modern thinkers knew and wrote about classes. Class concepts are imbedded in the analyses of Plato and Aristotle, whether we are looking at Plato's just polis as one that harmonizes and balances classes or whether we watch Aristotle's worry that without a sizeable middle class, the rich and poor will fight endlessly. Observing that the turmoil resulting from class conflict in the early Roman republic was healthy for good laws and public liberty, Machiavelli asserted that all political orders will have tension between the few and the many, the rich and the poor, patricians versus plebeians. It is in his *History of Florence*, so much admired both by Tocqueville and Marx, that Machiavelli used so brilliantly the analytical concepts of class, party, and faction. Nevertheless, despite the fact that earlier thinkers did use class analyses, they were almost always unsophisticated. Consider the emperors whom Tacitus described. How did they rule? Aside from controlling the military, what classes or factions or interest groups supported or opposed them? Or finish reading Machiavelli's *Prince*, and try and describe the structure of his power? Did he have a cabinet? Was someone in charge of commerce? Did he rely on certain classes or economic interests? We have no idea. It seems as if he stands alone like a musical conductor directing a tyrannical symphony.

Marx changed all that dramatically. In analyzing the governments in his time, he saw the French monarchy under Louis Philippe in 1830 as a "bourgeois monarchy," and he claimed that the Second Republic of 1848 "revealed that here *bourgeois republic* signifies the unlimited despotism of one class over other classes" (Marx 1963, 23–24). Because we take arguments for and against this kind of class analysis for granted—which just goes to show how much Marx has influenced social science—we are apt to miss what an astonishing break he was making with the past. No longer was he sorting governments, as had thinkers from Plato to Montesquieu, into whether rule was by the one, the few, or the many, because all of these forms of government—monarchies, aristocracies, democracies—were in reality open or hidden class rule, indeed class tyranny.

Perhaps his most famous proclamation, that the nineteenth century had simplified class struggle into the bourgeoisie versus the proletariat, is his most unfortunate and most easily refuted. "Society as a whole is more and more splitting up into two great hostile camps, into two great classes directing facing each other: Bourgeoisie and Proletariat" (Marx and Engels 1978, 222). Marx and Engels were here simplifying the class struggle for their extraordinary pamphlet *The Communist Manifesto*, depicting a startling and appealing Manichean worldview of good struggling against evil, useful for organizing but woefully weak for analysis.

Marx knew this. In his own political and historical analyses, he often examined the roles played by five or even ten classes. (It is worth noting that, unable to define what a class is, Marx memorably broke off the third and last volume of *Das Kapital* just as he began to make a systematic effort to clarify what we mean by the word *class.*) Consider just a single passage taken from his famous study of the political and class struggles leading up to Louis Napoleon's coup in 1851. "The bourgeois republic triumphed [after June, 1848]. On its side stood the aristocracy of finance, the industrial bourgeoisie, the middle class, the petty bourgeoisie, the army, the *lumpen proletariat* organized as the Mobile Guard, the intellectual lights, the clergy and the rural population. On the side of the Paris proletariat stood none but itself" (Marx 1963, 23). This is a sophisticated analysis that is a qualitative leap ahead of Aristotle, Tacitus, Machiavelli, and Montesquieu. If we count every group that Marx mentions as a class, then we see him mentioning ten classes in two sentences. If they are not all classes, then he is analyzing interest groups or perhaps factions of classes.

It doesn't matter. Marx's political and historical investigations led him to discover that every tyranny has a structure, what Weber will later call a structure of domination, and Marx was analyzing the interplay between those classes, factions, and groups that support the tyranny and those that oppose it. To be accurate, Plato first had the remarkable insight that every society is an interrelated whole, which was why he could claim that to alter the music is to change the regime fundamentally. Borrowing from Montesquieu and Hegel, Marx saw all the key elements of society—politics, economics, law, technology, religion, family, habits, customs, literature, art, and so on—as dynamically interrelated. One will hardly find egalitarian families or democratic religion or progressive political ideas in monarchies and tyrannies. Ambiguous as his discussion of classes was, Marx changed forever the vocabulary with which we discuss tyranny. Who after Marx could seriously argue that any tyrant ruled alone, without allying himself or herself with key classes or factions of classes or groups such as the military—or twentieth century communist parties—that sometimes resemble privileged classes?

SOMETHING NEW IN TWENTIETH CENTURY GENOCIDE: SYSTEMATIC GENOCIDE

Ralph Lemkin, a Polish Jewish émigré who taught at Yale law school, invented the word *genocide* in 1944. By 1948, the United Nations adopted the Genocide

Convention that defined genocide in part as "acts committed with the intent to destroy, in whole or in part, a national, racial, or religious group" (Totten and Parsons 2000, 24). Certainly massacres and mass murders have existed since recorded history, for example, the destruction of Carthage by Rome or the massacres of whole cities that refused to surrender by Genghis Khan. Conquered by the Spanish beginning in 1519, Mexico lost some 11 million people by 1600 from mass killings, overwork, and disease (Gellately and Kiernan 2003, 21). In 1492 there were approximately 5 million Native Americans in what is now the United States, but by 1900 there were only about 250,000 (Gellately and Kiernan 2003, 22). Similarly, the population in the Belgian Congo fell from about 20 million to about 10 million from 1885 to 1920 due to murder, overwork, and disease (Gellately and Kiernan 2003, 25). How many millions did the slave trade kill? As a result of these and other human catastrophes on a large scale, some scholars do not see genocide as new to the twentieth century. They instead see continuity. Nevertheless, other scholars—and I agree with these—see something new in the twentieth century when genocide became "more frequent, more extensive, and more systematic," (Weitz 2003, 71) in part because of new technologies and in part because of the bureaucratic efficiency of the modern state and the military (Hull 2003, 143, 160; Gellately and Kiernan 2003, 9).

Certainly, it seems that the Nazi Holocaust was an event of a new kind both in the extent (6 million Jews and others) and in the rapidity with which the murders took place and also in the systematic and efficient way in which it was carried out, applying the latest administrative techniques and scientific innovations. And yet the Nazi pattern was simply a more systematic and extensive extermination that followed in many ways from a pattern established by the Turkish genocide of Armenians of 1915. Undeniably, the Holocaust was the most important genocide of the twentieth century. But I want to show that there are parallels between the Holocaust and the Turkish genocide of Armenians of 1915 as well as the genocides of the Khmer Rouge in 1975–1979. In addition, I will try to demonstrate that these twentieth genocidal tyrannies are somewhat new in history.

So what factors were new to the twentieth century that allowed for what I will call *genocidal tyrannies*? First, new technologies brought novel ways to communicate with people, manipulate people, transport people, and kill people. Second, a fervent nationalism that dates back to the late eighteenth and early nineteenth centuries, but which became virulently powerful in the twentieth century. Third, racial or ethnic ideologies that emphasized, sometimes romanticized, and always justified the actions by those in power, especially action to increase the extent of land for one's people and kill en masse supposedly inferior ethnic groups. Finally, efficient action by the state and its bureaucratic administrations, which had become much more powerful by the twentieth century. Arguing that racism, ideology, and bureaucracy were all central in the genocides of the twentieth, Arendt is the pioneer in studying the causes of genocidal tyrannies (Boesche 1996, 419–454).

Turkish Genocide against the Armenians

It is important to note that the Armenian genocide took place during World War I, which was making killing on a vast scale more acceptable (Weitz 2003, 71–72.) On the night of April 23–24, 1915, exactly the night that allied troops landed at Gallipoli, hundreds of Armenian leaders—professionals, businessmen, clergy members, journalists, and so on—were seized from their homes and massacred, effectively removing much of the Armenian leadership. Armenians serving in the Ottoman army were soon after taken out and killed, thus eliminating the bulk of Armenian men who might have resisted. Also, in April of 1915, the Turkish government, the so-called Young Turks, had begun a program of "relocation"—notice the corruption of language—of nearly every Armenian in Turkey by railroad cars (sometimes 90 people for a car designed for 6 horses or 35 soldiers) (Balakian 2003, 190) to supposedly new homes in the deserts of Syria and northern Iraq, which were south of Anatolia but part of the Ottoman Empire. Although in theory the Armenian population was to live in these Mesopotamian deserts and then return home after the war ended, in reality there were no homes waiting in the deserts, and this was a deliberate policy of extermination. On the long trips that sometimes went the length or breadth of Turkey, the trains carrying mostly Armenian women and children—teenage boys and any men were usually killed early in the deportations—stopped intermittently and various Turkish killing squads (*chetes*) composed of ex-convicts and some army officers (Balakian 2003, 182–83)—sometimes organized by the government and sometimes the result of local citizen participation in the genocide—raped, tortured, and killed those who had been in the trains. Tens of thousands of Armenians were also taken from their homes and made to walk to the deserts in forced-march caravans. Along the way, there were what Turkish officials called "way stations"—whose conditions were "so fiendish that the most cruel of the Mongols could not have imagined them" (Dadrian 1995, 242)—where further massacres and outrages by the killing squads took place. The state set up a group called the Special Organization—and this was an early example of bureaucratic efficiency or "the skill with which the Turks used the bureaucracy" (Balakian 2003, 180) and units of this group were to kill and harass Armenians on the trains, in the caravans, and in the way stations (Dadrian 1995, 236, 196). Citizens from local towns hired thugs and criminals to kill, rape, and humiliate Armenians on trains and in caravans, so much of the Turkish population was complicit in the genocide (Winter 2003, 210). Those Armenians who actually arrived in the Mesopotamian deserts—and these were mostly just women and children—died of sand, starvation, and disease, and were still subject to rape and killing by these death squads (Adalian 2000, 40–48; Dadrian 1995, xvii–xix, 240–43; Melson 1992, 144–45; Winter 2003, 206–12; Hovannisian 1994,123–26; Balakian, 2003: 192). The uprootings and deportations destroyed Armenian communities; said one woman who was nine when deported in 1915 to Syria: "It is a sense of emptiness, of belonging nowhere, of isolation, desertion" (Keshgegian 2002, 46). Before 1915, there were approximately 2 million Armenians living in Turkey, and estimates as to how many died in the period from 1915–1922 range from 600,000 to 2 million, with the United Nations estimating "at least one million" (Hovannisian 1994, 125). Recent scholars estimate from 1 to 1.5 million Armenian were killed in this genocide, although we will never know for certain (Balakian 2003,180; Adalian 2000, 40). This genocidal killing was "legal," as the authorities passed legislation for the "relocation" and for the appropriation of Armenian wealth and property, so that the appearance of legality and constitutionality was intact (Balakian 2003, 186–89).

The deportations and massacres could not have taken place and been coordinated without the telegraph, and much of the transportation relied on railroads and cattle cars. Propaganda promulgated by newspapers was also important, so new technologies played a key role (Adalian 2000, 44, Dadrian 1995, 220). In disseminating propaganda, the Young Turks—and this was a tyranny without one identifiable tyrant—delineated a racist ideology claiming that they wanted to "Turkify" the country and move away from the multiethnic ideal of the Ottoman Empire. It is important to note that all of this took place in an atmosphere of war, and the elites could say that Armenians were an enemy within, "agitators," and threats to the national security of the country (Dadrian 1995, 259, 197). Said one bit of propaganda, "The Armenians are in league with the enemy. They will launch an uprising" (Balakian 2003, 181) and another said that the relocation of Armenians was vital to prevent "the decay of the Turkish race" (Dadrian 1995, 196). One German general wrote approvingly saying that "the Armenian is just like the Jew, a parasite" (Dadrian 1995, 259). Racism combined with religion, because Armenians were Christians in a Muslim Turkey, provided a powerful impetus to killing (Kiernan 2003, 29).

And all of this was swept up in what one author calls ultranationalism (Hovannisian 1994, 122) and an urge to "Turkify" the nation (Adalian 2000, 41). The chief ideologue of the Young Turks, Yusuf Akcura, declared that Turkey needed an empire of "Turkishness" that would build a foundation on a "brotherhood born of race" (Kiernan 2003, 30). Among other measures,

Turkification included schools teaching only in Turkish and "the compulsory use of Turkish as the language of business" (Adanir 2001, 77). Some Young Turks dreamed of a "Pan-Turanian" or Pan-Turkish empire, and wanted to call the Ottoman Empire "Turkestan," allowing the empire to spread wherever there were Turkish people, well into central Asia. Like the Nazis later who wanted *lebensraum*, the Turkish nationalists wanted to expand the borders to obtain more land and a golden empire for all Turks (Kiernan 2003, 33–34; Melson 1992, 163–64).

Class interests supported the state. Even though Armenians were only 10 percent of the population, they "controlled 60% of the import business, 40% of the exports, and 80% of the domestic trade." In short, Armenians, Jews, and Greeks were a great part of the Turkish bourgeoisie (Adanir 2001, 77) and within Ottoman society, the Armenians had become "better educated, wealthier, and more urban" (Melson, 1996: 158). So when the state confiscated property and wealth of the Armenians, it got richer, and so did the now growing middle class of Turks. "In effect, the Turks wanted the Armenians out of the way; they also wanted Armenian wealth and were prepared to kill, torture and maim to get it" (Winter 2003, 209–10; Dadrian 1995, 222).

Pol Pot and Genocide in Cambodia

Scholars agree that without the Vietnam War there would have been no genocide in Cambodia. While dropping 540,000 tons of bombs on Cambodia and causing an estimated 150,000 Cambodian deaths, the United States military provided fertile ground for Pol Pot and the Communist Party of Kampuchea (CPK) or Khmer Rouge to recruit followers amid the killing and chaos (Kiernan 1994, 194; Kiernan 2002, 18–19). The rule by the Khmer Rouge lasted from April 1975 to January 1979, when the Vietnamese army invaded, routed the CPK, and put an end to the killing. The Khmer Rouge probably killed just under 2 million people out of the Cambodian population of 8 million, although some estimates are as low as 750,000 dead and others as high as 3 million (Kissi 2003, 307; Clayton 1998, 2; Lapidus 1997, 31).

When the Khmer Rouge took over Phnom Penh in April 1975, they immediately ordered an evacuation of that city and all others in Cambodia, probably an action unprecedented in history. Long lines of Cambodians walked west, south, and east for a few days or up to six weeks (Kiernan 2002, 48). But why? Perhaps the CPK feared retaliatory bombing by the United States, and perhaps they wanted Cambodians to be closer to the food grown in the countryside, but more likely, the Khmer Rouge hated cities that promoted immoral and bourgeois habits and also they knew it would be easier to control the population if the cities were emptied. Cities offer public space in which to deliberate and organize. By contrast, if everyone is isolated in separate villages, it is impossible to organize (Kiernan 2002, 52, 62, 64; Kiernan 2001, 90). To prevent any opposition, the Khmer Rouge operated an elaborate system or spies and informers, so that an individual was afraid to speak sincerely to anyone, including friends and family (Kiernan 2002, 172). At any rate, the Khmer Rouge maintained tight control over individuals who were afraid, exhausted, hungry, and constantly watched. "While proclaiming a communal ideal, the CPK atomized its citizens to assure maximum social control. It succeeded" (Kiernan 2002, 167). Pol Pot controlled the CPK with his friends, family, and in-laws (Kiernan 2002, 186), but the party and state controlled the people. "Despite its underdeveloped economy, the regime probably exerted more power over its citizens than any state in world history. It controlled and directed their public and private lives more closely than government had ever done" (Kiernan 2002, 464).

An extraordinary ideology—a mixture of Leninism, Maoism, agrarianism, and Khmer nationalism—led to emptying the cities and trying to set up cooperative farming in the countryside. In May 1975, the CPK met and established the basic principles that they would act on over the next years. These included evacuating the cities, abolishing all markets, eliminating money, defrocking Buddhist monks and making them work, executing members of the previous regime headed by Lon Nol and supported by the United States, establishing cooperatives and communal eating, expelling all ethnic Vietnamese, and dispatching troops to protect the borders (Kiernan 2002, 55). The communist element of this ideology is clear. A Khmer Rouge radio broadcast said the following in 1975: The "new Cambodian society is a community in which man is no longer exploited by man. It is a community without oppressed or oppressors. It is an equal society where there are no rich or poor and all are equal and harmoniously united in the common effort to increase production, defend, and build their beloved fatherland" (Clayton 1998, 4). Ironically, by emptying the cities, by focusing only on agricultures, and by producing no factory goods for export (Abuza 1993, 1017), this supposedly Marxist-Leninist society left no workers, no proletariat. They did, however, talk about factories and industries for the future.

In attempting to follow their own unique brand of communism, the Khmer Rouge abolished markets and money. Said one Khmer Rouge leader, "If there are markets and money, there was property" (Kiernan 2002, 57). And they wanted to do away with a society in which the rich had property and the poor did not. This Khmer communism also led to attempts to form cooperatives. At first, cooperative farming took place among fifteen to thirty families, but soon each village was to be a cooperative unto itself with collectivized agriculture (Kiernan 2002, 58–59). These kind of ideological schemes could only be communicated and then carried it out if the CPK had a centralized control over the country, which they did with some 50,000 party members, the only people living in Phnom Penh (Kiernan 1994, 205; Clayton 1998, 7)! Once more, the technology of radio communication was vital.

The Khmer Rouge's first victims were those who worked for and fought for Lon Nol, the previous government's officials, soldiers, and supporters (Kiernan 2002, 173). Pol Pot's communist party also divided the country into "new" people and "base" people. Whereas "new" people were city dwellers who had been contaminated by international influences and bourgeois ideas, habits, and desires, "base" people were the pure peasants who did not have corrupt ideas (Kiernan 2001, 87). There was a bit of distorted communism here, because urban workers were also "new" people as were people in the middle class such as teachers, intellectuals, doctors, those who knew a second language, those with property, and so on. These latter were slaughtered indiscriminately (Clayton 1998, 7–8). There was also a hint of distorted Maoism in the fact that the peasantry remained "pure," and therefore city dwellers could learn from the peasants. However, the peasants were hardly in charge, and they were probably more praised for lacking any polluting influence and therefore being easily indoctrinated in political meetings and criticism and self-criticism meetings (Clayton 1998, 12, 14). In other words, the peasants were not necessarily good, but just ignorant and therefore ready to receive and absorb as if they were sponges soaking up CPK ideology.

Underneath all this unique Khmer communism was actually a powerful Khmer nationalism and racism. While a student in Paris, Pol Pot called himself the "the original Khmer" (Kiernan 2001, 85) not the original communist man. (Note that he and other high officials of the CPK were foreign educated intellectuals killing all other intellectuals, including journalists, teachers, professors, and doctors.) Says Ben Kiernan, "The motor of the Pol Pot program was probably Khmer racist chauvinism" (Kiernan 2001, 87). Pol Pot and the Khmer Rouge were fascinated with the great Khmer kingdoms of earlier centuries (Chirot 1994, 214). And indeed, aside from killing city dwellers—the so-called "new" people—the Khmer Rouge killed people because of their ethnicity. "The Cambodian case is notable for its combination of totalitarian political ambition and a racialist project of ethnic purification" (Kiernan 2001, 87). Toward the end of the reign of the Khmer Rouge, they called for the "defense of Cambodian territory and the Cambodian race" (Kiernan 2001, 90).[2]

The Vietnamese suffered first. When Lon Nol came to power in 1970, there were some 400,000 ethnic Vietnamese in Cambodia. Lon Nol expelled some 200,000, the Khmer Rouge expelled another 100,000, and the remaining were murdered (Kiernan 1994, 198). Cambodians living near the eastern border with Vietnam suffered terribly; some were "relocated" to the northwest of the country and forced to wear blue scarves, much as Jews under Hitler wore yellow stars. They were eventually murdered without exception (Kiernan 1994, 201). The CPK also focused much energy on destroying the ethnic Cham population who were Muslims, and through their religious organizations, the Chams were more capable of resistance. They tried to destroy these Cham communities by breaking up villages, by killing leaders, by making them eat pork and raise pigs, and ultimately killing them. Some 100,000 of the total 250,000 persons of the Cham population perished (Kissi 2003, 314; Kiernan 1994, 199). Buddhists were also attacked directly. From eight monasteries with 2680 Buddhist monks, only 70 survived (Kiernan 1994, 197). Buddhism was eradicated from Cambodia in roughly the first year of rule by the Khmer Rouge (Kiernan 1994, 198), which does not mean that every single Buddhist was killed, but that monks and monasteries all disappeared. Finally, ethnic Chinese were attacked both for their ethnicity and also because so many had been city dwellers with property or professions. About one half of the 430,000 ethnic Chinese died under CPK rule, although a high proportion died of "hunger and diseases like malaria" (Kiernan 2002, 295). It is very difficult to know how many people were murdered deliberately and how many died of disease or starvation, because some 15 percent of the "base" or Khmer peasant population died (Kiernan 1994, 201). The killing seemed to be accelerating toward the end as Pol Pot's speeches talked more and more about killing "enemies," "traitors," and "ugly microbes" (Kissi 2003, 314).

CONCLUSION

History has certainly had tyrants who have committed mass murders and the destruction of cities, but these examples of systematic Turkish genocide against its Armenian population and also the systematic murders of the Khmer Rouge against both supposed class enemies and ethnic enemies would, I believe, astonish Aristotle, Tacitus, and Machiavelli. In each case, these twentieth-century genocidal tyrannies made good use of new technologies, an organized and efficient bureaucratic state or communist party, a fervent nationalism, and a justifying racial ideology.

NOTES

1. I find myself disagreeing with Leo Strauss who claimed that modern thinkers seeking to understand the tyrannies of Hitler and Stalin were "relieved when they re-

discovered the pages in which Plato and other classical thinkers seemed to have interpreted for them the horrors of the twentieth century." See the second paragraph of Nathan Tarcov's essay in this book.

2. In Waller R. Newell's essay in this book, he correctly notes that tyrannical regimes motivated by ideology—in this case an ideology of communism, nationalism, and racism—often ignore basic economic self-interest and greed.

SOURCES

Abuza, Zachary. 1993. "The Khmer Rouge Quest for Economic Independence." *Asian Survey* 33 (10): 1010–21.

Adalian, Rouben. 2000. "The Armenian Genocide." In *Ethnic Violence*, ed. Myra H. Immell, 40–49. San Diego, CA: Greenhaven Press.

Adanir, Fikret. 2001. "Armenian Deportations and Massacres in 1915." In *Ethnopolitical Warfare: Causes, Consequences, and Possible Solutions*, ed. Daniel Chirot and Martin E. P. Seligman, 71–82. Washington, DC: American Psychological Association.

Aristotle. 1941a. *Nicomachean Ethics*. Trans. W. D. Ross. In *The Basic Works of Aristotle*, ed. Richard McKeon. New York: Random House.

———. 1941b. *Politics*. Trans. B. Jowett. In *The Basic Works of Aristotle*, ed. Richard McKeon. New York: Random House.

———. 1984. *The Athenian Constitution*. Trans. J. Rhodes. New York: Penguin.

Balakian, Peter. 2003. *The Burning Tigris: The Armenian Genocide and America's Response*. New York: Harper Collins.

Boesche, Roger. 1996. *Theories of Tyranny: From Plato to Arendt*. University Park, PA: Penn State Press.

Chirot, Daniel. 1994. *Modern Tyrants*. New York: The Free Press.

Clayton, Thomas. 1998. "Building the New Cambodia: Educational Destruction and Construction under the Khmer Rouge, 1975–1979." *History of Education Quarterly* 38 (1): 1–16.

Dadrian, Vahakn N. 1995. *The History of the Armenian Genocide*. 3rd rev. ed. Providence, RI: Berghahn Books.

Drescher, Seymour, ed. and trans. 1968. *Tocqueville and Beaumont on Social Reform*. New York: Harper & Row.

Engels, Friedrich, and Karl Marx. 1969. *Germany: Revolution and Counter-Revolution*. Ed. E. Marx, no trans. given. New York: International Publishers.

Gellately, Robert, and Ben Kiernan. 2003. "The Study of Mass Murder and Genocide." In *The Specter of Genocide: Mass Murder in Historical Perspective*, ed. Robert Gellately and Ben Kiernan, 3–26. New York: Cambridge University Press.

Hovannisian, Richard G. 1994. "Etiology and Sequelae of the Armenian Genocide." In *Genocide*, ed. George J. Andreopoulos, 111–140. Philadelphia: University of Pennsylvania Press.

Hull, Isabel V. 2003. "Military Culture and the Production of 'Final Solutions' in the Colonies: The Example of Wilhelminian Germany." In *The Specter of Genocide: Mass Murder in Historical Perspective*, ed. Robert Gellately and Ben Kiernan, 141–162. New York: Cambridge University Press.

Keshgegian, F. A. 2002. "Defining Testimonies: Narrative Remembrances by Armenian Survivors of Genocide." *Proteus* 19 (2): 43–48.

Kiernan, Ben. 1994. "The Cambodian Genocide: Issues and Responses." In *Genocide*, ed. George J. Andreopoulos, 191–228. Philadelphia: University of Pennsylvania Press.

———. 2001. "The Ethnic Element in the Cambodian Genocide." In *Ethnopolitical Warfare: Causes, Consequences, and Possible Solutions*, ed. Daniel Chirot and Martin E. P. Seligman, 83–92. Washington, DC: American Psychological Association.

———. 2002. *The Pol Pot Regime: Race, Power, and Genocide under the Khmer Rouge, 1975–1979*. 2nd. ed. New Haven, CT: Yale University Press.

———. 2003. "Twentieth-Century Genocides: Underlying Ideological Themes from Armenia to East Timor." In *The Specter of Genocide: Mass Murder in Historical Perspective*, ed. Robert Gellately and Ben Kiernan, 29–52. New York: Cambridge University Press.

Kissi, Edward. 2003. "Genocide in Cambodia and Ethiopia." In *The Specter of Genocide: Mass Murder in Historical Perspective*, ed. Robert Gellately and Ben Kiernan, 307–24. New York: Cambridge University Press.

Lapidus, David. 1997. "Rethinking the Khmer Rouge." *Harvard International Review* 20 (1): 30–33.

Machiavelli, Niccolò. 1950. *The Prince and the Discourses*. Trans. L. Ricci, E. R. P. Vincent, and C. E. Detmold. New York: Modern Library.

———. 1965a. "A Discourse on Remodeling the Government of Florence." In *Machiavelli: The Chief Works and Others*, ed. and trans. Allan Gilbert, 3 vols. Durham, NC: Duke University Press.

———. 1965b. *A History of Florence*. In *Machiavelli: The Chief Works and Others*, ed. and trans. Allan Gilbert, 3 vols. Durham, NC: Duke University Press.

Marx, Karl. 1963. *The Eighteenth Brumaire of Louis Bonaparte*. No trans. New York: International Publishers.

Marx, Karl, and Friedrich Engels. 1978. *The Communist Manifesto*. In *The Marx-Engels Reader*, ed. Robert C. Tucker, 2nd ed. New York: W. W. Norton.

Melson, Robert. 1992. *Revolution and Genocide: On the Origins of the Armenian Genocide and the Holocaust*. Chicago: University of Chicago Press.

———. 1996. "Paradigms of Genocide: The Holocaust, the Armenian Genocide, and Contemporary Mass Destructions." *Annals of the American Academy of Political and Social Science* 548: 156–68.

Montesquieu, Baron de. 1949. *The Spirit of the Laws*. Trans. T. Nugent. New York: Hafner.

Tacitus. 1970. *The Agricola and the Germania*. Trans. H. Mattingly and S. A. Handford. New York: Penguin.

———. 1975. *The Histories*. Trans. K. Wellesley. New York: Penguin.

———. 1977. *The Annals of Imperial Rome*. Trans. Michael Grant. New York: Penguin.

Tocqueville, Alexis de. 1945. *Democracy in America*. Ed. P. Bradley, trans. H. Reeve, F. Bowen, and P. Bradley, 2 vols. New York: Vintage Books.

Totten, Samuel, and William S. Parsons. 2000. "Preventing Genocide." In *Ethnic Violence*, ed. Myra H. Immell, 23–28. San Diego, CA: Greenhaven Press.

Weitz, Eric D. 2003. "The Modernity of Genocides: War, Race, and Revolution in the Twentieth Century." In *The Specter of Genocide: Mass Murder in Historical Perspective*, ed. Robert Gellately and Ben Kiernan, 53–74. New York: Cambridge University Press.

Winter, Jay. 2003. "Under Cover of War: The Armenian Genocide in the Context of Total War." In *The Specter of Genocide: Mass Murder in Historical Perspective*, ed. Robert Gellately and Ben Kiernan, 189–214. New York: Cambridge University Press.

Chapter 5

Failures of Autonomy: A Hegelian Diagnosis of Modern Tyranny

Douglas Moggach

Prior to the revolutions of 1848, the Hegelian school in Germany develops a powerful analysis of modernity and of its political tendencies toward freedom, but also toward new forms of domination and misrule. Among these thinkers, Bruno Bauer proposes a specific concept of freedom as conscious, formative activity, both on the self and on the external world. The origin of this idea is Hegel's concept of the free and infinite personality, the typically modern capacity to dwell in multiplicity and tension of social roles and self-definitions, while still returning to unity with others in rational political institutions. Hegel contrasts this modern capacity with the solidity of ancient communities, in which the interests of citizens are far less differentiated. Bauer's critique of modernity takes aim at the inability of modern subjects to realize this ideal of the free and infinite personality. Instead, they often choose heteronomy, or determination by another, over autonomy, or self-rule. They remain mired in domination by unexamined forces and interests, notably those of private property, which tend to constrict political involvement, or to inflect it away from the general good. Bauer distinguishes himself from his contemporary socialists because he seeks not to abolish property, but to limit its political influence in the name of active citizenship. The failure of subjects to practice autonomous self-determination assumes its political expression in a modern tyranny of state and market.

According to Hegel, the Enlightenment discovers the central truth that everything exists for the subject (Hegel 1971, 332–33). It thus effects a dramatic shift away from the heritage of classical antiquity, a legacy persisting, in various forms, till the dawn of the modern age: the idea that there are fixed, objective orders and values in nature and society. This Copernican revolution in philosophy, culminating in Kant, causes a reorientation toward subjective thought and action, with profound political consequences. Modernity holds out the promise of emancipation from traditional roles and relationships and endows the subject with the right to challenge and to validate political, social, and cultural norms and institutions. This is a tremendous liberation in respect to traditional social structures, but it also exposes subjects to extraordinary risks. Through the new division of labor, accelerated production, and exchange relationships, modern civil society refines and multiplies particular interests and allows them unprecedented scope. One of the results of this process is the emergence of what Hegel calls a culture of diremption or fragmentation, based on entrenched oppositions among subjects emancipated from traditional bonds (Hegel 1964, 88, 90–91). In Hegel's account, the prospect for a genuine modern freedom depends on reconciling these diverse interests without suppressing them, allowing for the fulfillment of personal objectives, but also for the emergence and recognition of common interests. The task of the rational state is to achieve this complex reintegration of disparate elements, to unite universal and particular interests in political structures that promote self-determination across the whole range of social life. The figure of achieved modern unity Hegel calls the free and infinite personality (Hegel 1991, 20–21), highly individualized in its own pursuits and purposes, but also capable of reflexively examining these ends and of generating new kinds of connections to others as a mutual enhancement of freedom. He invokes a specifically modern capacity to dwell in a multiplicity of roles and interests, but still to return to a conscious unity in rational political relations, and thus to secure autonomy. Far from advocating authoritarianism, as frequently alleged (Popper 1973, 27–28, 59), Hegel is a vigorous proponent of the freedom that the modern world uniquely makes available (Marcuse 1960; Avineri 1972; Collins, ed. 1995; Patten 1999), while also being alert to its dangers.

After Hegel's death, his school fractured into two rival parties, supporters of religious and political orthodoxy, and advocates of republican transformation of state and society. The analyses of modern freedom and of the forms of its denial are among the major themes of left-Hegelian thought in the 1840s, as it confronts the consequences of the Enlightenment and the French Revolution, and the prospects for future development. One of its contributions is an analysis of the tendencies in modern life toward new forms of political domination, a concern that connects this body of thought with recent research in the history of republicanism (Skinner 1998; Pettit 1997), but also with discussions of the problem of tyranny. Much of this contemporary reflection on tyranny takes its inspiration from Plato (Strauss 2000; Newell 2000; Lilla 2001). Hegel's republican followers offer another model, stressing the differences between the ancient and the modern.[1] Focusing on the incompleteness or failure of the modern project to realize its emancipatory potential, they show how subjects unwittingly generate new forms of domination, or specifically modern forms of tyranny, as an effect of the culture of diremption. Bruno Bauer is a representative of this critical Hegelianism (Moggach 2003). Bauer defines freedom as conscious, creative activity, transforming the objective world in the image of subjectivity and reason; but he sees this potential as imperiled by a new kind of tyranny rooted in the practices and understanding of modern freedom itself.

ANCIENTS AND MODERNS

For Hegel, the fundamental distinction between antiquity and modernity can be illustrated by two conceptions of personhood and community. The ancient idea, best represented by Platonic thought, is that of "beautiful individuality," exemplifying a predetermined set of values or excellences, which harmoniously integrate the person into a relatively undifferentiated community (Hegel 1991, § 356, 378–79).[2] The community here can be described through the philosophical idea of substance, or immediate unity. Toward this community, its particular members stand in the relation of accidents or aspects, sharing the attributes of the whole, which, as Aristotle says, is prior to its parts.[3] Viewed as substance, the ancient community is a kind of organism, attributing functions to its members in order to maintain the whole; they do not freely establish their place within it, but find their station prescribed. Nor had the idea of critical self-awareness and subjective probing of the validity of institutions yet dawned. When it emerges with Socrates, it presents a mortal danger to this form of life. In Hegel's assessment, Plato recognizes the threat, and far from carrying out the Socratic program, seeks instead to suppress subjectivity and free choice in his ideal polis. Hegel contends that there is nothing utopian in Platonic thought, but rather the clear expression of the principle of substantiality and fixed relationships upon which the Greek city-state reposed. Subjectivity would ultimately triumph, as the Enlightenment perceived, and with it the principle of the modern world would be established.

The modern idea of the free and infinite personality requires highly diversified, flexible, and (in principle) self-ascribed social roles. It entails, further, the refashioning of objectivity in light of subjective ends, and the recognition of autonomous moral conscience. Collective ends are to be legitimated by processes of free choice, and not by tradition or a putative natural order.[4] According to Hegel, the rational modern state, whose outlines can be detected in the aftermath of the French Revolution, accommodates this diversity in a new and more conscious unity (Hegel 1991, § 260, 282–83). It is possible to misconstrue this unity after the model of liberal instrumentalism, where the new community emerges through a social contract to protect prepolitical rights; but Hegel is critical of the more extreme versions of modern subjectivity that remove the individual from constitutive relations to others. He concurs that modernity contains a practical imperative of emancipation: to replace merely given forms and values with rationally sanctioned relations. In this process, the traditional community is dissolved. Modern solidarities must be constituted by acts of freedom and recognition that express the new understanding of the self and its relations, embodying it in new, complex configurations. The properly structured modern state, recognizing the unfettered inner freedom of moral choice and a legitimate sphere of private right, makes possible the effective realization of the Kantian concept of autonomy or fully rational freedom (Kant 1964, 98). Participation in political institutions can broaden the scope of freedom and confirm the independence of persons as citizens, not only as consumers or bearers of private rights.

Yet if modernity contains these emancipatory tendencies, Hegel also acknowledges opposing movements, which undermine the potentiality for rational autonomy. This culture of opposition or diremption, of unreconciled particular interests, is the terrain on which modern tyranny grows. Hegel's republican followers trace out these opposing tendencies in their own account of modernity.

MODERN TYRANNY AND CIVIL SOCIETY

The investigation of a newly emerging form of tyranny takes as its point of departure a specifically modern experience of freedom. This line of thought is initiated, before Hegel, by Herder, who sees modern tyranny as the result of standardization, the eradication of the rich multiplicities of popular life. Herder describes ancient Greek society as organic and vibrant, in contrast to the drabness, divisiveness, and mechanical interactions of the moderns. He particularly stresses the contrast between modernity and the medieval world. He argues for the greater diversity of medieval communities, with their textured and variegated relationships. The premodern specialization of craft work among artisans differs from the current manufacturing model, because it was guided by broadly Platonic injunctions to develop personal artistry and discipline, and to stress quality over quantity. Herder argues that compared with this former distribution of tasks, society is now becoming less, not more, differentiated through the modern organization of labor. Simplification, repetitiveness, and loss of skills in manufacturing result in workers that are reduced to identical, interchangeable units, no longer self-directing but responding to pressures from without (Herder 1877, 534–64), like parts of a mechanism. Tyrannical rule is inherent in modern society as connections and relationships break. Deprived of communal support and the buffering of corporate bodies, isolated individuals are thrust back on their own resources and narrow self-interest, and encounter the naked power of state. Herder deems deplorable the situation that Hobbes had rather prescribed in *Leviathan* as a restraint upon modern individualism, the elimination of intermediate agencies between the individual and the sovereign being one of the conditions for the exercise of power in civil society (Herder 1965, 27–145). Herder thus anticipates elements of Hannah Arendt's critique of totalitarianism. Unlike the authoritarianism to which some German romantics later succumb, and to which Herder's thought has been incorrectly likened, he favors a broad diffusion of power rather than centralization and hierarchy, but tends to idealize the popular life of the medieval commune and village.

As Bruno Bauer takes up the argument, the disappearance of mediating structures poses the problem of modern tyranny, but also the possibility of its overcoming. It is impossible to revert to the old structures of society and economy; instead, theorists must trace out the dialectic of the new, post-Enlightenment order to diagnose the modern malaise, and to envisage its possible solution. The direct and unmediated relation of individual and state must be reconceived so that the state is not an independent, transcendent power, but an agency of republican self-rule. One of the conditions for emancipation will be met if the universal interest that the state claims to represent is rendered immanent through popular sovereignty, and not enshrined in a separate institutional sphere divorced from concrete social life or from active direction by its members.[5] Further, however, individuals are to realize this universal interest in their own lives, becoming agents of critical self-consciousness. This idea of active citizenship implies a constant readiness to transform relations and institutions in the light of new experiences, to oppose fixity, privileges, and exclusiveness of all kinds. It implies processes of social creation,[6] whereby ever-new spheres of life are to be governed by relations of right, reciprocity, and justice. The sphere of right does not authorize a permanent clinging to private interest, but an ongoing revision of institutions. A stringent ideal of self-transformation underlies Bauer's republican vision in the 1840s, but also an awareness of the intrinsic difficulty of the ideal, and of the forces that oppose its implementation.

Bauer's thesis is that modernity contains a dialectic of freedom and its denial. The issue is framed in Bauer's thought as the opposition between formative self-consciousness and inert, undifferentiated substance. The disappearance of the old mediating structures like guilds and corporations, and the elimination of irrational privileges and of estates endowed with differential rights were necessary and historically progressive developments. These changes were effected theoretically by the Enlightenment, and practically by the French Revolution and the emergence of modern civil society. This historical movement is the precondition for new forms of republican governance, though these were still only present as a tendency, an imperative, and an emancipatory drive. Bauer's distinctive argument is that modernity also tends to engender a new form of the substantiality relation, to deny the autonomy that it promises. He defines this substance as a conformist, mass society, without true inner differentiation, and without critical self-consciousness of freedom and autonomy. He thus redraws Hegel's image of the culture of diremption. Bauer sees it not as highly diverse, but as monotonously identical: not as dynamic and versatile, but as stagnant and complacent. His depiction anticipates John Stuart Mill's arguments on the dangers of conformism, and on the value of individuality, critical self-consciousness, and experimentation for historical progress, though Bauer does not share Mill's utilitarianism, even in the more refined intellectual stance that Mill assumes in respect to Bentham. The new form of substance, mass society, is particularly favorable to the growth of tyranny, though ancient substantiality did not have this political outcome as its necessary expression. In antiquity, tyranny emerges when the forces of integration break down: it is a pathology of the polis. Modern tyranny is the essential expression of the new substantiality, and not a deviation. In its political application, the substantial represents a constriction or underdevelopment of the spontaneity and rationality of subjects. Bauer's explanation of tyranny follows the lines of Hegel's philosophy of history, as the history of freedom. In the classical world, the social whole represented a kind of achieved rationality, integrating parts for whom the perspective of individual freedom was not yet available. This harmonious unity cedes to tyranny only exceptionally, when unity is under severe stress. In the light of the historical progress of reason and freedom, the show of deficient rationality on the part of modern subjects is now a *parekbasis* or deformity, because higher standards are available. The whole and the part fall into disjunction: the pretended universal, or the state, seeks its own aims of power and dominance, while the particulars remain locked in their own narrow confines.

MODERN REPUBLICAN FREEDOM

Bauer defines substance as unshaped or relatively undifferentiated matter, and ascribes to self-consciousness the power of formal causality. Modern societies may opt to follow one or the other route. Modern freedom consists in critique, in examining and transforming the given so that all irrational relations and institutions are expunged. Inwardly, the modern free and infinite personality emerges through critical reflection on its own particular interests. It does not allow these to define its ends without self-assessment and critique, but questions and transcends them in free self-creation. This is Bauer's version of Rousseau's general will. The rational will is spontaneous in its independence of causes that might determine it without its own compliance. It is self-causing, because it admits the rules or maxims that are to determine its action, rather than being simply determined by external pressures or unexamined inner drives. It is self-legislating, by adhering to rationally justifiable criteria. The ends of political action require universalistic sanction: they must be valid and permissible for everyone, not just for special interests or identities, and they must not simply appeal to personal advantage or appetite where this conflicts with a broader general good. This universality, the equivalence of the positions of all subjects in the light of duty, is the true expression of modern equality. Bauer takes this Kantian moral premise as a basis for political and juridical action, too, advocating what can be called a republican rigorism (Moggach, forthcoming). No distinctions of rank or status, no differential rights or special privileges (*privileges*), are admissible in the court of reason.

The spontaneity and rationality of the will underlie Bauer's ideas of freedom and subjectivity. He intends his doctrine of universal self-consciousness to be a restatement of the idea of free and infinite personality, stressing personal responsibility and permanent change, rather than a stable institutional matrix. Autonomous individuals are those who have subjected their life to critical examination, testing their motives and commitments, and seeking the general welfare. They have thus purged or elevated their particular characters, taking them not as fixed, but as determinable or malleable according to rational standards. Subjects acquire autonomy by freeing themselves from private interests when these are incompatible with duty and republican virtue. They must also repudiate transcendent universals, namely those religious and political institutions that cannot meet the test of rational freedom, and that appear to derive from principles divorced from subjective activity. By making the general interest immanent in their activities, they thus achieve a genuine dialectical synthesis of universality and particularity (Hegel 1969, 618–19).

Only by transforming their own limited particularity can individuals become the organs through which a genuine, immanent universal interest attains historically effective form. By assimilating the principle of universality, recognizing a common interest with others, and performing the necessary historic tasks to make this interest a reality, subjectivity changes its own character, liberating itself from the impress of heteronomy and the confines of particular interest. Without this universal interest, the dissolution of ethical life is an impending threat.

MASS SOCIETY AND TYRANNOUS MODERNITY

Mere particularity is the principle of what Bauer calls modern mass society, whose attribute is private interest, or thoughtless acquiescence in the existing order. Its unreflective existence violates the normative demands of modern self-determination (Taylor 1991, 109–21; Pippin 1997, 31–53). Yet the mass is an extremely modern phenomenon. The French Revolution had hastened and validated the dissolution of the traditional order of estates, with their differential rights and privileges, leaving in its place a society that might either fall victim to massification, or utilize its newly acquired equality and freedom to build a better order. Tyranny is an inevitable consequence of mass society and modern substantiality, but it is not inevitable that modern society should so misconstrue its own freedom, or that it should do so permanently. Before the revolutions of 1848, at least, Bauer believes that the mass can transform itself into a politically active people, in propitious circumstances like France in 1789—though it can equally fall back into torpor and impotence. The modern project remains open and undetermined.

Bauer distinguishes historical forms of substantiality that oppose or limit free self-determination. The modern form is not to be confused with the substantiality relation of ancient society, persisting in various degrees up to the time of the French Revolution; here individuals have not yet fully emerged to assert their rights to critical examination of norms and institutions. The pre-Revolutionary ancien régime, with its hierarchies of privilege and irrational exclusions, still maintained something like the ancient political order in its organic discrimination among estates. The new form of substantiality is the result of the peculiarly modern failure of autonomy that Bauer sees in mass society. In this case, individuals have been wrenched from their embeddedness in traditional relations, but they are unable to define themselves by autonomous action and critical reflection. They succumb instead to particularity, in the form of acquiescence in the status quo, and determination of the will by exclusive proprietary interests. Here each subject seeks to exclude the other, but each is identical to the other in the acquisitive mainsprings of its action.

Hegel had examined this situation of merely apparent diversity in his *Logic*. He identifies, among kinds and degrees of difference, the special case where each particular is defined by the presence of the same attribute, and thus reveals itself to be indistinguishable from all others (Hegel 1969, 173–74). Herder, in a historical vein, had also contested the seeming differentiation of the modern division of labor, which reduces workers to interchangeable cogs in a machine.

Bauer applies the Hegelian logic of spurious difference when he describes modern mass society as largely undifferentiated, because in it all subjects are identical as possessive individualists, subordinate to the demands of accumulation. Like Herder, he emphasizes the uniformity of civil society, though he recognizes it as a historical necessity, and as a possible ground for further progress in freedom. For Bauer, it is not property itself that is illegitimate; he will vigorously contest this issue with Marx (Moggach 2003, chap. 8). It is rather the tendency of property to usurp the political domain, or to evacuate it, abandoning it to the free play of ruling groups. In this distinctively modern form of heteronomy, subjects fail to exercise the power of self-reflection and self-shaping that modernity uniquely makes possible. Freedom is instead disfigured into pure particularity, and so ethical relations among subjects dissipate, allowing the state and other agencies to pursue a course of action determined by the interests of the ruling cliques.

The modern form of substantiality conditions a type of tyrannical political order distinct from that of the past. It is in the wake of the French Revolution, with its enormous liberating possibilities and its signal failures, that the roots of modern tyranny lie. The susceptibility of mass, conformist society to tyranny, indeed their correspondence, arises from the renunciation of the political project of citizenship, in favor of the rule of self-interest, both among the rulers, and among the dominated, politically passive subjects, themselves preoccupied solely with their immediate, largely economic, concerns. According to Bauer, this relation prevails within various political structures, even where the franchise is broadly available. Formal institutional democracy is not a sufficient safeguard against it if it does not promote a critical attitude toward all existing relationships, and if it limits participation and citizenship to the assertion of private, exclusive rights.

Just as the Platonic account of tyranny directs us to regard the inner dispositions of political subjects, so too does Bauer, but his diagnosis is based on a Hegelian understanding of freedom. His psychology of the tyrannized presents the problem not as an expansive hubris or overstepping of legitimate bounds, as Plato does, but as a self-imposed constriction within the limits of private, proprietary interest. Tyranny is an exacerbated form of heteronomy, deriving from subjects' lack of courage, insight, and critical self-awareness. Its basis is the failure of subjects to attain the potential offered by modern culture, to achieve the promise of autonomy implicit in the ideal of free and infinite personality. A transcendent or false universal, a state that undermines the capacity of its members to achieve rational freedom or autonomous self-determination, is the necessary complement to truncated particulars. Modern tyranny promotes and consolidates this narrowly individualist attitude as a condition of its own power. Plato had observed the dangers of self-interest, and saw an acquisitive society as a breeding ground for tyranny; but this problem becomes central to the modern experience of freedom and subjectivity in left-Hegelian accounts. Bauer contends that the universal interest will be appropriated and deformed by another agency if individuals do not actively concern themselves with its realization (Bauer 1841, 465–79; Bauer 1842 (anonymous), 589–96; Bauer 1843a, 163). The self-confinement of the particulars in the narrow scope of their private interests—their idiocy in the literal Greek sense—allows the sphere of the universal, the state, to escape their control, whereby it assumes distorted shapes and pursues irrational or merely sectional objectives, sanctioning new types of juridical and economic privilege, and violating universal rights. The split between a transcendent universal and a mass of particulars bereft of self-determination defines the conditions of modern tyranny. The tyrannical state thwarts the emancipatory drive of its people, repressing critical thought and the possible emergence of alternative visions. Its subjects remain mired in domination, first by their own products, and then by the pseudopolitical order.

Bauer argues that the triumph of mass society would lead to increasingly tyrannical political forms. The Restoration state was still marked with elements of the old, pre-Revolutionary society and did not manifest the tendencies toward a fully modern tyranny in all its purity. A new situation arises with the spatial extension of modern mass society and the market, which cannot be confined within the compass of a single state or continent. Inevitable contact with other cultural zones, up till now relatively untouched by modern interests, breaks down the barriers among both European and non-European states, inaugurating globalizing tendencies that Bauer detected as early as the mid-nineteenth century.

TYRANNY AND GLOBALIZATION

Examining the failure of the liberal, republican, and socialist movements in the revolutions of 1848 across Europe, Bauer concludes that the future belongs not to the sovereign, republican people, as he had previously predicted (Bauer 1843a, 185),[7] nor to individual countries or separate national destinies. He now foresees imperialism on a world scale, as the universalization of mass society and of perfected modern tyranny, anticipating Karl Kautsky's theses on supranational or "ultra" imperialism (Kautsky 1915). Bauer does not believe that this movement will reduce the causes of armed conflict in the world. In Bauer's version, ultraimperialism spawns large-scale wars to dominate the world's resources and peoples. Contenders for hegemony are no longer states but agglomerates of political and corporate power cut off from accountability and control. The emerging world order is framed not by the defense of national interests, but by a struggle for transnational supremacy among factions with no local attachments. The historic result of this globalizing movement will be the crushing of particular, historically inherited interests and national identities,[8] creating the basis for a possible cosmopolitan rebirth after a long period of internecine wars, though the outcome cannot be predicted with confidence. History does not necessarily end with worldwide mass society, but may possibly enjoy a new and higher phase, though the later Bauer is increasingly pessimistic. In his analyses, Bauer downplays the significance of nationalism as a political force; it does not motivate the elites, though it may have its subordinate political uses in mobilizing the masses, who will serve as fodder in the wars. This globalizing trend corresponds to what Bauer calls the culmination of political pauperism (Bauer 1882a, 17), a generalized disability to intervene in political affairs. The problem for the future is how to reverse this enervating tendency, and to unite equality with personal autonomy rather than with passivity and uniformity. In Bauer's view, this will be the key to any possible cultural revival (Bauer 1882b, 3).

Until such a renewal might occur, the rivalry among imperialist powers and agencies would perfect the form of modern global tyranny and usher in a world cultural, political, and economic crisis of uncertain resolution. For Bauer it is clear, however, that these conflicts for hegemony do not stimulate but hinder economic growth, since permanent insecurity and military mobilization undermine or misdirect productive activity (Bauer 1882a, 17). Yet the sustaining force of modern imperialism and tyranny is the abandonment of the political and the complete self-absorption of individuals in their private affairs. Militarism works against the very economic conditions that promote it. Bauer here reproduces the distinction he had proposed in his early work, between the development of the productive forces (Bauer [1848] 1972, 530) and the pathology of the market, the anxious clinging to property that circumscribes the political involvement of the modern liberal-bourgeois consciousness (Bauer 1844, pt. 1, 6). This dialectic now operates on the global scale.

These are prescient conclusions, though Bauer may have misconstrued important aspects of the developments he describes. He misjudges, perhaps, the abiding force of nationalism beyond its merely instrumental possibilities; he recognizes, but insufficiently analyzes, the workings of interimperialist rivalries in the West, without close attention to specific forms, to shifting patterns of alliances and rivalries, or to types of economic interests. Nonetheless, he aptly portrays significant phenomena of the ongoing globalization process, which he dates from the mid-nineteenth century: the conjunction of private interest or the ideological triumph of the market, with the strong, expansionist, and militaristic state. As we enter an era of wars in which neomercantilist efforts at monopoly of supply, and massive corporate subsidies, disguise themselves behind the rhetorical celebration of the free market, Bauer's analysis of modern tyranny seems almost prophetic. His critique alerts us to forms of domination and heteronomy concealed in contemporary economic and military globalization but holds out the prospect that history may not end in tyranny and mass culture. Genuinely republican options, renewals of citizenship and political community, might still be open. As Bauer puts it in an optimistic moment, "Nothing is impossible for spirit" (Bauer 1843b, 195).

NOTES

The author gratefully acknowledges the support of the Social Sciences and Humanities Research Council of Canada for this project.

1. Arendt (1973, 419, 460–61) stresses that ancient and modern tyrannies are incommensurable, being based on underlying conceptions of society that are fundamentally different. On the nature of these differences, however, the present account does not adopt Arendt's description of modern society.

2. The ancient community expresses, however, an inner conflict between human and divine law, state and family. See the analysis of the *Antigone*, in Hegel (1967, 466–90). Hegel (1991, 356) also stresses the exclusionary character of the Greek community, where only some are free.

3. This integration involves acculturation, or *paideia*. See Aristotle (1985, Book 3, 1–5) on *prohairesis*, the choice of a way of life, not as an existential choice by a deracinated individual, but as a result of habituation.

4. Tenets of authentic subjectivity are outlined in Taylor (1991, 81–91).

5. Previously, orthodox religion and absolutist politics had produced this separation in their respective spheres, and Bauer argues that a new, more informal separation emerges from modern, apolitical mass society. His argument here can be seen as completing the Lutheran revolution by rendering the absolute immanent politically, not only ecclesiastically. The primacy of the Enlightenment in heralding modernity must thus be qualified by acknowledging preceding moments, such as the Renaissance and Reformation. See, for example, Andrew (2001).

6. For a similar view in Fichte, see Maesschalck (1996).

7. Bauer's work after 1848 is highly problematic in several respects, notably a vociferous anti-Semitism. His analysis of the emerging world market can bear critical scrutiny independently of this view.

8. On his earlier views of the crushing of particularity by the state, see, for example, Bauer (1840, 19–33).

SOURCES

Andrew, Edward. 2001. *Conscience and Its Critics: Protestant Conscience, Enlightenment Reason, and Modern Subjectivity*. Toronto: University of Toronto Press.

Arendt, Hannah. 1973. *The Origins of Totalitarianism*. New York: Harcourt Brace Jovanovich.

Aristotle. 1985. *Nicomachean Ethics*. Trans. T. H. Irwin. Indianapolis, IN: Hackett.

Avineri, Shlomo. 1972. *Hegel's Theory of the Modern State*. Cambridge: Cambridge University Press.

Bauer, Bruno. 1840. *Die evangelische Landeskirche Preußens und die Wissenschaft*. Leipzig: Otto Wigand.

———. 1841. "Theologische Schamlosigkeiten." *Deutsche Jahrbücher für Wissenschaft und Kunst* 117–20 (November 15–18): 465–79.

———. Anonymous. 1842. "Bekenntnisse einer schwachen Seele." *Deutsche Jahrbücher* 148–149 (June 23–24): 589–96.

———. 1843a. "Rezension: Die Geschichte des Lebens Jesu von Dr. von Ammon." In *Anekdota zur neuesten deutschen Philosophie und Publizistik*, ed. Arnold Ruge, vol. 2, 160–85. Zürich und Winterthur: Verlag des literarischen Comptoirs.

———. 1843b. "Die Fähigkeit der heutigen Juden und Christen, frei zu werden." In *Einundzwanzig Bogen aus der Schweiz*, ed. G. Herwegh, 56–71. Zürich und Winterthur: Verlag des literarischen Comptoirs.

———. 1844. *Die Septembertage 1792 und die ersten Kämpfe der Parteien der Republik in Frankreich*. Charlottenburg: Egbert Bauer.

——— [1848] 1972. "Erste Wahlrede von 1848." In Ernst Barnikol, *Bruno Bauer: Studien und Materialien*, ed. P. Riemer and H. M. Sass, 525–31. Assen: van Gorcum.

———. 1882a. *Disraelis romantischer und Bismarcks socialistischer Imperialismus*. Chemnitz: Ernst Schmeitzner.

———. 1882b. "Vorwort." *Schmeitzner's Internationale Monatsschrift* 1: 1–17.

Collins, Ardis B., ed. 1995. *Hegel on the Modern World*. Albany: SUNY Press.

Hegel, G. W. F. 1964. *Vorlesungen über die Ästhetik, I, Sämtliche Werke*. Ed. H. Glockner. Vol. 12. Stuttgart: Fromann-Holzboog.

———. 1967. *Phenomenology of Mind*. Trans. J. B. Baillie. New York: Harper & Row.

———. 1969. *Science of Logic*. Trans. A. V. Miller. London: Allen & Unwin.

———. 1971. *Vorlesungen über die Geschichte der Philosophie, III, Werke*. Vol. 20. Frankfurt/M.: Suhrkamp.

———. 1991. *Elements of the Philosophy of Right*. Ed. Allen W. Wood, trans. H. B. Nisbet. Cambridge: Cambridge University Press.

Herder, J. G. 1877. *Auch eine Philosophie der Geschichte zur Bildung der Menschheit, Sämtliche Werke*. Vol. 5. Berlin: Weidmann.

———. 1965. *Ideen zu einer Philosophie der Geschichte der Menschheit, Erster Band*. Berlin: Aufbau Verlag.

Kant, Immanuel. 1964. *Groundwork of the Metaphysics of Morals*. Trans. H. J. Paton. New York: Harper & Row.

Kautsky, Karl. 1915. *Nationalstaat, imperialistischer Staat und Staatenbund.* Nürnberg: Fränkische Verlagsanstalt.

Lilla, Mark. 2001. *The Reckless Mind: Intellectuals in Politics.* New York: NYRB.

Maesschalck, Marc. 1996. *Droit et création sociale chez Fichte: Une philosophie moderne de l'action politique.* Louvain: Éditions de l'Institut supérieur de philosophie Louvain-La-Neuve et Éditions Peeters.

Marcuse, Herbert. 1960. *Reason and Revolution.* Boston: Beacon Press.

Moggach, Douglas. 2003. *The Philosophy and Politics of Bruno Bauer.* Cambridge: Cambridge University Press.

———. Forthcoming. "Republican Rigorism and Emancipation in Bruno Bauer." In *The Left Hegelians: New Philosophical and Political Perspectives,* ed. Douglas Moggach. Cambridge: Cambridge University Press.

Newell, Waller R. 2000. *Ruling Passion: The Erotics of Statecraft in Platonic Political Philosophy.* London: Rowman and Littlefield.

Patten, Alan. 1999. *Hegel's Idea of Freedom.* Oxford: Oxford University Press.

Pettit, Philip. 1997. *Republicanism.* Oxford: Clarendon Press.

Pippin, Robert. 1997. "Hegel, Freedom, the Will." In *Grundlinien der Philosophie des Rechts,* ed. Ludwig Siep. Berlin: Akademie Verlag.

Popper, Karl. 1973. *The Open Society and Its Enemies, Vol. 2, Hegel and Marx.* 5th ed. London: Routledge.

Skinner, Quentin. 1998. *Liberty before Liberalism.* Cambridge: Cambridge University Press.

Strauss, Leo. 2000. *On Tyranny.* Revised and expanded edition. Ed. Victor Gourevitch and Michael S. Roth. Chicago: University of Chicago Press.

Taylor, Charles. 1991. *The Malaise of Modernity.* Concord, ON: Anansi.

Chapter 6

What Is "Tyranny"? Considering the Contested Discourse of Domination in the Twenty-first Century

Simon Tormey

At one level, it seems odd to be asking the question, what is tyranny? Surely, it might reasonably be said, we know what tyranny is. We know what tyrants look like and how they behave. We know what tyrannical practices are and how they impact those subject to them. The world is replete with reminders of tyranny and tyrannical regimes. After a century marked by tyranny of the most cruel and genocidal kind, this century opens with the overthrow of a tyranny, and the threat of further interventions against a host of others (the "Axis of Evil"). Why, then, do we need to think about the nature and meaning of "tyranny"?

Firstly, there is a question of comparison. One of the objectives of this volume is after all to compare existing tyrannies with past tyrannies and to ask whether and to what extent they are the same. Is the tyranny of Oedipus or Solon the same as that of Saddam Hussein or Kim Jong-Il? Are the tyrannies of the ancient world analogous to the sophisticated totalitarian systems of North Korea or the late USSR? There is the question of continuity of logics, technologies, and characteristics. This is an entirely legitimate exercise, but comparison is only possible where the terms of the comparing are relatively stable and "trusted." We can compare kinds of dog because the term "dog" is itself relatively uncontested and taken for granted. But this is not the case for "tyranny." Here, by contrast, we are confronted not merely by a term the *application* of which is in question (are modern tyrannies the same as the tyrannies of antiquity?), but whose *meaning* is both contested and inherently political. Evil and, by extension, tyrannical states are to be opposed and confronted. Free, democratic regimes are those with whom the rest of the free, democratic world is happy to "do business." Up to 1941, Soviet Russia was widely described as a tyranny. After the German invasion of June of that year, the USSR was converted into a "friend" and "ally," and the principle long established in realpolitik that the enemy of my enemy is my friend was reconfirmed. The term "tyranny" was banished from official briefings, newspaper reporting, and academic writings on the nature of the system confronting the Nazis—that is, until the onset of the Cold War in 1945, when the USSR reemerged as a "totalitarian" regime, and thus as a tyranny (Gleason 1995; Tormey 1995).

Does all of this mean, however, that the term "tyranny" is in current usage merely arbitrary, a kind of boo word to be flung against those whom, for whatever temporary or contingent reasons, we happen not to like, whom we don't get on with or have sympathy for? It is of course a boo word, in that most of us are keen to avoid living in a tyranny and will happily go along with actions that diminish their proliferation or establishment. But this alone does not make the term *arbitrary*, which is to say without settled definition or agreed qualities. The term is not arbitrary, but rather loaded with a set of meanings that resonate in a very particular way, indeed in much the same way as other terms in the lexicon of political science resonate, such as "liberty," "equality," or "justice." Such words are part of the armory of linguistic combat and of the hegemonic struggles between different conceptions of the world, between different notions of the good life, of how we should live. How we describe regimes and systems reflects in very direct terms our own normative preferences and ideals. The notion, for example, that contemporary tyrannies are the same as or similar to those of the ancient world is an essentially liberal or—following Kojève's critique of Strauss—perhaps even "aristocratic" viewpoint, concentrating as it does on the centrality of law and the "virtues" of the wise ruler to "just" rule (Strauss 1963, 146). As I think is evident, such a focus is perhaps useful for describing regimes of a premodern character, but much less so when it comes to analyzing contemporary forms of domination, with the much more complex patterns of dependence, power, and authority that we find in modern political systems. Whilst liberal accounts are undoubtedly "hegemonic," in that they inform "official" as well as "common sense" thinking about the nature of political systems, a more critical approach is one likely to yield not only a better sense of the distinctiveness of *both* classical and contemporary political systems, but it will also produce a "politics" that is more attuned to the nature and form of oppression under modern systems of governance—and an understanding of the nature of the resistances that arise against it.

CLASSICAL AND/OR LIBERAL "TYRANNY"

Since the pre-Socratics, "tyranny" refers to political systems in which power is used in an arbitrary manner by those who are unaccountable in direct—and usually indirect—ways to those who are subject to that power. To paraphrase from the short section supplied by Aristotle in *The Politics*, a tyrant is one who exercises a monopoly on the use of power and uses it to his own benefit or in his own interests. In other words, rule is exercised "as by a master" (Aristotle 1990, bk. 4, x).

Even on this minimal or baseline definition, what becomes evident is the importance of certain key terms. This is particularly so for the concepts of "power," "interest," "law," and "accountability." Tyrants cannot stand challenges to their power; they want all the power, and they want to monopolize it in such fashion that no other individual or office can come to undermine or query their position. Similarly, they do not recognize limitations on their actions. They do not want to be hindered by something outside of their own power and, in particular, the limiting influence of the law. Hence, of course, the source of Oedipus's rage and introspection. The fear of the powerful Other, those/that which lies outside of the subject, underpins the drama of Oedipus—a point brought out in Lacan's dramatization of the Oedipus complex as the quest for absolute power in the formation of the psyche (Stavrakakis 1999).

A key consideration is, therefore, the *visibility* of power, the fact that it does not hide itself or seek to dress itself up as something that it is not. The tyrant is someone separate and apart from the society over which he or she rules. Power is something naked, forceful—something that emerges out of a barrel of a gun or perhaps from the edge of a sword. But then, according to early liberal theory, so too does *legitimate* power. It was Hobbes, after all, who asserted that "Covenants, without the Sword, are but Words, and of no strength to secure a man at all" (Hobbes 1968, 223). *All* power, Hobbes tells us, is coercive. This is what makes it power. So what then is the difference between legitimate and illegitimate power, and how does this connect back to classical notions of the difference between tyranny and "just" rule?

We mentioned that the classical account of tyranny rotated around four intersecting concepts: power, interest, law, and accountability. According to Aristotle, the difference between a "'perfect" constitution such as kingship and an "imperfect" system such as tyranny lay in the particular configuration of these concepts. Under "perfect" conditions, power is exercised in the interest of all citizens, exercised in conformity to laws, and made accountable to the citizens by a mechanism such as voting or rotation of office. Power is used "virtuously" and "wisely," not imprudently or for the interests of the rulers alone. An imperfect constitution is one where power is used in interests of the one over the many, where law is subject to power rather than vice versa, and where the ruler or tyrant is unaccountable.

Hobbes' concern echoes this classical account almost exactly but with paradoxical results from the point of view of the analysis of modern systems. In

Leviathan, Hobbes restates that effective, or in Aristotelian terms, "perfect," government does not equate to democratic government. Far from it: effective government is legitimate government in that it is conferred by the *consent* of the governed, a principle that underwrites liberal constitutionalism in Locke and the work of the Founding Fathers. Hobbes insists that consent can be divined through the operation of a hypothetical contract between rulers and the ruled, thereby improving (so it seems) on the rather more *ad hoc* judgments of observers of classical political systems seeking to establish the "worth" or "virtue" of rulers. This is to say that the existence of consent can be inferred through the willingness of subjects to obey a sovereign power. In obeying the sovereign, we in effect manifest the existence of a "contract" between governed and governor. Contractual governance contrasts with tyranny in that both parties behave as if bound by the terms of an agreement made between them. Leviathan is thus posited, curiously, as a "representative" of the people, as opposed to the tyrant who remains in the state of nature vis-à-vis his own "subjects" (Hobbes 1968, 228). "Representative" governance mirrors the idea of "just" governance in classical commentary in being based on the affirmation of the people, on their voluntarily recognizing the legitimacy of the ruler or ruling group.

The shortcomings of such an account when transferred to the analysis of modern regimes are too obvious to need to be restated at length here (see Macpherson 1962; Plamenatz 1963). Suffice to say that the "difference" Hobbes establishes between the Leviathan and the counterfactual tyrant are more apparent than real. In practice, the citizen of such a state is subject to an absolute power which is by definition unaccountable and unlimited. The only means of redress against the Leviathan is the fabled witch's test of "revolution" that was to be such a useful means of underpinning Locke's "tolerant" liberalism and the legitimating rhetoric of the Founding Fathers. Government is legitimate as long as it is not overthrown. If it is overthrown, then, self-evidently, it is no longer "government." In the meantime, anyone resisting the Leviathan can be and should be "put to death, by the command of the Sovereign Power" (Hobbes 1968, 265). It is upon such sophisms that the liberal doctrine of consent and in turn the distinction between legitimate constitutional authority and tyrannical power rested and, arguably, continues to rest. Here, too, is the origin of the difficulty of the liberal paradigm as a basis for reading the nature of contemporary political systems whose oppressiveness frequently lies beneath the surface of daily life. If a society appears to be at peace with itself, then at one level it is legitimate. For the main, liberal commentary remains wedded to the classical notion of domination as the open and coercive use of power against an unwilling body of individuals. Tyrannies are "self-evidently" coercive, oppressive regimes. Nothing is hidden.

TYRANNY AND MODERNITY

Here, matters become more complex because not all tyrannies have this nakedly coercive character, and not all coercive regimes are tyrannical. Indeed we might hazard the hypothesis that as modernity has developed, so the correlation between the overtly coercive nature with which power is exercised and the degree to which a system or leader can be regarded as "tyrannical" has steadily *diminished* to the point where we now have a contested field of signifiers jostling for supremacy. To take the example of the USSR again, during the early years of the Soviet regime, power was classically tyrannical in the sense that power was on open display. Enemies real or imagined were rounded up and killed in open displays of power designed quite explicitly to signal the despotic nature of the regime. Trotsky argued in *Terrorism and Communism* that the open use of violence was useful, not only for terrorizing opponents, but for serving as a reminder to supporters of the need for vigilance and discipline (Trotsky 1975, 78). It goes without saying that the period of War Communism and the civil war over which Trotsky presided was tyrannical in the extreme. Yet by the 1960s, the Soviet regime had become more subtle and less confrontational in its methods, so much so that many commentators were given to redescribing the Communist regime as one built on some form of consensus between those who "govern" and those who are "governed" (see, for example, Hough and Fainsod, 1979). It was argued that, logically, communist regimes were not so different from the liberal democracies with which they had long been contrasted, a move recognized by a growing literature devoted to the "convergence" of industrial societies along a continuum. What, it was asked, makes communist systems tyrannical when all *overt* signs of the arbitrary and open use of power of the sort we have so far been describing are absent—or absent from the eyes of the casual observer? If communist and capitalist regimes were at one level "alike" (law governed, industrial, consensual), why should they be treated as fundamentally "different"?

It is here that we encounter the crux of the difficulty in transferring the classical image of tyranny to the setting of modern states and situations. To be clear, this is not to say there are no regimes that display tyrannical qualities of the classical kind. The point is rather that this overt coercive character is, arguably, a function of their *lack* of modernity, that is, a lack of sophistication in developing forms of coercion, control, and discipline that are consonant with modern systems of governance. Saddam Hussein's regime may at one level have been modern in the sense that it embraced nationalism as opposed to religious fundamentalism, and secularism over revealed knowledge—both hallmarks of "modernity." It was also clearly tyrannical: power was exercised in a savage and coercive manner against all manner of individuals and groups, including large ethnic minorities such as the Kurds. This implies that in assessing modern as opposed to premodern regimes, what is relevant is not what is open or on the surface, but what is tacit and hidden. Domination is no longer easily legible, that is, lying on the "surface" of regimes and systems. It lies hidden beneath outward displays of conformity, of everyday habits of thought and expression, of daily interactions. Because in a sense domination and coercion lie out of view (there is less "jackboot" in view), whether a given system can be regarded as tyrannical is a matter of piecing together the evidence of expressions of dissent, of deciphering what in this connection James Scott aptly terms the "hidden transcripts" of domination (Scott 1992). How, then, to render this difference more evident?

One of the most penetrating accounts of the nature of contemporary oppression and thus of contemporary forms of tyranny is supplied by Vaclav Havel in a remarkable essay, "The Power of the Powerless," written as a dissident in Communist Czechoslovakia (Havel 1985). The essay rotates around the analysis of the following vignette of life under Communist rule. A greengrocer displays in his window a sign saying, "Workers of the World, Unite!" At one level, that is, at the level of the "open" transcript, little seems to be amiss. The greengrocer is displaying his loyalty or fidelity to the system in much the same way that someone singing the British national anthem or saluting the American flag is demonstrating his or her "pride" at being British or American. Except that, as Havel goes on to explain, the sign actually meant the opposite. Its subliminal meaning is, "I, the greengrocer, XY, live here and know what I must do, I behave in a manner expected of me. I can be depended upon and am beyond reproach. I am obedient and therefore I have the right to be left in peace" (Havel 1985, 28). The sign is a talisman, an attempt to ward off difficulties and problems through an overt display of loyalty to the system. It is thus the product of fear rather than contentment or consent, of the pragmatic concern to keep out of harm's way rather than to risk the wrath of the authorities. The greengrocer puts the sign in the window because he thinks by doing so he will appear loyal to those around him, to officials and ultimately to the police. It helps him slip quietly into the "panorama" of daily life. The issue of relevance for our concerns is, how did Havel know that this is what the sign meant—as we now know it did? More generally, what does such a reading tell us about the nature of contemporary forms of power and domination?

What Havel's example shows us is that the terms used to describe tyranny under contemporary conditions are barely relevant and need to be rethought. In particular, we have to revisit the idea of domination as the open and coercive use of power against subject groups, a definition that serves for classical and premodern societies but not, as the example above shows, for more advanced societies and systems of domination. Here it will be useful to touch upon the work of Michel Foucault, as it complements Havel's analysis while making clear the analytic properties of power in differing periods of historical and social development. Foucault's work serves as an important counterpoint to the liberal understanding of power and indeed to the liberal account of domination that takes as its cue the classical interpretation of tyranny outlined above.

FOUCAULT, POWER, AND "TYRANNY"

At one level, Foucault's investigation of the nature of power can be taken as a direct critique of what might be termed the physicalist conception of power underpinning Hobbes's account—though it is more often discussed in relation to other critical conceptions of power such as that articulated by Marx in relation to class society. To Foucault, modernity can be equated to the elaboration of forms of power that are radically distinct from those of antiquity and the medieval period. Such an account, if valid, in turn necessitates the reappraisal of the nature and meaning of "tyranny" itself.

As he makes clear in a number of places, modernity witnesses the supplanting of the physicalist conception of power with one focused on the disciplinary and constitutive nature of power (Foucault 1977, 2001). This would equate to the generation of a model that sees power not merely as operating against a passive and preconstituted subjectivity (as in Hobbesian methodology—the subject that "like a mushroom" springs fully formed into the world), but as a positive element in the constitution of subjectivity itself. As we have had occasion to mention, the classical model of tyranny presupposes the prior existence of the subject as citizen who is then aggressed upon by a usurping power, the tyrant. This creates the familiar dynamic analyzed by Aristotle, namely "the instability of the polis." Those who are used to being free do not take kindly to having their freedom taken from them by an agent who seeks to maximize his own benefit. It is for this reason that tyrannical rule is unstable in Aristotle's view. It can last only as long as people feel sufficiently threatened that they go along with the regime. The moment fear recedes or people perceive a weakness in the tyrant, they will seek to remove him. So much for Aristotelian political science. The point is that power is used against something, which in turn resists and creates a dynamic relationship, albeit of a one-dimensional kind (as long as the tyrant possesses a sufficient quantum of power, he will be able to maintain himself in power against those who seek to resist). According to Foucault, such a characterization of the relation between the various agencies of power does not survive into the modern era. Why not?

What impresses Foucault in his extensive studies of differing domains of activity—the family, prisons, hospitals, and governmentality more generally—is the shift from the overt and coercive use of force against transgressing or "failing" subjects toward forms of internal disciplinarity and regulation. Instead of treating the subject as an "externality" that has to be punished, branded, hounded, and harassed, the various microagencies of governmentality produce a subject that is complicit in its own domination, and thus which does not need to be treated as an "outsider," as a hostile power to be tamed through the overt or explicit use of coercive power. Through an extension of the logics and apparatuses of control, a subject could be fashioned in accordance with the requirements of the particular system, institution, or regime into which he or she is inserted. The transitional motif Foucault deploys to describe such a shift is what he terms "panopticism."

The panopticon is a device invented by Bentham (who is in turn regarded as the quintessential "modern" figure by Foucault) to resolve the problem of creating perfectly acquiescent subjects—initially in the context of the prison, but more generally in asylums, schools, and indeed in any context where the subject is required to conform to a particular kind of behavior in the interests of the stability of the local system or regime (Foucault 2001, 58–59). Bentham's design places a central control tower at the center of a given space in which all subjects are permanently bathed in light. Each subject occupies a given space or room that can be watched over by the occupants of the control tower, who are themselves hidden behind shutters or spyglasses. Thus every subject can be watched over, whilst the watcher himself remains hidden from view. Without even being present, the watcher maintains a "presence" for each of the subjects, who by virtue of the design of the panopticon, can never be certain *when* they are being watched. By this simple device, Bentham ensured that the distinction, real or metaphoric, between the public and the private, the inner and outer world, was eliminated—to the "benefit of society." Surveillance and control displace coercion and compliance.

As Foucault sees it, panopticism is no mere utilitarian fantasy, but rather a literal description of how power operates under modern conditions (Deleuze 1988, 72–76; Foucault 2001, 58). What impresses Foucault is how the physical operation of power experienced as something external to oneself has been displaced by a series of interlacing and interlocking regimes of discipline, surveillance, and control. From seeing the subject as something external to governmentality and the disciplines it imposes, subjectivity became the object of governmentality—specifically the manufacturing of subject types that would conform to the logic of the system itself. Prisons are transformed from a site of punishment to a site of rehabilitation and "treatment." Asylums are transformed from sites of enforced exclusion from the rest of society, becoming instead sites of control and reconstitution of the hapless malleable subject.

As Foucault was at pains to make clear, none of these developments were in response to the demands of a clear identifiable agent: a governing class, or even less a state or leader. They were the responses to the emergence of modernity in turn shaping and constituting the modern itself. The transition from feudalism to factory production necessitates a new kind of subject, but in turn this new subject necessitates changes in the nature of now anachronistic institutions and processes. At one level, therefore, what Foucault is describing is what others describe as "socialization"—the coming to be of the subject within a given social context. Yet his point is that there is an "outside" of such processes, in turn implying that they are more or less coercive, evincing more or less resistance. Such resistances are rarely the kind we associate with resistance to tyrannical regimes. They are rarely in the form of large-scale or organized uprisings of the kind that punctuates the history of tyrannies in the ancient world, in turn helping Aristotle to formulate his conclusion that such systems of rule were inherently "unstable" (Aristotle 1990, bk. 5, xi–xii). What they evince is, rather, a set of what may be termed "petty" resistances of a kind that are hidden beneath the surface of everyday life. They are hardly resistances to "the system," for as Foucault makes clear, it no longer makes sense under modern conditions to talk about "the system" as if there were one overarching governmentality located in one space or place—as there is in classical and even early modern systems of rule. There is no sovereign power—or rather there is, but sovereignty is now largely fictive or illusory, helping to paper over the "functional" character of the modern state and its officeholders. As he mordantly puts it, in political theory, "we need to cut off the king's head" (Foucault 2001, 122). What we term "the system" is rather a multiplicity of interlocking governmentalities, regimes, institutions, and processes, some linked by an obvious underpinning rationale (e.g., "neoliberal governance," "communism," "homeland security"), others not. From this point of view, it is futile to think of power as something that is used or wielded like a weapon (or "the sword," in Hobbes' sense). Parties and governments *manage* a system; they do not invent or construct it. The site of "power" is not the state but the *discursive* mechanisms that underpin the operation of the various elements composing the social system. These elements construct and reconstruct a particular kind of subject, in turn maintaining the functioning of the whole. The firm produces the obedient worker who will fulfill her allotted tasks—or, better, "identify" so completely with "the brand" that she sees herself as a mere cog in the machine of "economic productivity" and "global competitiveness." The university, which once offered a critical intellectual grounding in a discipline, now offers a "training" in "transferable skills" as a return on the student's "investment." In each domain, a subject type or position is immanent to the system itself, requiring conformity to its disciplinary logic. How does Foucault's account impact on the question of the nature of tyranny?

- In modern systems, power is dispersed throughout the system rather than being concentrated in one locale or one office (the leader/*fuehrer*). It is located in sets of interlocking practices and institutions that themselves are multiple and heterogeneous, that is, not reducible to a governing ideology that could be displaced with another "ideology." Although there are leaders and ruling groups, classes, and castes, power is not possessed or controlled by such groups. They *have* power, or rather powers; but power as the ensemble of relations and practices determining the formation and direction of subjective preferences and behavior is not reducible to the actions or demands of such groups.
- In earlier forms of tyranny, domination is experienced collectively, if not en masse. Slaves were oppressed as a group; the Jews were *collectively* oppressed by the Nazis; the "kulaks" (an almost entirely artificial category) were "liquidated as a class"—as Stalin characteristically put it. Now the diffuse and constitutive character of power means that the subject's sense of "being dominated" is, where appropriate, felt as a rupture between herself and dominant values, beliefs, practices, and even linguistic forms. This produces a sense of dislocation, of rupture and anomie. Oppression is highly individualized, often experienced as neuroses, depression, feelings of helplessness, and a mute desire for an "outside" (flight, exile, emigration).
- Resistance is in turn something that stems, initially at least, from highly individualized rejection of particular practices, processes, and procedures. Revolts rarely take place against "the system" or totality itself (1968 was perhaps the last great collective revolt of this kind). Resistances are rather "petty" and isolated. Workers subvert or undermine the workplace by failing to carry out instructions, by stealing from the office or factory, or by turning up late. Youths in the inner city spray graffiti, smash up telephone boxes, and shoplift. Patients forget to take their medicine, disrupt the functioning of the ward, attempt to distract the nurses and staff, and abuse the system of exeats and visiting hours (e.g., McMurphy in *One Flew Over the Cuckoo's Nest*). Resistance is concrete and "local" rather than being directed against "the state" or "the ruling class." Resistance often translates as a kind of "antisocial" behavior, one that threatens "the decent law-abiding majority."

This latter point illustrates a key consideration in relation to the notion of domination underpinning Foucault's analysis, namely that it is no longer possible or meaningful to think in terms of certain modern societies as "tyrannical" and certain others as unproblematically "free" or "democratic." Whether any given setting is oppressive or "tyrannical" (to continue with the archaisms) is a matter of what might be termed one's "positioning" relative to the dominant "majoritarian" ethos upon which modern societies are built. Here the work of Gilles Deleuze and Felix Guattari may be of service to us because they articulate in perhaps clearer terms (as Foucault himself suggests) what is at stake in such an assessment of the modern experience (Foucault in Deleuze and Guattari 1984, xi–xiv). As they argue in *A Thousand Plateaus*, whether one regards the operation of modern systems of power as oppressive depends on whether one subordinates one's identity and sense of self to the dominant value and belief system—that of the fictive "majority" that provides the constituency and basis of support for the system itself (Deleuze and Guattari 1988).

Here of course is an echo of Hobbes and Locke, though the conclusions they draw are radically opposed to both. For the latter "consent" to the system of governance is fictive, virtual, or "tacit." It is never or very rarely expressed, and indeed there are no occasions whereupon it *could* be expressed except through the swearing of an oath of allegiance—and even this is often under a form of duress (as for example in the case of economic migrants). Yet the "consent" is said to be real where we are happy to subordinate ourselves to an already existing power: to identify with the crown, constitution, nation, or people. The point is that an act of identification with a collective subject is required in order to permit us to speak in terms of the existence of "consent." We have to subordinate our sense of ourselves as "univocal" or distinct to a larger aggregate identity in order for the superstructure to operate. Where that sense of distinctiveness—what might ordinarily be termed independence of thought—is asserted, then our perspective alters. We come to see the "majoritarian" relations around us as inhibitive, repressive, and oppressive. We come to see the system in which we live as, if not tyrannical, then one that inhibits criticism, independence, and freedom of thought and action—all qualities we associate with living under tyrannical rule. Such a process equates to what Deleuze and Guattari term "becoming-minor," which is to say coming to see oneself as an autonomous entity within a system that can only be maintained by a radical *heteronomy* of thought and action, a surrendering of the critical and interrogative power that the autonomous individual preserves (Deleuze and Guattari 1988, 291–92). We find ourselves on a collision course with particular practices, laws, and institutions, and eventually with the governing logics of the system itself. Such an imperative is one built into contemporary society on the unquestioning acceptance of certain imperatives: the necessity for "development," "the clash of civilizations," the desirability of "normality," heterosexuality, working hard, "getting on," and "living healthily"—all euphemisms for a particular kind of discipline that remains "tacit" and understood by "the majority." To those who are excluded by this fictive consensus, to those who are in some way—or perceive themselves to be—"minor" (e.g., homosexuals, the psychologically different, the "idle," the "unhealthy," those of mixed race, the "antisocial," those who are reluctant to "identify with the brand"), such imperatives and the world of practices and procedures associated with them may well come to seem "tyrannical" and may (and do) elicit their own forms of resistance—though we will need to dig beneath the surface of everyday life to find them (see, for example, Fantasia 1988; Cohen and Taylor 1992; Scott 1992; McKay 1996).

How does all of this connect to the discussion above? Modernity has at one level rendered the question of "tyranny" redundant. This is not the same as saying that there are no tyrannies in the world—there are many. What it means is that with modernity comes a change in the nature of power and thus a change in the nature of our relationship to power, a change in the nature of ruler and ruled that makes the discourse or lexicon of political analysis increasingly questionable. This is particularly the case for what we have been terming "physicalist" conceptions of power based on a simple and simplistic equation of power as "power over" others. As Havel's discussion of the greengrocer demonstrates, power is much more insidious than such a description allows. It is less open than concealed and fluid, operating to form and reform relations between agents and structures. This requires us to look beneath the surface binary of state-society relations, beneath rulers and ruled, beneath governors and those who are governed. It requires us to look at the hidden transcripts: the subtle, undramatic, particularistic, spontaneous resistances of everyday life. It also requires us to recognize that the dichotomies propping up political science (e.g., perfect/imperfect constitutions, free/unfree) are largely redundant, even if they retain their hegemonic or "political" force. If "tyranny" has relevance for us, then it has to reflect the multiplicity of ways in which the subject is "tyrannized."

Havel's greengrocer was one among many who "lived the lie," as Havel put it. Life in contemporary society is by and large more complex than a matter of truth and lies, good and bad, tyranny and democracy. It is more a matter of a multiplicity of forms of power, and thus of resistances and transgressions against what, with Foucault, we might term microtyrannies (or "micro-fascisms" to borrow directly from Deleuze and Guattari). There is the tyranny of being "an effective and productive member of society," or a "decent law-abiding citizen"; there is the tyranny of "common sense" and of "moral majorities." Some of these "tyrannies" are no doubt easier to cope with than others, and some of them induce mere "rebellions" against the majoritarian fads of "the age." Yet some of them are more than this, serving to expose the necessity for thinking outside or beyond of modern systems of power no matter how "democratic," consensual, or stable they may seem.

SOURCES

Aristotle. 1990. *The Politics*. Trans. T. A. Sinclair. London: Guild Publishing/Penguin.

Cohen, Stanley, and Laurie Taylor. 1992. *Escape Attempts: The Theory and Practice of Resistance to Everyday Life*. London: Routledge.

Deleuze, Gilles. 1988. *Foucault*. Minneapolis: University of Minnesota Press.

Deleuze, Gilles, and Felix Guattari. 1984. *Anti-Oedipus: Capitalism and Schizophrenia*. London: Athlone Press.

———. 1988. *A Thousand Plateaus: Capitalism and Schizophrenia*. London: Athlone Press.

Fantasia, Rick. 1988. *Cultures of Solidarity: Consciousness, Action and Contemporary American Workers*. Stanford: University of California Press.

Foucault, Michel. 1977. *Discipline and Punish: The Birth of the Prison*. Trans. A. Sheridan. London: Penguin Books.

———. 2001. *Power*. Trans. R. Hurley. London: Penguin Books.

Gleason, Abbott. 1995. *Totalitarianism: The Inner History of the Cold War*. Oxford: Oxford University Press.

Havel, Vaclav. 1985. *The Power of the Powerless*. London: Hutchinson.

Hobbes, Thomas. 1968. *Leviathan*. London: Penguin.

Hough, Jerry F., and Merle Fainsod. 1979. *How the Soviet Union Is Governed*. Cambridge, MA: Harvard University Press.

Macpherson, C. B. 1962. *The Political Theory of Possessive Individualism: Hobbes to Locke*. Oxford: Oxford University Press.

McKay, George. 1996. *Senseless Acts of Beauty: Cultures of Resistance*. London: Verso.

Plamenatz, John. 1963. *Man and Society*. London: Longmans.

Scott, James C. 1992. *Domination and the Arts of Resistance*. New Haven, CT: Yale University Press.

Stavrakakis, Yannis. 1999. *Lacan and the Political*. London: Routledge.

Strauss, Leo. 1963. *On Tyranny*. Ithaca, NY: Cornell University Press.

Tormey, Simon. 1995. *Making Sense of Tyranny: Interpretations of Totalitarianism*. Manchester: Manchester University Press.

Trotsky, Leon. 1975. *Terrorism and Communism: A Reply to Karl Kautsky*. London: New Park Publications.

Chapter 7

Postcolonial African and Middle Eastern Tyrannies: Combining the Worst of the Classical and Modern Traditions

Daniel Chirot

On Saturday, March 20, 2004, the *New York Times* carried a front-page story about an obscure backwater, Equatorial Guinea. This very small Africa country merited such treatment for three reasons. First, it claimed to have been the target of a bizarre coup attempt involving mercenaries from Europe, Central Asia, America, and Africa; and second, in recent years it has become a major oil exporter. What truly piqued the interest of the *Times* editors, however, was clearly something more: the perverse nature of its vicious and utterly corrupt tyranny run by and on behalf of president Teodoro Obiang Nguema Mbasogo's extended family. Michael Wines, the *Times* reporter, wrote,

> The coup attempt . . . features a dysfunctional ruling family, a Lamborghini-driving, rap-music producing heir apparent and a bitter political opponent in exile who insists that Equatorial Guinea is run by a gonad-eating cannibal. (Wines 2004, A1, A5)

After explaining the confusing and contradictory accounts of the coup attempt and the immense poverty of the country, where oil royalties have been almost entirely stolen by the ruling family, the article provides some details about how the government tortures and murders its potential opponents, abuses its people, and is subject to real, imagined, or invented coup attempts quite routinely. It closes with a cryptic remark:

> After all, the sole successful coup here occurred in 1979 when Mr. Obiang himself, then a lowly lieutenant-colonel [my note—he was actually the commander of the army], overthrew and executed the self-proclaimed "Unique Miracle," Francisco Macias Nguema. Mr. Nguema was his uncle. It was a family affair.

Though little known to the outside world, this country, its ruling family, and its awful history have been explored by a few good scholars and even a famous novelist.[1] The full details are even worse than the *Times* story, which gives the impression that this is somewhat of a comic opera. There is nothing comic about it at all. Macías Nguema, the only other president since independence, prohibited the use of the word "intellectual" and proscribed writing letters to foreign destinations, going so far as having the right arms of some offenders cut off for doing so. He gave himself extraordinary titles, not only the aforementioned "Unique Miracle," but others such as "Grand Master of Education, Science, and Traditional Culture." His clan came from the African mainland (Rio Muni), and he slaughtered tens of thousands of islanders (the other, richer, more developed part of the country is the island formerly called Fernando Poo, now Bioko, and the small island of Annobon) to stay in power. He particularly disliked the small educated elite, hundreds of whom he had tortured to death. He usually had his victims' legs broken before proceeding with more torture. He was deposed by his family when it became evident that he had gone too far and risked being overthrown. His successor's soldiers were too frightened of his reputed witchcraft powers to execute him, so France arranged to have Moroccan troops flown in to do the deed, and Moroccans have been presidential guards since then. After 1979, Equatorial Guinea, which then was not an oil exporter, received substantial French aid. It was incorporated in the French monetary (CFA) zone and returned to being a seminormal African kleptocracy as described by economist Robert Klitgaard in his aptly named book *Tropical Gangsters*.

Suetonius' descriptions of Caligula and Nero might have been the models for the ruling Caesars of Equatorial Guinea, though it is unlikely that either of its two presidents were influenced by the classics. When Macías Nguema's residence was inspected after his overthrow, what was found in his bedroom were some of the works of North Korea's Kim Il Sung in Spanish.[2]

WHY ARE THERE SO MANY AFRICAN TYRANNIES?

If Equatorial Guinea is one of the most grotesque examples of this kind of governance, it is, unfortunately, only a bit more gruesome than many other postcolonial African cases. Everyone remembers the late Idi Amin who destroyed Uganda, engaged in mass murder and torture, and eventually stripped his economy so bare that he could no longer pay off his soldiers and so had to invade Tanzania looking for more loot. This resulted in a counterinvasion by Tanzania that overthrew him. (Young 2002, 445–63).

There was also Emperor Bokassa of the Central African Empire (now, once again, the Central Africa Republic) who was at first humored by the French and then was overthrown by them when he also went too far by murdering over one hundred school children who had not purchased the required school uniform (made by Bokassa's personal factory) (Titley 1997). The bemused Bokassa later would express his surprise about being condemned for this by saying, "I killed fewer children than they said, and they were older than they said" (Le Honde 1979).

Then there was the late President Mobutu, the "walking bank account wearing a leopard skin cap," as Bernard Kouchner characterized him, who ruled over the Congo (Zaire) for thirty-five years and systematically plundered it, leaving its economy and infrastructure in ruins (Young and Turner 1985). There has been a whole series of corrupt and sometimes vicious military dictators in Nigeria, the genocidal regimes in Rwanda and Burundi, the long-lasting rule of President Eyadema in Togo that has seen that country decline from being a putative "Switzerland" of Africa to another ruin, and many others. The most recent cases to catch international attention have been Robert Mugabe, who has managed to transform one of Africa's richest economies into one where two-thirds of the population is malnourished and where there would be mass starvation without international aid; and the Arab Government of the Sudan, which has conducted a genocidal campaign of ethnic cleansing against the black people of Darfur.[3]

The conventional ideological left-right distinctions are not the issue. Haile Mengistu Meriam of Ethiopia and Sékou Touré of Guinea (Conakry) were responsible for thousands of deaths (perhaps over a million in Ethiopia) and brought ruin to their people while trying to implement socialist development schemes. The Dos Santos clan in Angola, the inheritors of Agostinho Neto's left-socialist regime, has turned into one of the most kleptocratic of all governments. Somalia was dominated by a brutal dictatorship that was first pro-Soviet and then pro-Western, that made war on its neighbor, that set clans against each other to stay in power, and that left behind a complete ruin. On the other side, the capitalist, pro-Western regime of Félix Houphouët-Boigny in the Ivory Coast, which was one of Africa's shining success stories, entered a long period of economic stagnation in the 1980s, and after Houphouët's death in 1993, it turned into an ethnically based, corrupted autocracy beset by military coups. Since 2002, it has experienced a civil war that has divided the country. The government is run by a former socialist, Laurent Gbagbo, who now bases his rule on his ethnic kin, uses death squads to eliminate his opponents, and sanctions the disenfranchisement of northerners to win rigged elections. Nor are the rebels who control the northern part of the country better. Were they to gain control, they would probably run the same type of regime.[4]

There are some more benevolent countries in Africa: Mali, Senegal, Benin (whose dictator allowed free elections and is now back in power), Ghana (whose dictator also allowed free elections and a measure of economic reform),

Uganda (under its present relatively enlightened dictator), Tanzania, Mozambique (since it gave up its attempt to impose socialism and since the arrival of full democracy in South Africa ended outside interference that had been supporting an antigovernment guerrilla war), Botswana, and a few others, such as Niger, which is more democratic and less corrupt than it was under the rule of various military dictatorships in the 1990s. There is, of course, the South African exception, but that is so different in so many ways that it has to be excluded from this analysis. All the positive cases, however, are either very fragile democracies or autocracies that rely on having enlightened despots to keep them functioning at a reasonably, but only very relatively decent, level.

It is worth highlighting one of Africa's most notable contemporary success stories, Ghana. After a quarter century of economic decline, coups, and internal violence, it set out on a different path. Democratic reforms were gradually introduced; the inflated, corrupt, and inefficient state sector was pared down; and a somewhat fairer, more open legal system encouraged renewed investment. Over the past twenty years, Ghana has almost regained the economic level it had at independence in 1957. Jeffrey Herbst's analysis, however, emphasizes the fact that this was rendered possible by Ghana's military dictator, Jerry Rawlings, who changed his mind in power and shifted from being a socialist autocrat to a reform-minded capitalist one, and who then voluntarily relinquished power. Ghanaians know that Rawlings remains in the background, ready to seize power once more if he so decides (Herbst 1993).

What this brief overview suggests is that more often than not the fate of African countries depends heavily on whether they are ruled by a "good" autocrat or a "bad" one, and in cases such as Robert Mugabe's, it depends on whether the autocrat is in a "good" or a "bad" period of his rule. That is more than a little reminiscent of the past, when in all agrarian polities it was never autocracy as such that was judged to be tyrannical, but only the more abusive autocrats who ruled badly. Caligula and Nero were tyrants, but Trajan and Hadrian were not, even if the latter two were perhaps even more solidly autocratic than the earlier Caesars who still had to watch out for the Senate (Grant 1975).

We do not, however, live in an age of agrarian empires and kingdoms, so we are obliged to go beyond the "good king/bad king" distinction. Black Africa's governance problems, even in its better-off cases, are too systemic and widespread to be passed off as the fault of this or that individual politician or ruling party, much less as ideological wrong turns to the left or right by past governments. Besides which, one has to recognize that the "bad" rulers have been far more numerous than the "good" ones.

Even in the classical sense of the word, "tyranny" as the rule by an individual or small clique that has low legitimacy with the population, that is abusive and corrupt, and that has damaged the well-being of most of those it rules, the average postcolonial African regime has been tyrannical. Indeed, today the average African country has a lower per capita GDP than at the moment of independence. This includes countries with very large quantities of exportable resources such as Angola and Nigeria, and corruption has kept poverty high even in little countries with huge resources, like Gabon. Far too little of what wealth there has been has been invested in infrastructure, health, or education; the investment climate for both domestic as well as foreign capitalists has been almost uniformly dismal, and human rights abuses have been extraordinarily widespread. The few exceptions have barely been able to recoup earlier losses inflicted by prior regimes.[5]

The reasons for this sad state of affairs are many, and analysts differ about which are the main reasons. For a long time, "dependency" and neoimperialist theories were popular. They claimed that Africa was systematically "underdeveloped" by exploitative colonialism and neocolonialism. There is no doubt that foreign interference has often hurt African countries. The Soviets supported repressive tyrannies in Mozambique and Ethiopia, as did the West in Congo (Zaire). France has been particularly kind to some genuine monsters such as Bokassa, and even worse, to the Hutu tyranny that it armed and abetted, only to abandon it at the start of the 1994 genocide (Prunier 1997). France supported Mobutu even after the United States dropped its toleration for that regime when the Cold War ended. The civil war in Angola was fed by Soviet aid and Cuban troops on one side, and American and white South African arms, money, and men on the other. At the height of the Angolan civil war, big Western oil companies paid royalties to the repressive and corrupt "pro-Soviet" government while Cuban troops protected oil installations from the "pro-Western" UNITA rebels led by Jonas Savimbi, who was receiving American aid. The fact that Savimbi himself began as a Maoist revolutionary who never abandoned his harsh autocratic ways did not prevent his becoming the darling of conservative Americans. The presence of exportable oil or diamonds has increased corruption, not helped. Shady Lebanese, Israeli, and European diamond dealers have been involved in some of Africa's worst civil wars and tyrannies, as in Sierra Leone and Liberia.[6]

This kind of explanation, however, falls far short of being sufficient. The almost universal corruption and kleptocracy has its roots in something much deeper, the fact that Africa has been ruled by what Max Weber would have called patrimonial regimes. These are governments whose support is based on their being able to pay their armed supporters to buy their loyalty, and whose chief goal is to collect enough booty, legitimately or not, to do this. Such regimes are essentially little more than bandits. Their leaders surround themselves with relatives or ethnic kin who presumably can be trusted somewhat more than pure mercenaries. Being associated with the ruling group, such kin understand that if their clan loses power, they lose everything, including, quite possibly, their lives.

Mancur Olson has emphasized the important difference between "roving" and "stationary" bandits (Olson 2000). The former will strip the land bare as they seek simply to carry off as much loot as possible. The latter will be more cautious as they hope to stay in place a long time, and to utterly ruin their taxable base would leave them unable to pay off their troops, as happened to Idi Amin, or more recently, Charles Taylor in Liberia. That is why, according to Olson, most successful agrarian states throughout the world ruled by patrimonial regimes had hereditary rulership. Not only did this keep power within the family, but also such regimes tended, over time, to become less tyrannical and more committed to their people for the simple reason that they thought about the longer term. That commitment, however, was fragile and went overboard as soon as resources became insufficient to pay off the fighters who kept the regime in power.

Agrarian states developed all sorts of techniques to increase their legitimacy and thus reduce the costs of ruling. Turning kings into gods or representatives of gods and promoting legitimizing religions were, in the long run, effective in stabilizing patrimonial rule. The problem was that creating such legitimacy took a long time, and it never secured ruling dynasties from their internal high-class rivals, often from related families, who knew that the king was just an uncle or cousin, not a god. Nor was it sufficient to keep away jealous neighboring tribes and kingdoms who wanted the loot and hardly cared about this or that king's divinity.

Jeffrey Herbst has explained that precolonial African states were weak. Either there was little or no state structure, or else states ruled populations that could easily escape taxation. This had much to do with Africa's geography, which has few natural barriers and low population densities. Thus states, where they existed, tried to control people through clientelistic arrangements, but did not have fixed boundaries. The rulers' clients received military aid from the center in return for tribute (goods or slaves), and states tended to live by exploiting their peripheries in order to maintain control over a center that provided military might. In other words, these were weak and typically unstable patrimonial states (Herbst 2000).

Colonialism weakened whatever African state structures existed by harnessing them to the alien rule it imposed, but left weak modern structures in their place. At their best, colonial regimes had few trained functionaries, ruled for only two or three generations, and did little to help Africans catch up to the technological lag from which the continent suffered. The only major exceptions were in white settler colonies, most notably, South Africa, and to some extent Southern Rhodesia (now Zimbabwe), though the advantages bestowed on those countries by the whites were substantially negated by the marginalization of their black population.

It is, therefore, not surprising that postcolonial Africa reverted to patrimonial regimes intent on maintaining themselves in power by paying off their core supporters at the expense of their own peripheries. This was the basis of independent Africa's most glaring and widespread policy failure. As Robert Bates so clearly showed, from the start, politicized urban centers were subsidized by seizing crops from politically fragmented peasants at disastrously low prices. This ruined agriculture and turned what had been a largely self-sufficient or agricultural exporting continent into one that increasingly relies on foreign food aid (Bates 1981). Yes, the promotion of cash crops over food was started by colonial masters more interested in tropical exports than in food production, but as cases such as Ghana demonstrate, even export agriculture (in this case, cocoa) could be ruined by extracting the crop at prices below production cost to squeeze out profits in order to support urban constituencies and fanciful, prestige-development schemes. This is what led to the ruin of Ghana in its first twenty-five years of independence. In 1957, it had a per capita income higher than South Korea's or Taiwan's, and by 1983, it had a per capita income much lower than in 1957. This was not the fault of imperialism or neoimperialism but was a rational political strategy designed to keep the elite in power even as it ruined the majority rural population.

As resources from which to extract revenues decayed, patrimonial regimes were forced to rely on ever-narrower bases, and thus to become ever more predatory, leading to downward spirals that made regimes increasingly brutal and corrupt. As payoffs declined, only those closest to the ruling clique could be trusted, making nepotism worse. As revenues declined, fewer parts of the country could garner any benefits at all from the corruption, causing ethnic and regional discontent to increase.

Many of Africa's woes have been blamed on the artificial boundaries its states inherited from colonial days. These pay little or no attention to cultural boundaries and thus worsen the problem of creating legitimate state structures. As Herbst has pointed out, however, this argument is backward. In fact, respect for the international boundaries laid out in the late nineteenth and early twentieth centuries by the colonial powers has been one of the few sources of stability in Africa. If these cease to be respected, as is starting to happen with civil wars that now spill over borders throughout much of the continent, instability will grow, the time horizon of rulers will decrease, and "roving" banditry will increasingly replace the "stationary" kind.

The Ivory Coast is a dramatic case of this process. At first, because of its relative prosperity, it created a kind of "Ivoirian" loyalty. In the growing desperation to control a resource base that was no longer expanding, "Ivoirian" in the 1990s came to be defined as "southern Ivoirian," and largely Christian. That split the country. Now, the south itself is dividing along ethnic lines, and underneath the international posturing of its president, the regime is starting to behave ever more autocratically and corruptly. Were it not for the presence of French and (soon) UN troops enforcing a precarious truce, the Ivory Coast would fragment into a set of local fiefdoms ruled by warring patrimonial bandits, as has happened to both Congos, Sierra Leone, Liberia, Angola, Chad, and to some extent Sudan.

Under such conditions, what does the concept of "tyranny" contribute to an understanding of what is happening? If we look at Africa in a broad historical and comparative way, the concept can actually tell us a lot, though not in a reassuring way.

As some analysts are beginning to point out, and as the noted Weberian scholar Guenther Roth claimed decades ago, rulership in Africa is not sui generis because patrimonialism is neither new nor specifically African. Rather, Africa today in some ways resembles early medieval (postimperial) Western Europe. Weak, tribally based states then sought to assert control, but they were, at first, little more than roving bandits. As they stabilized, their rulers tried various techniques to make their rule more permanent (Roth 1968, 581–91). They claimed to be inheritors of Rome, they used Christianity and the largely Roman church hierarchy to sanctify their positions, and they sought to control their clients by granting them land in return for military service. For centuries, this failed to produce stable polities. After the fragmentation of Charlemagne's Empire, Western Europe became little more than a crowd of local regimes extracting what they could from their peasants and fighting each other as their resource bases shrank. We rarely think of tenth-century Europe as a set of little, unstable chiefdoms, but that is what they were. Rome's cities and roads were neglected, trade shrank, and the claims to broader legitimacy by Europe's kings were more fictional than real. That was why, as Marc Bloch observed, its kings tried to claim magical powers and get themselves anointed by the Christian God in hopes of securing their rule (Bloch 1924). Ultimately, however, these were entirely kin-based systems of rule in which squabbles within and between powerful families dominated the political process.

Were these little local tyrannies? By modern democratic standards, that is exactly what they were. They paid no attention to the wishes of their largely peasant populations; they were ruthless, violent, nepotistic, and autocratic. Some local rulers were better than others, and these, presumably, were viewed as "good" kings, dukes, or barons by their subjects. Others were particularly cruel or inept and were "bad" rulers. Few of their subjects thought that a different kind of governing system was possible, though revolts could and did occur whenever rulers extracted so much that the peasantry was threatened with starvation. Tyrants, then, were the "bad" rulers who overtaxed or were particularly vicious. "Good" rulers were just as autocratic, just as patrimonial, and just as ruthless as tyrants, but they did their job better. They were Mussewenis (the present ruler of Uganda), not Idi Amins.

In fact, this kind of autocracy characterized Rome and other empires as well, though if they were stable enough, empires developed religious and philosophical legal traditions that defined the difference between tyranny and legitimate rule more broadly. Greek and Roman tradition did this, as did the classical Indians and Chinese, but these restraints were somewhat of an illusion because the essence of imperial rule was always kin-based patrimonialism. Thus, essentially, "tyrants" (or their equivalent in various civilizations) were "bad" emperors, while equally autocratic ones who ruled over periods of prosperity and peace, or whose military exploits protected their core populations from harm, were not tyrants.

After the nearly total breakdown of the Roman imperial tradition in Western Europe, it took a long time for a new set of restraints to come into being. Eventually, local hereditary lords and the Church gained enough stable power to force kings to follow certain rules about how much and under what circumstances they could extract revenue, and some kings, in England, France, Castille, and a few other places, were able to lay serious claim to having some authority over larger and more stable states. As trade revived after the tenth century and towns grew more important, urban elites also obtained enough bargaining power to force lords to respect property rights and markets as a way of enhancing their revenues. The rule of law and civil society developed where the rich and powerful were able to secure their own rights against predatory kings, but where these kings were able, nevertheless, to retain some sway over their kingdoms. Kings and nobles developed competing interests in protecting their peasants to maintain a stable base of taxation. If local lords overexploited them, peasants could rely on kings, while if kings overtaxed them, they could rely on their local lords. Only very late—in the seventeenth and eighteenth centuries—did the notion develop that rulers were bound by a social contract to serve all the people, and even later, in the nineteenth and twentieth centuries, did majorities get to have much political say at all, thus insuring that state power had to take into consideration the general welfare, not just the interests of its rulers (Poggi 1978).

The history of the idea of tyranny roughly (though not precisely) mirrors these changes. In classical Greek theory, Plato, Socrates, and Xenophon defined the tyrant as a ruler who transgressed the law to gain or keep power, and then abused his power. Aristotle added that oligarchies and even democracies can be lawless and arbitrary, and thus tyrannical. In the European Middle Ages, however, as Mark Lilla has pointed out, rulership came to be vested once again entirely in the hands of war chiefs, so that the term "tyrant" came to mean little more than just a bad king. Only with the Renaissance, and more, with the Enlightenment, did the Greek notion of tyranny as nonlegitimate rule come back. Nevertheless, both conceptions of tyranny, of a "bad king" and of an arbitrary and lawless kind of rule, are similar. They both emphasize the immoral quality of the tyrant, the tyrant's (or the tyrannical clique's) depravity, and most of all, the damage this does to the abused general population (see Lilla's essay in this volume).

Only in relatively recent times has a different kind of tyranny emerged. By no stretch of the imagination could Stalin, Mao, Hitler, Pol Pot, or other revolutionary leaders who tried to transform their societies be considered simply "bad kings" or mere "usurpers" who did not follow the law. They were, instead, revolutionaries who tried to thoroughly transform their societies in ways never tried before, and, in fact, to reshape human behavior. If there is any premodern aspect to them, it is because they are akin to religious fanatics who thought they could extirpate sin by converting some and exterminating the others. Perhaps Cromwell in Ireland, where his armies used the Book of Joshua's descriptions of mass extermination of the Canaanites as a model, or the Taiping Rebellion in nineteenth-century China are premodern examples of this kind of tyranny (Fox 1992, 232; Spence 1997; Wareman 1975, 143–56).

To return to Africa, the situation is in some ways what it was in Western Europe in the centuries after the fall of Rome. The process of imperial disintegration that began forty years ago is still accelerating. The postcolonial states all tried to inherit the mantle of colonial legitimacy, with the languages, boundaries, and administrative systems bequeathed by the empires. (The only multiethnic postcolonial black African state to have made an African language its main official language is Tanzania with Swahili.) It has not worked because these are no more national states than France was under its Merovingian or Carolingian rulers, so they do not come with any inherent, built-in legitimacy (Geary 2002). African nationalists could unite in their wish to be rid of white rulers, but not far beyond that.

With low legitimacy or loyalty and weak tax bases, almost no African government had adequate resources to maintain its ruling cliques in power except through patrimonial clientelism that extracts resources from majorities to arm and feed the minority rulers. This means that whatever legal systems may have been bequeathed by the colonial powers and whatever weakened forms of traditional African legitimacy survived the colonial period, both get repeatedly violated by the new African autocrats. Everyone who has worked in any of these societies in recent years (and here I am thinking of my own experiences in 2003 and 2004 in the Ivory Coast) knows that the populations in these countries have few illusions about what goes on. Governments and politicians are regarded as largely corrupt, arbitrary, and illegitimate except by the small circle of their direct beneficiaries, and of course, by the closest clan or tribal allies of the rulers. There are, therefore, many bad African rulers, tyrants in the classical sense. As the Greek political philosophers and Machiavelli understood, however, it is not simply a matter of this or that king being bad, but of a structural situation in which the basis for a legal order and stabilized, legitimate rule are very weak.[7]

The analogy between modern Africa and post-Roman Europe is useful but can also be misleading. The reason we do not normally think of all of early medieval Europe as a set of vicious little tyrannies is that little good was expected of governments in those times. In a modern world dominated by Western Europe and North America, where norms of governance are very different, where the state is supposed to serve the needs of its people, and where kin-based patrimonial rule by stationary (much less by roving) bandits is not considered "normal" under any circumstances, standards are much higher. Not only do Westerners know this, but so do Africans. Many Africans have emigrated to the West; many more watch its movies and television programs; and most hear about pronouncements made in international forums about democracy and justice. If that were not enough, the rest of the world is moving away from patrimonial autocracy and purely bandit regimes. In East Asia, there exist old nations whose states have an inherent stability and legitimacy lacking in Africa and who have been gradually, if not always steadily, democratizing. India, for all its faults, is a functioning democracy. Its much longer period of colonial rule left it an effective high civil service, a cultural unity that reinforced its ancient pan-Indian commonalities, and a substantial, highly educated, Westernized elite. Most Latin American countries that began as patrimonial, ineffective semi-bandit states in the nineteenth century no longer tolerate the patrimonial kleptocracies that once ruled them.

This is what makes so much of Africa tragic. Its people expect much more than what they are getting from their governments, and they know that they are ensnared in unjust tyrannical political systems. Even their "good" kings are not entirely reassuring, because, like Robert Mugabe, they can change very quickly, and who knows about their successors or potential rivals?

If Africa can be explained in these terms, the problem would seem to be different if we turn our attention to the Middle East. There, tyranny has been common, and the nontyrannical rulers remain dictatorial autocrats; yet, the Middle East began its own postcolonial period with far more advantages than Africa.

WHY ARE THERE SO MANY MIDDLE EASTERN TYRANNIES?

It does not take a very deep knowledge of the Arab Middle East to notice that it has no functioning democracies, though it has had a record of impressive political stability over the past three decades. Whether one is looking at the monarchies in most of the Arabian peninsula (Yemen is the only state there that is not a monarchy) and Morocco, at the Ba'athist dictatorships (Syria, and Iraq until 2003), or at other secular dictatorships (Tunisia, Egypt, Algeria, Libya), none have been overthrown in more than three decades, except by outside invasion: Kuwait (temporarily) and Iraq (by the United States). Lebanon has in some sense been more democratic, but that was based on an uneasy coalition of different religiously defined tribes. That coalition foundered in a civil war ended only by the Syrian military occupation of Lebanon (sanctioned by the United States and Israel in return for Syria's nominal participation in the anti-Iraqi coalition during the first Gulf War of 1991.) Limited democratic elections in such places as Kuwait, Jordan, Morocco, and Egypt have not really determined who is in power, and parliaments get dismissed if they displease the monarch or president. Elections that really threaten the regime, as in Algeria in the early 1990s, are suppressed, and in that case, this led to a decade-long, bloody civil war that killed over 100,000 people (Ajami 199).[8]

Almost all Arab regimes have generated some opposition, often a great deal, and all have experienced internal political disputes within the elite; but in one way or another, they have maintained regime stability by being brutally repressive whenever necessary. At the same time, despite their stability, their records for promoting economic growth and social justice have ranged from merely fair to awful, they have been corrupt and nepotistic, and by liberal modern standards, they have all been at least somewhat, and in many cases extremely, tyrannical. Almost all these states' regimes have been able to draw on enough legitimacy (religious, traditional monarchical, as champions of "third world" socialism, or through Arab nationalism) to sustain themselves better than the majority of postcolonial African regimes, but that has not obviated the need for violent repression as well (Barnett 1988).

The first observation to make is that, on the whole, the states ruled by more or less traditional monarchies have had to be less brutal than most of the more "modern" presidential dictatorships. Algeria, Libya, Syria, and Iraq have had the most brutal regimes in the Arab world, though Tunisia's and Egypt's secular dictatorial presidencies have ruled with a lighter touch. The monarchies, on the other hand, have been repressive and autocratic but have not had to resort to the extreme bloodiness and slaughter of tens of thousands of dissidents that have characterized Algerian, Syrian, and Iraqi rule. None of the Arab monarchies have as bad a record as those three, or even as bad as Qaddafi's rule. The champion, of course, was Saddam Hussein's Iraq, though Hafez Assad's Syria in the 1980s and Algeria's military regime in the 1990s also killed on a very large scale and terrorized their populations, and in Libya the population was impoverished by their ruler who for a long time jailed and killed his opponents and savagely repressed dissent while spreading war and terrorism throughout much of Africa.

In other words, whatever their original revolutionary pretensions, the more extreme secular regimes have reverted to being quite classical tyrannies, with frightened, abusive rulers who became increasingly isolated from their people and who resorted to very high levels of brutality. Here, Xenophon's explanation of why a tyrant, for all his power, is necessarily an unhappy man is apt. Hiero the tyrant, lamenting his situation, says to Simonides the poet,

> I will tell you of another harsh affliction . . . which tyrants have. For although they are acquainted with the decent, the wise, and the just, no less than private men, [the tyrants] fear rather admire them. They fear the brave because they might dare something for the sake of freedom; the wise, because they might contrive something; and the just, because the multitude might desire to be ruled by them. When, because of their fear, they do away secretly with such men, who is left for them to use save the unjust, the incontinent, and the slavish? (Strauss 1991, 12)

The reason for this appears to be that once the modernizing project of Arab socialism, in the form of the Ba'athism, of Algerian Third Worldism, of Nasserism, or of Qaddafi's odd mixture of all of these, failed, there was no basis left to legitimize these regimes. They were therefore forced to rely on narrowing circles of the "unjust, the incontinent, and the slavish," and of course on their ethnic and religious kin whose support was assured by showering them with benefits (Ajami 1991).[9]

Gamal Nasser probably died just in time in Egypt in 1970, as his aggressive nationalism and socialist schemes had bankrupted his economy and led him from one disaster to another. He died while still popular, but one can wonder how he would have fared had he lived another ten or twenty years. It was Sadat who reaped the hatred of both the radical left and the growing Muslim extremism, and his successor, Mubarak, who has been forced to complete the retreat from any ideological pretension, combined with harsh selective repression to cement his rule (Kepel 1993).

Saddam Hussein, the most ambitious of the post-Nasser Arab nationalists, was at one time popular, but after causing two wars (against Iran and Kuwait) and losing both, he was able to hold on only through the use of massive repression and a descent into a grotesque kind of corrupt, classical tyranny (Makiya 1989, 19, 93).

The Assad regime in Syria, the other Ba'athist revolutionary party in power, held on to its ambitious nationalist program as it went from failure to failure, lost its legitimacy, and also resorted to extreme brutality to stay in power against a revolt of the Sunni Islamic Brotherhood (Ma'Oz 1988). It is a de facto monarchy whose new king inherited the presidency from his father.

The story was much the same in Algeria, once the shining image of revolutionary Arab socialism. As its transformation of the Algerian economy led to economic disaster and corruption, it lost its legitimacy, and an Islamic movement grew, gained widespread popular acceptance, and had to be repressed in blood by the ruling clique of army officers.

In all of these cases, what had been revolutionary programs regressed into tyrannical rule by a small clique. In the case of Syria and Iraq, these cliques were supported by tribal and religious minorities, Sunnis from around Tikrit and adjoining areas in Iraq, and Alawites from northwestern Syria. In Algeria, though the regime has been Arab rather than Berber, the ruling minority is not tribally or religiously based but consists of the military elite that took power after independence and their immediate successors. In Libya, Qaddafi's rule is much more based on his particular clan's support than is commonly understood, or admitted by the regime itself (Anderson 1990, 288–302, esp. 297–300). So, in a sense, these once ideological regimes transformed themselves into exactly what postcolonial African regimes are, namely narrowly based, corrupt patrimonial states increasingly obliged to rely on their privileged clients and kin to brutally stay in power. Their ideological pretensions, once used to justify their "modernizing" tyrannies, have been exposed as hollow. They have managed to set their societies on the wrong path by practicing modernizing, transformative tyranny and then combining this with the old-fashioned, corrupt kind, thus creating the worst of both.

The Arab monarchies, even those that are recent (twentieth century) creations such as Jordan's are not, however, tyrannies if they are judged by classical standards. This is not to say that they are liberal or democratic, but only that they have avoided many of the excesses of the secular tyrannies. Their kings have claimed power on the basis of tradition, and in some cases, notably in Morocco and Jordan, on the supposed descent of their dynasties from Muhammad. Many have had relatively "good" kings who have spread as much as possible the benefits of whatever riches they controlled. Saudi Arabia's and Kuwait's royal families, like those of the other Gulf states, may be corrupt and wasteful, but they have built vast numbers of schools, roads, and hospitals, and they have created huge welfare operations for their citizens. By avoiding overly ambitious nationalist or modernizing programs, they have not led their societies to ruin, as did Saddam Hussein and Qaddafi. They do not need to resort to large-scale torture and killing to stay in power, and they have managed to buy a certain level of legitimacy and considerable stability, even if they are autocratic. Morocco's monarchy has buttressed its legitimacy by resorting to nationalism and the occupation of the former Spanish Sahara. Jordan finds legitimacy and stability by relying on its Bedouin tribesmen and by skillfully trying to accommodate the wishes of its Palestinians as much as possible. Saudi Arabia's monarchy has allied itself to an eighteenth-century puritanical Islamic sect. In other words, these regimes are really quite similar to the more stable, legitimized monarchies of the past, judged on whether or not they are ruled by "good" or "bad" kings, not by the fact that by liberal standards they are patrimonial autocracies. Most of them have also had sufficient resources to stabilize their rule, unlike the newer, less legitimate, less traditional African patrimonial states.

In effect, the same is true of the more benign presidential regimes. Presidents Mubarak in Egypt and Ben Ali in Tunisia are also "good" kings broadly acceptable to their populations. Avoiding grand ideological dreams, supporting sham democracies, and ruling like old-fashioned autocrats who manage, however, to deliver both order and enough economic growth to quiet their masses, they are more like classical successful monarchs than like either modern or classical tyrants. As long as they deliver these modest benefits, their regimes can survive.

What has characterized the Arab monarchies as well as both Tunisia and Egypt is that their leaders have abandoned (as in Egypt) or never had drastic revolutionary ideological programs. They have tried to be accommodating and to promote gradual economic reforms and modernization rather than grand transformations. They have not done very well except in those monarchies with few people and a lot of oil, but they have not ruined their societies with unrealistic and lofty ambitions.[10]

Such moderation, however, will never satisfy the idealists, be they fervent Arab nationalists, Islamicists, or leftists who think that they can revolutionize their societies and turn them into avenging great powers who will get rid of Western domination and eradicate Israel. Therefore, for the extremists waiting in the wings, neither the monarchies nor the monarchical regimes in Egypt and Tunisia are legitimate. This means that if moderate progress stalls, these regimes will be faced by the choice of either collapsing or turning themselves into brutal tyrannies in order to survive.

In a way, this makes no real sense. Arab societies had long experience with complex statecraft well before the arrival of the European colonizers. They had ancient traditions of literacy, and in most cases linguistic unity. Despite the many different strands of Islam and the presence of Christian and Jewish minorities, they had Muslim majorities and a high degree of cultural unity, except perhaps in Lebanon. They also had at least a century or more of exposure to European modernization and had many more modern social and economic structures than African societies when they emerged from colonialism.

So why have Arab states reverted either to brutal tyranny or, in the more successful cases, to patrimonial monarchies (in actual name, or merely de facto in Egypt and Tunisia) with fragile legitimacy? Why is it that even their most stable and least tyrannical regimes remain autocratic and patrimonial and are also hated by their more idealistic religious and secular citizens? What will happen to the reasonably stable monarchies if they have a "bad" king? Or if there is another disastrous war against Israel? Or if a world economic crisis sweeps away their modest prosperity? We can look back at the fate of the Iraqi monarchy in 1958 and the case of nearby Iran in 1979 and find our answer—bloody revolution, the victory of extremism, and a descent into a modern kind of ideological tyranny that will degenerate into yet one more patrimonial, corrupt, but more familiar old-fashioned kind of tyranny.[11]

Because the Arab Middle East began with more advantages than sub-Saharan Africa, its poor performance and prospects are harder to explain. This, of course, brings us back to the much larger problem of why certain societies adapt better to modernization than others. Without trying to answer such a complex question completely, however, it is possible to look at the social basis of many of the Middle Eastern Arab states and find a partial answer that may be startling.

On close inspection, much of the Arab Middle East is only a few generations removed from the tribal and clan systems that underlay the large but somewhat superficial empires ruled by Mamlukes and Ottomans. Only at their centers were these empires genuine bureaucratic and stable states. Outside of the more sophisticated cities dependent on administration and trade, it was the tribes who dominated the landscape. Theirs was a world of intense feuds where the only trustworthy allies were close kin (Gellner 1990, 109–26; Tibbi 1990, 127–52).

One of the most shocking aspects of the chaos that has descended upon Iraq, supposedly one of the most modernized and nationalistic of the Arab states, is the discovery that underneath it all are tribes, clans, and religious sects that have little basis for any kind of national union except a common dislike of infidel occupiers. Syria, another relatively modernized society, is quite similar. The old tribal system has been gravely weakened by modernization, as in Africa, but not replaced by national solidarity. Tribal, clan, and sectarian politics still dominate.

It may be pure coincidence, due to the proclivities of their relatively benign rulers, that the two stable autocratic, but less abusive, less tyrannical, Arab Middle Eastern nonmonarchical states are Egypt and Tunisia. Albert Hourani has noted that these two were well-established bureaucratic states with strong armies and sufficient revenues from taxes and trade to maintain themselves as such for centuries before their exposure to the West (Hourani 1990, 303–11, esp. 303). The rest of the Arab world did not have this advantageous tradition. Therefore, in a sense, the basis of lasting political solidarity and loyalty to a national ideal existed when Egypt and Tunisia emerged into full independence from French and British rule. Those Arab societies still ruled by traditional monarchies also have a kind of traditional legitimacy. Those that deposed their tribal rulers but did not have old unified state traditions became quasirevolutionary tyrannies that degenerated into classically corrupt ones.

More legitimate, unified national entities have an easier time modernizing their state structures and can count on greater stability than ones where old tribal alliances are disintegrating but have not yet been replaced by strong national ties. Despite the appearance of greater modernity, many of the worst Arab tyrannies have, in fact, reverted to the kind of corrupt patrimonial rule that prevails in much of sub-Saharan Africa.

PROSPECTS FOR FUTURE REFORM: CAN THE LEGACIES OF TYRANNY BE OVERCOME?

The immediate prospects for the future in both Africa and the Arab Middle East are exceedingly bleak. There is little on the horizon to suggest that in Africa fundamental political reform will have enough of a base to succeed. African states will continue to rely on relatively "good kings," who may, if enough of them succeed each other, build a more stable, more benign kind of governance. Unfortunately, relying on such luck is dangerous, and a return to tyranny is always possible. As for the Arab Middle East, there is every indication that rising Islamic rage against past tyrannies, against the more stable monarchies and quasimonarchies, and against the West (represented most of all by Israel and, now, the United States) will result in greater repression, internal wars, and, in some cases, the establishment of religious tyrannies. These will no longer be classical tyrannies but modern ones with totalitarian, transformative revolutionary ideologies. Where they gain power, these religious ideologies will undoubtedly fail, as their Ba'athist and socialist predecessors did, but that will only produce a reversion to corrupt tyranny.

Are there alternatives? Turning back to history suggests that there may be, if only we pay attention to the ways in which a Western European democratic tradition evolved. What Africa needs is for its local elites, the local feudal lords, so to speak, the traditional chiefs and notables whose power was badly eroded by colonialism and delegitimized by efforts to turn colonies into modern states, to regain enough power to create stable barriers against whoever happens to be their king. Elite democracy of this sort was the basis for the construction of modern Western democracies, and it astounds me that very few of those trying to help Africa remember this. Over time, the local elites can become committed to the idea of a stable nation if their interests are protected, and as their own local powers often depend on at least the tacit support of their tribes, they can bring larger segments of the population into the nation as well. Given the rapid urbanization throughout Africa, cities should also be taken into consideration, but these consist largely of agglomerations of crowded villages, with various districts heavily dominated by immigrants from single regions and related ethnic groups. Cities have their own notables, as well as professionals, civil servants, and entrepreneurial elites. Forcing democratic elections on these states is a bad strategy because they are seen as winner-take-all events, thus inviting abuse of the electoral process. But remembering that in the West the rise of civil society was a matter of growing elite self-organization, not a mass movement, suggests that this is what African states need as well.

The recent experience of Iraq suggests that much the same process also might be better adapted to combating future tyrannies in the Arab Middle East. Jordan's monarchy has survived by catering to its various kinds of notables, from tribal Bedouin chiefs to prominent Palestinian families, much more than to mass demands or electoral democracy. The same holds for the Moroccan monarchy, and of course for the Saudi one as well, though in the latter case the growing Islamic radicalism of its religious elite threatens to bring down the monarchy. Assemblies of notables, not general elections, and the decentralization of power into the hands of regions, urban quarters, and the remnants of tribal and clan structures do not seem very modern or democratic, but they may well be the only way to avoid future tyranny.

The classical theorists who defined tyranny and who were also quite suspicious of democracy would have understood the situation better than most of our political analysts and policy makers. Whether or not there is still time to try to build, or rebuild, civil society institutions through a kind of reversion to democratic elitism in either Africa or the Middle East, however, is a big question. Also, if few active political thinkers in these regions, or their leaders, or the Western powers who have the capacity to influence them reach that conclusion, it is unlikely to happen. Are there better alternatives? Probably not. Unfortunately, not many understand this.

NOTES

1. Robert Klitgaard's *Tropical Gangsters* (1990) is about the earlier days of the present regime. Samuel Decalo's *Psychoses of Power: Africa Personal Dictatorship* (1989) concerns Macias Nguema, Idi Amin, and "Emperor" Jean-Bédel Bokassa of the Central African "Empire" (now Republic). Frederick Forsyth's book *The Dogs of War* (1976) is a fictionalized account of what actually was a bungled attempt to over-

throw Macias Nguema in which Forsyth himself participated before he became a well-known fiction writer.

2. The overthrow of Macias Nguema and subsequent events were well covered by *Jeunes Afriques*, the leading Francophone African news magazine, published in Paris. See issue 979, October 10, 1979, pp. 24–25, and issue 988, December 12, 2004, pp. 42–43.

3. Robert H. Jackson and Carl G Rosberg (1982) grasped the phenomenon a long time ago. More recently, Jeffrey Herbst (2000) has explained the weakness of African states and the resulting political disorder. The essays on Africa in Beissinger and Young (2002) provide examples, and two recent articles by Samantha Power detail events in Zimbabwe and Darfur Province in Sudan: "How to Kill a Country: Turning a Breadbasket into a Basket Case in Ten Easy Steps the Robert Mugabe Way" and "Dying in Darfur: Can Ethnic Cleansing in Sudan Be Stopped?" The best accounts of Rwanda and Burundi's genocides are, respectively, Gérard Prunier (1997) and René Lemarchand (1996).

4. On Côte d'Ivoire, see Daniel Chirot, "What provokes violent ethnic conflict? Timing, the international situation, and political choice in one African and two Balkan cases" (2005).

5. The African Development Bank's *African Development Report* (2000) tries to put as positive a spin as possible on African economics by pointing out that in the late 1990s macroeconomic performance was generally better than in the prior four decades. However, it cannot hide the facts that for four decades, per capita decline was more common than growth, and that some recent improvements are bounces from catastrophically dismal performances in the past.

6. Some of these stories are told by William Reno in *Warlord Politics and African States* (1998) and "Mafiya Troubles, Warlord Crises," in Beissinger and Young (2002).

7. It is in *The Discourses* particularly that Machiavelli speculates about the causes of tyranny, going from blaming particular individuals like Caesar to recognizing the general structural changes that produced unending abuses in Rome. See, for example, pp. 141–45, chap. 10, in the first book of *The Discourses*. Pierre Manent's (1995, 16) discussion of Machiavelli points out Machiavelli's faith in the wisdom of common people to overcome the inherent evil of politics, and in that sense calls him the first modern political analyst.

8. See also the very thoughtful review of this book by the economist Timur Kuran in *Independent Review* 3, no. 1 (1998), 111–23.

9. On third worldism in general and the tragedy of Algeria, see Robert Malley (1996).

10. There is a vast literature on these individual countries, but a good summary of the relationship between different types of regimes, politics, and economic development is Clement M. Henry and Robert Springborg (2001)

11. On Iraq, see Makiya (1989). On Iran, see Tim McDaniel's provocative comparison of the Iranian Revolution of 1979 with the Russian one of 1917: Autocracy, *Modernization, and Revolution in Russia and Iran* (1991).

SOURCES

Ajami, Fouad. 1999. *The Dream Palace of the Arabs*. New York: Vintage Books.

Anderson, Lisa. 1990. "Tribe and State: Libyan Anomalies," in *Tribes and State Formation in the Middle East*, ed. Philip S. Khoury and Joseph Kostiner, 288–302. Berkeley: University of California Press.

Ayubi, Nazih N. 1995. *Over-stating the Arab State: Politics and Society in the Middle East*. London: I. B. Tauris.

Barnett, Michael N. 1998. *Dialogues in Arab Politics: Negotiations in Regional Order*. New York: Columbia University Press.

Bates, Robert H. 1981. *Markets and States in Tropical Africa*. Berkeley: University of California Press.

Bloch, Marc. 1924. *Les rois thaumaturges*. Strasbourg: Librairie Istra.

Chirot, Daniel. 2005. "What provokes violent ethnic conflict? Political Choice in one African and Two Balkan Cases." In *Ethnic Politics after Communism*, ed. Zoltan Barany and Robert G. Moser, 140-65. Ithaca, NY: Cornell University Press.

Decalo, Samuel. 1989. *Psychoses of Power: Africa Personal Dictatorship*. Boulder, CO: Westview.

Forsyth, Frederick. 1976. *The Dogs of War*. New York: Viking Press.

Fox, Robin Lane. 1992. *The Unauthorized Version: Truth and Fiction in the Bible*. New York: Alfred A. Knopf.

Geary, Patrick J. 2002. *The Myth of Nations: The Medieval Origins of Europe*. Princeton, NJ: Princeton University Press.

Gellner, Ernest. 1990. "Tribalism and the State in the Middle East," in *Tribes and State Formation in the Middle East*, ed. Philip S. Khoury and Joseph Kostiner, 109-26. Berkeley: University of California Press.

Grant, Michael. 1975. *The Twelve Caesars*. New York: Scribner's.

Henry, Clement M., and Robert Springborg. 2001. *Globalization and the Politics of Development in the Middle East*. Cambridge: Cambridge University Press.

Herbst, Jeffrey. 1993. *The Politics of Reform in Ghana, 1982–1991*. Berkeley: University of California Press.

———. 2000. *States and Power in Africa*. Princeton, NJ: Princeton University Press.

Hourani, Albert. 1990. "Tribes and States in Islamic History." In *Tribes and State Formation in the Middle East*, ed. Philip S. Khoury and Joseph Kostiner, 303–12. Berkeley: University of California Press, 1990.

Jackson, Robert H., and Carl G. Rosberg. 1982. *Personal Rule in Black Africa: Prince, Autocrat, Prophet, Tyrant*. Berkeley: University of California Press.

Kepel, Gilles. 1993. *Muslim Extremism in Egypt: The Prophet and the Pharaoh*. Berkeley: University of California Press.

Klitgaard, Robert. 1990. *Tropical Gangsters*. New York: Basic Books.

Kuran, Timur. 1998. "Review of *Over-stating the Arab State: Politics and Society in the Middle East*." *Independent Review* 3 (1): 111–23.

Lemarchand, René. 1996. *Burundi: Ethnic Conflict and Genocide*. Cambridge: Cambridge University Press.

Liniger-Goumaz, Max. 1988. *Small Is Not Always Beautiful: The Story of Equatorial Guinea*. London: Hurst.

Ma'Oz, Moshe. 1988. *Asad: The Sphinx of Damascus*. New York: Weidenfeld and Nicholson.

Machiavelli, Niccolò. 1950. *The Prince and the Discourses*. New York: Modern Library.

Makiya, Kanan. 1989. *The Republic of Fear: The Politics of Modern* Iraq. Berkeley: University of California Press.

———. 1993. *Cruelty and Silence: War, Tyranny, Uprising and the Arab World*. New York: W. W. Norton.

Malley, Robert. 1996. *The Call from Algeria: Third Worldism, Revolution, and the Turn to Islam*. Berkeley: University of California Press.

Manent, Pierre. 1995. *An Intellectual History of Liberalism*. Trans. Rebecca Balinski. Princeton, NJ: Princeton University Press.

McDaniel, Tim. 1991. *Autocracy, Modernization, and Revolution in Russia and Iran*. Princeton, NJ: Princeton University Press.

Olson, Mancur. 2000. *Power and Prosperity: Outgrowing Communist and Capitalist Dictatorships*. New York: Basic Books.

Poggi, Gianfranco. 1978. *The Development of the Modern State*. Stanford: Stanford University Press.

Power, Samantha. 2003. "How to Kill a Country: Turning a Breadbasket into a Basket Case in Ten Easy Steps the Robert Mugabe Way." *Atlantic Monthly*, December: 86–94.

———. 2004. "Dying in Darfur: Can Ethnic Cleansing in Sudan Be Stopped?" *New Yorker*, August 30: 56–73.

Prunier, Gérard. 1997. *The Rwanda Crisis: History of a Genocide*. New York: Columbia University Press.

Reno, William. 1998. *Warlord Politics and African* States. Boulder, CO : Lynne Rienner.

———. 2002. "Mafiya Troubles, Warlord Crises." In *Beyond State Crisis: Postcolonial Africa and Post-Soviet Eurasia in Comparative Perspective*, ed. Mark Beissinger and Crawford Young, 105-27. Washington, DC: Woodrow Wilson Press/Johns Hopkins University Press.

Roth, Guenther. 1968. "Personal Rulership, Patrimonialism, and Empire-Building in the New States." In *State and Society*, ed. Reinhard Bendix, 581-91. Boston: Little, Brown and Company.

Spence, Jonathan. 1997. *God's Chinese Son: The Taiping Heavenly Kingdom of Hong Xiuquan*. New York: W. W. Norton.

Strauss, Leo. 1991. *On Tyranny*. New York: The Free Press.

The African Development Bank's African Development Report. 2000. Oxford: Oxford University Press.

Tibbi, Bassam. 1990. "The Simultaneity and the Unsimultaneous: Old Tribes and Imposed Nation-States in the Modern Middle East." In *Tribes and State Formation in the Middle East*, ed. Philip S. Khoury and Joseph Kostiner, 127-52. Berkeley: University of California Press.

Titley. E. Brian. 1997. *Dark Age: The Political Odyssey of Emperor Bokassa*. Montreal: McGill-Queen's University Press.

Wakeman, Frederic. 1975. *The Fall of Imperial China*. New York: The Free Press.

Wines, Michale. 2004. "Where coup plots are routine, one is not." *New York Times*, March 20: A1, A5.

Young, Crawford. 2002. "After the Fall: State Rehabilitation in Uganda." In *Beyond State Crisis: Postcolonial Africa and Post-Soviet Eurasia in Comparative Perspective*, ed. Mark Beissinger and Crawford Young, 445-463. Washington, DC: Woodrow Wilson Press/Johns Hopkins University Press.

Young, Crawford, and Thomas Turner. 1985. *The Rise and Decline of the Zairian State*. Madison: University of Wisconsin Press.

Chapter 8

Tyranny and Tragedy in Nietzsche: From the Ancient to the Modern

Tracy B. Strong

> What kind of man must one be in order to set one's hand on the wheel of history?
>
> —Max Weber, *Politics as a Vocation*

We tend to think of tyranny as a politically unhealthy situation. Plato warns against it and in the *Republic* sets it up as the polar opposite of the best state. Aristotle, likewise, in Book 8.10 of the *Politics*, considers tyranny to be "the worst deviant form, . . . the contrary of the best." And a perusal of the major figures in Western political theory shows that almost all of them tend to repeat in one or another manner the Plato-Aristotle understanding. The tyrant is the person who exercises power "not [in] the interests of the whole body," as Hume put it in "That Politics May be Reduced to a Science," but in his own. Only Hobbes partially escapes the pattern when he declares in *De Cive* (chapter 7.1) that "A tyranny is not a diverse state from a legitimate monarchy."[1]

Hobbes was not entirely off the mark, however. The Greek word for "tyrant" (*turannos*) betrays what is to most of us a certain ambivalence. Inside the same text (i.e., the *Oedipus Tyrannos*), it is used to designate a king, an absolute ruler, and (if insolent) imperious or despotic behavior. In all cases it refers to a person not limited by law or constitution. Greek usage was reserved for supernatural beings until Archilochus applied it to Gyges in the seventh century. If we think of tyranny only as an unhealthy body politic, we might ask how is it that we have come to share the sense that has come down in the canon and lost the multiplicity of the original?

In notes written during the winter of 1883–1884, Nietzsche elaborates the idea in the context of establishing a hierarchy of those who have the ability to make appearance real. He establishes a hierarchy of "creative strength," which goes from "the artist, who makes a character from himself; (2) the poet, the artist, the painter; (3) the teacher (Empedocles); (4) the conqueror; (5) the lawgiver (philosopher)."[2] All those named in this list have in common that they construct, as we now say, reality—that is, they provide the terms (which could be in a work of art) by which we understand the world. In a real sense, the world that is understood in a particular set of terms *is* the world of those terms and thus, to some degree, also the world that the originator or origination of those terms gives us.[3] Not named in this first list is the tyrant; yet, as we shall see, the tyrant is cousin to those of "creative strength." In the last book of the *Genealogy of Morals*, Nietzsche draws up a similar list of those who create and shape a world. Here he is speaking of those whose role it is to take care of the slavish morality (they are themselves slavishly moral). They can be "a support, a resistance, a prop, a compulsion, taskmaster, a tyrant, a god."[4] The intensification in this sequence is one of world creation and maintenance.

Where and how, for Nietzsche, does the tyrannical make its appearance in human life? He finds it in areas with which we moderns would normally not associate it. In *Beyond Good and Evil*, he argues that the limitations of Stoicism come from the fact that they insisted on seeing nature as "stoic and that with time this became what nature was for them. . . . But this is an old everlasting story: what happened then with the Stoics still happens to-day, *as soon as ever a philosophy begins to believe in itself.* It always creates the world in its own image; it cannot do otherwise; *philosophy is this tyrannical impulse itself*, the most spiritual Will to Power, to the 'creation of the world,' to the *causa prima*."[5] There is no avoiding the creation of the world in one's own image—so much we might say is the lesson that Nietzsche draws from Kant—the difficulty comes when one comes to believe that the image that one has created is in fact the way that the world is.[6] Here Nietzsche designates the belief in the naturalness of what one understands the world to be as the essence of the tyrannical impulse and holds it to be a more or less natural consequence of any philosophy. Philosophy is or wants to be a creation of the world, but it also fatally takes the world it creates as its own world. To return to the hierarchy of world makers above, philosophy is in effect a form of law giving, of saying, "thus it shall be."[7]

Tyranny thus arises for Nietzsche from *the failure to remember* that we live in worlds that have been made:[8] tyranny is thus a forgetting of human agency, one might say. Much as the famous passage about "truth" as a "worn out metaphor," as an "illusion of which one has forgotten what it really is,"[9] there is thus a kind of built-in amnesia about tyranny, an amnesia that accompanies all acts of volition. The will, as Nietzsche notes in the chapter "On Redemption" in *Zarathustra*, "cannot break time."[10]

The point here, however, has to do with what tyranny *means*: it is in its essence the taking as accomplished the world that one has defined and the forgetting that the world in which one lives is one that one has made. It is for this reason that Nietzsche can write in *Beyond Good and Evil* that the "will to truth . . . is will to power."[11] It follows from this, however, that Nietzsche does not, and cannot, simply assume that one can at one's leisure forego this process. Why not? The most noteworthy characteristic of the tyrant is his (her?) belief in his own understanding of the world as simply and finally true and his failure to question that belief. Nietzsche does not think that one should simply *not* believe in what one does, but adopt, as it were, a kind of benevolent skepticism toward oneself.

To get a better idea of what this might mean, I propose that we read what Nietzsche has to say about tyranny in the context of two other sources. To do so will be to advance an argument about what Nietzsche had in mind when he wrote of (ancient) tyranny. There is an important family resemblance between what Nietzsche says about the tyrant and what has been and was being said about the genius.[12] Emerson, with whose dwelling Nietzsche was intimately acquainted, wrote of the genius:

> To believe your own thought, to believe that what is true for you in your private heart is true for all men, — that is genius. Speak your latent conviction, and it shall be the universal sense; for the inmost in due time becomes the outmost, — and our first thought is rendered back to us by the trumpets of the Last Judgment. Familiar as the voice of the mind is to each, the highest merit we ascribe to Moses, Plato, and Milton is, that they set at naught books and traditions, and spoke not what men but what they thought. A man should learn to detect and watch that gleam of light which flashes across his mind from within, more than the lustre of the firmament of bards and sages. Yet he dismisses without notice his thought, because it is his. In every work of genius we recognize our own rejected thoughts: they come back to us with a certain alienated majesty. Great works of art have no more affecting lesson for us than this.[13]

For Emerson, the following: (1) The genius knows what is true in his heart and knows this also to be true of all humanity; (2) It is a speaking of oneself that is in question; (3) Most men have this, but few recognize that they do; (4) Genius has the quality of allowing others to recognize themselves in it: it is thus creative of a community; (5) The fundamental mode of this is aesthetic.

It is important to realize that Emerson is here developing a thought that he learned, one suspects strongly, from reflection on his reading of Kant's *Critique of the Power of Judgment*. Kant had posed the problem of aesthetic judgment as that of the relation between what appears to be a subjective individual judgment and the claim that that judgment was valid generally. He had argued that the aesthetic quality is free from "all constraint by arbitrary rules."[14] It appeared as natural—that is, as given in and of itself. Such is "beautiful art"—art which Kant argues is both purposive and without an end. As such, the origin of that which we experience as art must be without apparent foundation, as it is grounded in precisely the incomprehensible.[15] So the question naturally arises as to how the work of art comes into being, since such a work is the work of "subjective universality" (that is, it is made beautiful without referring to any concept).[16] Somewhat later in the section, Kant differentiates between the perceiver of beauty and its creator, and clearly thinks that accounting for the creation of beauty a more difficult matter. It is this that leads Kant to introduce the idea of genius.

The genius is "the talent (natural gift) that gives the rule to art."[17] The genius has the complete freedom of incomprehensibility. He (she?) "does not know himself how the ideas for [the beautiful work of art] come to him, and also does not have it in his power to think up such things at will or according to plan, and to communicate to others precepts that would put them in a position to produce similar products."[18] This is originality, which for Kant means that what the genius accomplishes cannot be confined to, nor explained by, any systematic understanding. In the *Anthropology*, Kant is clear that the word applies only to an "artist" and only to the artist who does something original. Later in that book, he can write that "Genius . . . glitters like a momentary phenomenon which appears and disappears at intervals, and vanishes again. It is not a light that can be kindled at will and kept burning for a period of one's choosing, but it is rather like a spark scattering flash which a happy seizure of the spirit entices from the productive imagination."[19] Here it is worth noting that even Newton does not make the cut, as it were, for what he did could be set out for all to understand and thus could in principle have been discovered by others.[20] Indeed, Kant thought that at times it might be hard to distinguish the genius from the madman.[21]

Kant does not in the *Critique of the Power of Judgment* provide criteria by which to differentiate the genius from the lunatic; nor, I think, can he. The mark of art is that it is always questionable, always fragile as art. The genius here, for both Emerson and Kant, is kin to the tyrant. He (she?) is the person whose belief in and actions from himself are such that the world he brings about becomes a world for everyone (a version one might say of the relation of the subjective and the universal that Kant saw as central to aesthetic judgments).

The genius and the tyrant thus function much in the same way, although it is not clear whether the amnesia that affects the tyrant also affects the genius. What can be done, though, about the impulse to forget? Nietzsche says that one of the cures that the Greeks apparently found for the amnesia inherent in tyranny was murder. Thus: "The tyrants of the spirit were almost always murdered and had only sparse lasting consequences (*Nachkommenschaft*)."[22] The solution may appear drastic, but Nietzsche holds it as part of the virtue of Greek politics that those who would fix once and for all the polis in their own terms were soon done away with. Thus in the first volume of *Human, All Too Human*, Nietzsche writes of ancient philosophers. Each of them, he says,

> was an aggressive violent tyrant. The happiness in the belief that one possessed the truth has perhaps never been greater—so also the hardness, the exuberance, the tyrannical and the evil of such a belief. They were a tyrant, that is, that which each Greek wanted to be and which each was when he could be. Perhaps Solon constitutes an exception; in his poems he speaks of how he spurned personal tyranny. But he did this out of love for his work, for his law giving, and the law-giver is a sublimated form of the tyrannical.[23]

This is pretty much the theme to which he will return in the passage from *Beyond Good and Evil* cited at the beginning of this essay. Inherent in philosophizing is a tyrannical element, which is the belief in the possession of the truth. The desire that what one believed in one's heart be true for all is both the essence of that element and a goal fervently sought after by ancient Greeks. It follows from this that the restraint on tyranny will not come from philosophy. This is not only because, as Alexandre Kojève wrote, "The philosopher's every attempt at directly influencing the tyrant is necessarily ineffectual,"[24] but because philosophy is in itself tyrannizing.

The additional element here is that law is understood as a form of violence, as a sublimation of the tyrannical impulse.[25] In addition, it is clear that the drive to tyranny is a necessary quality of thought. If all will is will to power, as Nietzsche will write later, then all will is the will to make the world in one's own image (whatever that image be) and is thus, as it were, a kind of passive categorical imperative. The praise that Nietzsche finds for this arrangement derives from the fact that precisely the competition set up by the desire of each to be tyrant produces a situation where nothing is lasting.

In this early period, what kept philosophy from tyrannizing? Here Nietzsche's answer is importantly political. The political system led to the killing of tyrants. Yet this solution—one that was later to be given a central place in Machiavelli's conception of political foundation—to tyranny cannot be complete. What if a tyrant is not killed? What if he constantly wins? This matter is not limited to what we would ordinarily name "philosopher." The paradigmatic case here is Homer, who is in effect a kind of philosopher-tyrant for Nietzsche. He writes:

> *Homer.*— The greatest fact about Greek culture remains the fact that Homer became Panhellenic so soon. All the spiritual and human freedom the Greeks attained

> goes back to this fact. But at the same time it was also the actual doom of Greek culture, for, by centralizing, Homer made shallow and dissolved the more serious instincts of independence. From time to time an opposition to Homer arose from the depths of Hellenic feeling; but he always triumphed. All great spiritual powers exercise a suppressing effect in addition to their liberating one.[26]

Homer, Nietzsche concludes, "tyrannizes."

Whereas Homer had in effect defined what it meant to be Greek, fatally that which was Greek then had difficulty in escaping from the constraints of the world that had come from Homer. (Here it is worth noting that Nietzsche does not attribute this achievement to a putative person, "Homer," but thinks that "Homer" became the name for what was achieved.)[27] The problem for Greece was to move away from the effective tyranny of Homer while remaining Greek. The point of his analysis of both the "pre-Socratics" and of the birth of tragedy was to explore how it was possible (for it was necessary) to redefine what it meant to be Greek in light of the developments (living in cities, commerce, breakdown of the preeminence of blood relations, development of currency, writing, etc.)[28] that had intervened.[29]

This was one of the central concerns of his early book, *Philosophy in the Tragic Age of the Greeks*. This book, which remained unpublished and indeed unfinished, is about philosophy and politics and tragedy, or about the possibility of philosophy and about the role of philosophy in making culture possible, about what that might mean in terms of a valuation of the everyday and as a possibility of the production of (one's own) genius.

It is well-known that Nietzsche argued in the *Birth of Tragedy* that tragedy had as its purpose the revitalization of common culture in Greece. A locus of collective participation, a common festival, it was the focus where the culture came together and pursued its understanding of itself. I have elsewhere investigated the working of tragedy in detail and will not repeat that analysis here.[30] But what is often not understood is the relation of tragedy to philosophy. And here Nietzsche's analysis is one of a failed opportunity—a failure that is nonetheless important for our understanding.

He had argued that the philosophers before Socrates had reformation in mind. They were, as he says at one point, *lauter Staatsmänner*.[31] But, he is clear also, the project of reformation fails: the "dawn remained almost only a ghostly appearance."[32] Even the one of these philosophers who came the closest—Empedocles—whose "soul had more compassions (*Mitleiden*) than any Greek soul [and] perhaps still not enough, for in the end, Greeks are poor at this and the tyrannical element became a hindrance in the blood of even the great philosophers."[33] This despite the fact that "something new was in the air, as proves the simultaneous emergence of tragedy."

The point of *Philosophy in the Tragic Age of the Greeks* is to explore the relation of philosophy and philosophers to tragedy. If one reads *Philosophy in the Tragic Age* together with *The Birth of Tragedy* (as Nietzsche had intended they should be read), the conclusion is that tragedy was necessary to put an end to the tyranny of Homer over Greece: that is, to solve the political problem of adapting to the new conditions that had arisen since Homer. What Nietzsche shows is that the unity of tragedy, philosophy, and politics that had been possible does not come off—in great part due to the effects of Socratism.

What had been possible? The forms of the philosophical voice as Nietzsche develops them in his diadochical analysis of the philosophers who make the tragic age possible, are the following.[34] What follows here, in other words, are the spiritual and epistemological presuppositions that make tragedy possible:

1. One must have a *scientific* (nonmythical) understanding of the world. (Here one should remember that Nietzsche considers himself (properly in German) to be doing science—*Wissenschaft*—in his philology.[35] The point however is not to ground the polity on science but to make possible, as he argues in the *Birth*, a regrounding on a mythic understanding. (I take a myth to be a story of which one accepts the authority while knowing that it is truthful rather than true.) This is a refoundation for the polis. *Thales* is Nietzsche's exemplar of this: he makes possible, Nietzsche notes, a pan-Hellenism that would have been the only way of preventing the Persian Wars.[36]
2. One must bring to the foreground an account of the centrality of change and contingency. Nietzsche finds this in *Anaximander*. Without such an account we will be kept from Dionysian knowledge, that is, the knowledge of the transitoriness of the worlds in which we live. Hamlet is the prototype of the Dionysian man for Nietzsche.
3. The third part of the philosophical voice is the realization that not only is all impermanent, but that as things come into being and pass away, that which is is always in conflict. Conflict is immanent in existence, and definiteness is thus a denial of existence. (In *Experience*, Emerson says, "Our love of the real draws us to permanence, but health of the body consists in circulation, and sanity of mind in variety or facility of association. We need change of objects."[37]) In Greece this voice is that of *Heraclitus*, for whom the world was a game "of the child Zeus" and of "fire with itself."
4. Next, we need to know that that which is comes not from that which is not, but only from itself. (A point Heidegger was to drive to the ground.) Truth is therefore not a predicate of phenomena, of that which appears. Here the voice was that of *Parmenides*.

5. With this, we must acknowledge the centrality of plurality, especially of value. The world is thus nonrational but nevertheless is one, and its unity lies in its appearance, in its beauty. This is the voice of *Anaxagoras*.

   The finished text of *Philosophy in the Tragic Age of the Greeks* breaks off here. We know from the notes that had Nietzsche finished it, he would have dealt with three other elements that speak in a philosophical voice:

6. *Democritus* holds to the necessity of an aesthetic understanding, that is, that our world is made and shaped. To Anaxagoras, Democritus adds the claim that the world is necessary and comprehensible and focused in this world, in the polis.
7. *Empedocles* holds that value, beauty, and reality are of and in the world only and that they result from, as well as lead to, different perspectival stances. Nietzsche calls attention to his political reforms and relates him to the Pythagoreans. He is a "democrat, who has social reform up his sleeve" and is identified with "love, democracy and communal property."[38]
8. It is not hard to find each of these elements as making possible the analysis of the *Birth of Tragedy*. All of this laid the necessary foundations for and could have supported a tragic age. But here things went awry. Instead of completing the process of making tragedy possible—thus curbing the tyranny of philosophy—the last of the philosophers puts an end to the possibility of tragedy. He is "the virtuoso of life," *Socrates*.[39] "With Empedocles," Nietzsche writes, "the Greeks were well on their way toward assessing correctly the irrationality and suffering of human existence; but thanks to Socrates, they never reached the goal." Socrates, Nietzsche goes on to note, "(1) destroys the ease (*Unbefangenheit*) of ethical judgment; (2) annihilated science; (3) had no feeling (*Sinn*) for art; (4) wrenched the individual from any historical bonds; (5) furthered dialectical verbiage and chatter."[40] In fact, "after Socrates it is no longer possible to preserve the common weal (*das allgemeine Wohl*)."[41] Tragedy would have provided the counter to the tyrannical elements of philosophy. In Nietzsche's analysis, the failed union takes the form of Socratic rationality, and this in turn permits the tyranny of a single philosophical voice.

What might an age of a marriage of philosophy and tragedy have made possible?[42] Part of the answer is to be found in Nietzsche's claim that only in Greece during the "immense" period between Thales and Socrates, has the philosopher been *at home*, and not a "chance random wanderer,"[43] "conspiring against his fatherland."[44] For a philosopher not to be a "comet," a culture is needed. His task, as he sets it, is "to describe the world, in which the philosopher and the artist are at home."[45] Thus Nietzsche writes that he wants "to know how philosophy behaves towards an existing or developing culture which is not the enemy."[46] In order to know this, "one must know that which we call his age."[47]

These early philosophers (whom we refer to as the "pre-Socratics" but whom Nietzsche usually calls the "pre-Platonics") can only be understood, he avers, if we "recognize in each of them the attempt and the initiation (*Ansatz*) to be a Greek Reformer."[48] The culture in which these philosophers were at home was the "tragic age." In other words, each of these philosophers embodied an element of what it meant to do philosophy, something that in Greece was done as the exponent and proponent of a culture. Philosophy and politics and tragedy are close to being co-terminal—or they should be. The focus on the tragic age has to do with whether or not the Greeks will successfully incorporate these elements into the world that issues from the Peloponnesian War. In a collection of fragments to which Nietzsche gave the general name *Science and Wisdom in Conflict*, we find: "One can describe these older philosophers as those who felt the Greek air and customs as a constraint and barrier: thus as self-liberators (the war of Heraclitus against Homer and Hesiod, Pythagoras against secularization, all against myth, especially Democritus. . . .). I conceive of them as the precursors of a reformation of the Greeks: but not that of Socrates. One set of occurrences carried all of the reforming spirits along: the development of Tragedy."[49] Tragedy in this understanding is a "means" to carry out a reformation and is to be seen as *made possible by* and as *a continuation of* the individual achievements of the philosophers. Thus *Philosophy in the Tragic Age of the Greeks* is an investigation of what lies behind and leads up to the developments discussed in *The Birth of Tragedy*. In the latter book, the elements of that which was "Greek" had remained unexamined. More importantly, *the role of philosophy in making tragedy possible and of tragedy in putting an end to a tyranny and in making the polis possible* had disappeared under the destructive Socratic enterprise. If philosophy is consequent to and evincing of the "human willingness to allow questions for itself which it cannot answer with satisfaction,"[50] thus of humanness itself, then Nietzsche's accusation against the effects of Socratism is that it makes such philosophy and the human impossible.

This is, as I understand it, the central message in Heidegger's analysis of the great choral ode in *Antigone* on the human.[51] Heidegger calls attention to he who is *hupsipolis*—which he translates as *hochüberragend*: standing high above, that is, not part of the polis. The polis, as Heidegger understands it, is the "historical place, the There *in* which, *from* which and *for* which history happens."[52] To be above this—as a tyrant—is to be *apolis*. This is why philosophy tempered with and by tragedy could have led to a "tragic age of the Greeks" and to political health.

Nietzsche in fact writes to Rohde in March 1873 that he is working on a book about Greek philosophy that he thinks he may call "the philosopher as the physician of culture."[53] He has hopes, in other words, to accomplish in his time that which Socrates obviated in Ancient Greece. However, that project—the joining of philosophy and politics in tragedy—failed in Greece, and we are for Nietzsche the inheritors of that failure. What, then, is the problem of tyranny in modern times? It makes a difference, says Nietzsche, whether it is "Homer, or science (*Wissenschaft*) or the Bible that tyrannizes."[54] But if it "makes a difference," the difference is not simply of the substitution of one tyrannical paradigm for another. It also makes a difference which paradigm it is that happens to tyrannize; there is a difference in the *kind* of tyranny. In the second volume of *Human, All Too Human*, he returns to his theme in a new context.

> *Tyrants of the Spirit.*— In our time we speak of each who would forcibly be the expression of a moral discipline, such as the characters in Theophrastus and Molière, as ill and speak of a "fixed idea" in that relation. The Athenians of the fourth century would appear to us as deluded madmen, if we could make a visit to them. Now the democracy of concepts rules every head:—the leader is many taken together: a single idea that wishes to become master is now called, as was said, a "fixed idea." This is our way of killing tyrants—we send them to an insane asylum.[55]

How has mankind passed from one to the other? What are we to make of that change? What is the nature of that change? These are all questions that concerned Nietzsche throughout his life. Indeed a preliminary answer is given already in the continuation of an earlier citation:

> The period of the tyrants of the spirit is past. In the spheres of higher culture there will always have to be a mastery, to be sure—but this mastery will hereafter lie in the hands of the oligarchs of the spirit. Despite their territorial and political divisions, they constitute a close-knit society whose members know and recognize one another, a thing which public opinion and the judgments of the writers for the popular papers may circulate as expressions of favor and disfavor. The spiritual superiority which formerly divided and created hostility now tends to unite: how could the individual keep himself aloft and, against every current, swim along his own course through life if he did not see here and there others of his own kind living under the same conditions and take them by the hand, in struggle against both the ochlocratic character of the half-spirited and half-educated and the attempts that occasionally occur to erect a tyranny with the aid of the masses? The oligarchs have need of one another, they have joy in one another, they understand their emblems—but each of them is nonetheless free, he fights and conquers in his own place, and would rather perish than submit.[56]

Nietzsche here differentiates between tyranny and oligarchy. He opposes *both* to ochlocracy, the rule by the mob. The nature of modernity is not only the replacement of tyranny by oligarchy but a transformation of the political system into one divided between a ruling elite and a potential mob. In *Politics as a Vocation*, Max Weber lamented the disappearance of what Nietzsche saw as the ancient mode. For the *Fachmenschtum* of the present, he wrote, "the price that has to be paid for having leaders . . . is only this stark choice: either a democracy with a leader together with a machine, or a leaderless democracy, in other words, the rule of professional politicians who have no vocation and lack the inner charismatic qualities that turn a man into a leader."[57] Charisma—the gift of grace—is of course the belief in oneself and in the universality (at least for a people) of one's voice. Paradoxically, the absence of those who take their own vision to be universally valid generates both stability and a mass-elite division. The present situation is one in which there is, as Nietzsche remarks in *Zarathustra*, "one herd and no shepherd," where everyone is the same and wants the same, and where anyone who feels differently is sent to the insane asylum.[58] Tyranny in the ancient world was a natural potentiality. The achievement of tragedy was to make tyranny impossible. But in the modern world, tragedy has disappeared. It has disappeared consequent to what Nietzsche calls Socratic rationalism: if we do not want to blame Socrates, we can at least see that the dynamic that he has identified is the same as what Max Weber called "the demagnification [*Entzauberung*] of the world through science." The modern world holds that there is an explanation for whatever happens, and persists in the pursuit of such explanations. But the conviction that there is an explanation to be had is itself a modern prejudice and leads not so much to tyranny as to a search for tyranny. But since this search can never accomplish itself, modern man is in the position of pursuing the unattainable—the consequences of which form the basis for Nietzsche's understanding of nihilism.

It is for this reason that Nietzsche insists that the philosopher-tragedian (poet) is a lawgiver, one who is able to say and to have acknowledged, "thus it shall be." In the period of the morality of custom, the lawgiver appeared necessarily as a "healer and in some manner a demi-God: that is to say that he was to create customs—a task both frightening and of a mortal peril."[59]

The lawgiver is, for Nietzsche, not a being having anything to do with nature. "Basic proposition: in nature there is no compulsion, no spirit outside that of the human and humanness, there is no miracle and no providence, no creator, no lawgiver, no sin, no punishment."[60] It is important to realize that Nietzsche does not think that any pronouncement of "thus shall it be" by any person will constitute the giving of a law. The point of the above analysis was to show that Nietzsche thinks that a lawgiver must have acquired certain qualities, qualities that he or she will have by training rather than by constitution. It is a matter of entitlement. This was the point behind Max Weber's question that serves as an epigraph to this essay.[61]

The matter is not as distant from us as we might like to think. What underlies law? Take the following case. In John Ford's *The Man Who Shot Liberty Valance*, the setting is a small Western town, on the edge of the world of law, established enough to have women and farmers, but not established enough to have churches and schools. The town is controlled by a cartel. Two characters set each other off: the one, Tom Doniphon (John Wayne), is a feared gunslinger who lives by his own law; the other, Liberty Valance (played by Lee Marvin), is also a gunslinger and enforces the will of the cartel. Both are men of skill and ability with the guns that allow them to live by their own will. Into the town comes Ransom Stoddard (James Stewart), a lawyer (whom Doniphon calls "tenderfoot" and "Pilgrim"). He helps the women, is seen in an apron washing dishes, and winds up in a duel with Liberty Valance, a task that he does not avoid though he has no skill with a gun. In the gunfight, Valance is shot dead. From the resultant fame, Stoddard is elected senator when the territory becomes a state, he breaks the power of the evil cartel that had controlled the area, and he institutes numerous progressive policies. He brings the rule of law. It turns out, though, that Valance was shot not by Stoddard but by Doniphon, from hiding. Doniphon had been in love with the woman whom Stoddard marries; knowing that her happiness would only come with civilization, he had broken his own code, murdering Valance by shooting him the back so that it would appear that Stoddard was a hero.[62]

The Wayne character, like the Marvin character, is beyond the law, beyond good and evil. The Marvin character can get away with it because he is strong; the Wayne character can get away with it because he is strong enough to impose law on himself, that is, to allow the existence of something other than the realization of his own will.[63] The effect of what Doniphon does in killing Liberty Valance (such is the price of human liberty under the law, as it were) is to make possible a legal and moral code. He makes it possible by killing Valance, but that possibility can only come about because it is not known that he kills Valance. In Ford's presentation, law and morality depend upon a veiling of origins, origins that have as their intent the bringing about of a moral and legal world.

There is, I think one feels, something admirable about what the Wayne character has done. Yet he has clearly acted beyond the law that makes civilization possible—being *hupsipolis*, he is *apolis*. Like the Marvin character, he is unto himself, but contrary to the Marvin character, while his actions are also beyond the law, they make law possible.[64] He knows that he does not matter, in the end. The fact that we admire him is an indication, I think, of what Nietzsche was getting at in his suggestion that law and philosophy will always have the quality of tyranny. The consequence for Doniphon is that he accepts his condition as *hupsipolis*—he makes human society possible by removing himself from it, by foregoing the fruits of his tyranny.

Something like this understanding is captured by Nietzsche in this passage, which can, then, serve as conclusion:

> *The tyrants of the spirit.*— The march of science is now no longer crossed by the accidental fact that men live for about seventy years, as was for all too long the case. Formerly, a man wanted to reach the far end of knowledge during this period of time and the methods of acquiring knowledge were evaluated in accordance with this universal longing. The small single questions and experiments were counted contemptible: one wanted the shortest route; one believed that, because everything in the world seemed to be *accommodated to man*, the knowability of things was also accommodated to a human timespan. To solve everything at a stroke, with a single word—that was the secret desire: the task was thought of in the image of the Gordian knot or in that of the egg of Columbus; one did not doubt that in the domain of knowledge too it was possible to reach one's goal in the manner of Alexander or Columbus and to settle all questions with a single answer. "There is a *riddle* to be solved": thus did the goal of life appear to the eye of the philosopher; the first thing to do was to find the riddle and to compress the problem of the world into the simplest riddle-form. The boundless ambition and exultation of being the "unriddler of the world" constituted the thinker's dreams: nothing seemed worth-while if it was not the means of bringing everything to a conclusion *for him*! Philosophy was thus a kind of supreme struggle to possess the tyrannical rule of the spirit—that some such very fortunate, subtle, inventive, bold and mighty man was in reserve—one only!—was doubted by none, and several, most recently Schopenhauer, fancied themselves to be that one.—From this it follows that by and large the sciences have hitherto been kept back by the *moral narrowness* of their disciples and that henceforth they must be carried on with a higher and *more magnanimous* basic feeling. "What do I matter!"—stands over the door of the thinker of the future.[65]

NOTES

1. Hobbes in *Leviathan*, chap. 46, writes also:

> From Aristotle's civil philosophy, they have learned, to call all manner of commonwealths but the popular (such as was at that time the state of Athens), tyranny. All kings they called tyrants; and the aristocracy of the thirty governors set up there by the Lacedaemonians that subdued them, the thirty tyrants. As also to call the condition of the people under the democracy, liberty. A tyrant originally signified no more simply, but a monarch. But when afterwards in most parts of Greece that kind of government was abolished, the

name began to signify, not only the thing it did before, but with it, the hatred which the popular states bare towards it. As also the name of king became odious after the deposing of the kings in Rome, as being a thing natural to all men, to conceive some great fault to be signified in any attribute, that is given in despite, and to a great enemy.

For Hobbes, tyranny is a kind of *attitude* toward government and not a quality of a particular government.

2. WKG VII-1 686: Die Grade der schaffenden Kraft/ 1) der Schauspieler, eine Figur aus sich machend . . . z.B./ la Faustin / 2) der Dichter / der Bildner / der Maler / 3) der Lehrer—Empedocles / 4) der Eroberer / 5) der Gesetzgeber (Philosoph) / überall ist erst der Typus noch zu finden, außer auf den niedrigsten Stufen: es ist noch nicht die Leidens- und Freudensgeschichte nachgewiesen. Die falschen Stellungen z.B. der Philosoph, sich außerhalb stellend—aber das ist nur ein zeitweiliger Zustand und nöthig für das Schwangersein.

Citations from Nietzsche are from either the *Werke Kritische Gesamtausgabe* (Berlin: Gruyter, ongoing) by volume (roman) and subvolume (arabic subscript), or from the *Kritische Studienausgabe* (Berlin: Gruyter, 1973) by volume and page number. If the text in question is from a text Nietzsche published, I give the text and its internal subdivision before the citations just noted.

3. Thus Yeats can write in *The Tower* that the effect of Locke was to undermine or eliminate the possibility of Eden and to initiate the Industrial Revolution.

"Locke sank into a swoon;
The Garden died;
God took the spinning-jenny
Out of his side."

4. *Genealogy of Morals* (=GM) iii 15, WKG VI-2 p. 390.

5. *Beyond Good and Evil* (=BGE) 9, KSA 5.21: Aber dies ist eine alte ewige Geschichte: was sich damals mit den Stoikern begab, begiebt sich heute noch, sobald nur eine Philosophie anfängt, an sich selbst zu glauben. Sie schafft immer die Welt nach ihrem Bilde, sie kann nicht anders; Philosophie ist dieser tyrannische selbst, der geistigste Wille zur Macht, zur "Schaffung der Welt", zur causa prima.

6. I have explored this in the context of an analysis of the will to power in chapter 8 of my *Friedrich Nietzsche and the Politics of Transfiguration*, 3rd ed. (Champaign: University of Illinois Press, 2001).

7. See the important discussion of the affinities between philosophy and tyranny in J. Peter Euben, *The Tragedy of Political Theory: The Road Not Taken* (Princeton, NJ: Princeton University Press, 1990), 248–50, 36–38.

8. Montesquieu gives a version of this when in the *Persian Letters* he understands tyranny as the unwillingness to allow anyone an existence other than that you permit them (Uzbek to Roxanne, for example).

9. *Truth and Lie in the Extra-Moral Sense*, KSA 1.875.

10. *Thus Spoke Zarathustra* (=Z) ii On Redemption, KSA 4.177.

11. BGE 211, KSA 5.144.

12. See the account in Jochen Schmidt, *Die Geschichte des Genie-Gedankens in der deutschen Literatur, Philosophie und Politik, 1750–1945*, 2 vols. (Darmstadt,

1985), which covers thinkers from Klopstock and Lessing, through Kant to Schopenhauer, Nietzsche, and the twentieth century, albeit not always unconventionally.

13. R. W. Emerson, "Self-Reliance," in *Essays*, series 1 (first paragraph).

14. I. Kant, *Critique of the Power of Judgment* (=CPJ) § 45 (185/5.396).

15. As Dieter Henrich writes, "We must . . . wonder how understanding, in its lawfulness, can enter a situation that cannot be elucidated by reference to the constitutive usage of the categories and that precludes general concepts," in *Aesthetic Judgment and the Moral Image of the World* (Stanford, CA: Stanford University Press, 1992), 47.

16. CPJ § 6 and p. 100.

17. CPJ § 46ff (186ff/5.307ff).

18. Ibid. 187.

19. I. Kant, *Anthropology*, 234n.

20. CPJ § 47 (5.309–187).

21. He betrays considerable anxiety about this, for the lack of preexisting criteria make it difficult to determine precisely the difference between the genius and the lunatic. In the *Anthropology*, he writes, "Such a patient [the lunatic] fancies that he comprehends the incomprehensible. . . . There is in this type of mental disturbance not merely disorder and departure from the laws which govern reason, but also a positive unreason, that is, a different rule, a totally different standpoint to which the soul is transported so to speak. From such a perspective the soul looks at objects in another way. . . . It finds itself transported to a faraway place" (para. 51).

22. KSA 8.42; cf. KSA 8.114.

23. *Human, All Too Human* (=HAH) I 261, KSA 2.214. Jeder von ihnen war ein streitbarer gewaltthätiger Tyrann. Vielleicht war das Glück im Glauben an den Besitz der Wahrheit nie grösser in der Welt, aber auch nie die Härte, der Uebermuth, das Tyrannische und Böse eines solchen Glaubens. Sie waren Tyrannen, also Das, was jeder Grieche sein wollte und was jeder war, wenn er es sein konnte. Vielleicht macht nur Solon eine Ausnahme; in seinen Gedichten sagt er es, wie er die persönliche Tyrannis verschmäht habe. Aber er that es aus Liebe zu seinem Werke, zu seiner Gesetzgebung; und Gesetzgeber sein ist eine sublimirtere Form des Tyrannenthums.

Nietzsche associates Solon with philosophers (KSA 7.385). He does also say that Solon wanted "moderation" (KSA 8.109) and that without Peisistratus the tyrant there would have been no tragedy.

24. This is from an exchange between Leo Strauss and Kojève in Leo Strauss, *On Tyranny: Including the Strauss-Kojève Debate*, ed. Victor Gourevitch and Michael Roth (New York: The Free Press, 1991), 165–66. See also my "Dimensions of the New Debate around Carl Schmitt," in Carl Schmitt, *The Concept of the Political* (Chicago: University of Chicago Press, 1996) and "The Sovereign and the Exception," introduction to Carl Schmitt, *Political Theology* (Chicago: University of Chicago Press, forthcoming).

25. See, here, Jacques Derrida, "Force of Law," *Cardozo Law Review* 11, nos. 5–6 (July–August, 1990), 919–1045, and John P. McCormick, "Derrida on Law: Or Poststructuralism Gets Serious, *Political Theory*, June 2001, 395–423.

26. HAH I 262, KSA 2.218: *Homer.* — Die grösste Thatsache in der griechischen Bildung bleibt doch die, dass Homer so frühzeitig panhellenisch wurde. Alle geistige und

menschliche Freiheit, welche die Griechen erreichten, geht auf diese Thatsache zurück. Aber zugleich ist es das eigentliche Verhängniss der griechischen Bildunggewesen, denn Homer verflachte, indem er centralisirte, und löste die ernsteren Instincte der Unabhängigkeit auf. Von Zeit zu Zeit erhob sich aus dem tiefsten Grunde des Hellenischen der Widerspruch gegen Homer; aber er blieb immer siegreich. Alle grossen geistigen Mächte üben neben ihrer befreienden Wirkung auch eine unterdrückende aus.

27. This was the subject of his inaugural lecture, *Homer and Classical Philology*. "We believe in a great poet as the author of the *Iliad* and the *Odyssey—but not that Homer was this poet*."

28. It is often overlooked that Nietzsche discusses all these things both in GT and GM as well as elsewhere.

29. See *Philosophy in the Tragic Age of the Greeks*; WKG IV-1 p. 180–81.

30. See my *Friedrich Nietzsche and the Politics of Transfiguration*, 3rd ed. (Champaign: University of Illinois Press, 2000), chap. 6.

31. *Wisdom and Science in Conflict*, WKG IV-1 pp. 178–79.

32. WKG III-4 p. 131.

33. Idem.

34. For a more detailed analysis, see my *Friedrich Nietzsche and the Politics of Transfiguration*, 152–161, chap. 6, passim. See also WKG III-4 pp. 50, 84–85, 107, 117, 119–122, 142–144, 173–174 and WKG IV-1 pp. 194–195.

35. See the discussion of science in Babette Babich's contribution to G. E. Moore and T. Brobjer, eds., *Nietzsche and Science* (London: Ashgate, 2004).

36. So also will Nietzsche later proclaim himself a "European."

37. Emerson, *Essays and Lectures* (New American Library, 1979), 476.

38. WKG IV-1 pp. 189, 195.

39. See the discussion in my *Friedrich Nietzsche and the Politics of Transfiguration*, 112–123, 168–185.

40. WKG IV-1 pp. 183–84.

41. WKG III-4 p. 10.

42. I do not think that I fantasize when I call attention to the fact that a modern attempt to make possible such a remarriage can be found in Stanley Cavell, *The Claim of Reason: Wittgenstein, Skepticism, Morality, and Tragedy*, new ed. (Oxford: Oxford University Press, 1999).

43. *Philosophy in the Tragic Age of the Greeks* i, WKG III-2 p. 303/33.

44. Ibid. 304/35.

45. WKG III-4 p. 5.

46. WKG III-4 p.141.

47. WKG III-4 p. 221.

48. WKG III-4 p. 131.

49. WKG IV-1 p. 180–81.

50. Stanley Cavell, *Themes Out of School* (Chicago: University of Chicago Press, 1984), 9. Cf. Heidegger's understanding of the human as the being for whom its being is in question.

51. See Martin Heidegger, *Einführung in die Metaphysik* (Niemeyer: Tübingen, 1976), 112–26, esp. 116–17.

52. Ibid., 117.

53. Nietzsche to Rohde *Gesammelte Briefe* (Berlin: Gruyter, 1979), iv, 136. That which Kremer-Marietti and Breazeale give under this title, following the Kroner edition, may be found in III 4 pp. 136ff.

54. HAH I 262, KSA 2.218.

55. HAH ii 203, KSA 2.657. *Tyrannen des Geistes.* — In unserer Zeit würde man Jeden, der so streng der Ausdruck Eines moralischen Zuges wäre, wie die Personen Theophrast's und Molière's es sind, für krank halten, und von „fixer Idee" bei ihm reden. Das Athen des dritten Jahrhunderts würde uns, wenn wir dort einen Besuch machen dürften, wie von Narren bevölkert erscheinen. Jetzt herrscht die Demokratie der Begriffe in jedem Kopfe, — viele zusammen sind der Herr: ein einzelner Begriff, der Herr sein wollte, heisst jetzt, wie gesagt, "fixe Idee." Diess ist unsere Art, die Tyrannen zu morden, — wir winken nach dem Irrenhause hin.

56. HAH I 261, KSA 2.215: Die Periode der Tyrannen des Geistes ist vorbei. In den Sphären der höheren Cultur wird es freilich immer eine Herrschaft geben müssen, aber diese Herrschaft liegt von jetzt ab in den Händen der Oligarchen des Geistes. Sie bilden, trotz aller räumlichen und politischen Trennung, eine zusammengehörige Gesellschaft, deren Mitglieder sich erkennen und anerkennen, was auch die öffentliche Meinung und die Urtheile der auf die Masse wirkenden Tages- und Zeitschriftsteller für Schätzungen der Gunst oder Abgunst in Umlauf bringen mögen. Die geistige Ueberlegenheit, welche früher trennte und verfeindete, pflegt jetzt zu binden: wie könnten die Einzelnen sich selbst behaupten und auf eigener Bahn, allen Strömungen entgegen, durch das Leben schwimmen, wenn sie nicht ihres Gleichen hier und dort unter gleichen Bedingungen leben sähen und deren Hand ergriffen, im Kampfe eben so sehr gegen den ochlokratischen Charakter des Halbgeistes und der Halbbildung, als gegen die gelegentlichen Versuche, mit Hülfe der Massenwirkung eine Tyrannei aufzurichten? Die Oligarchen sind einander nöthig, sie haben an einander ihre beste Freude, sie verstehen ihre Abzeichen, — aber trotzdem ist ein Jeder von ihnen frei, er kämpft und siegt an seiner Stelle und geht lieber unter, als sich zu unterwerfen.

57. Max Weber, "Politics as a Vocation," in *The Vocation Lectures*, ed. David Owen and Tracy B. Strong (Indianapolis, IN: Hackett, 2003), xx.

58. Z preface 5, KSA 4.18: Kein Hirt und Eine Heerde! Jeder will das Gleiche, Jeder ist gleich: wer anders fühlt, geht freiwillig in's Irrenhaus.

59. *Dawn of Day* 9, KSA 3.21.

60. WKG V1 442: "Grundsätze: es giebt in der Natur keine Zwecke, es giebt keinen Geist außer bei Menschen und menschenartigen Wesen, es giebt keine Wunder und keine Vorsehung, es giebt keinen Schöpfer, keinen Gesetzgeber, keine Schuld, keine Strafe."

61. See the analysis in David Owen and Tracy Strong, "Introduction" to Max Weber, *The Vocation Lectures* (Indianapolis, IN: Hackett, 2003).

62. When this comes out at the end in an interview between now Senator Stoddard and some reporters, one of them famously says, "When the facts and the legend conflict, print the legend," and thereby Ford deconstructs our myths for us the viewers without depriving them of their power.

63. I am indebted here to the analysis of this film in Stanley Cavell, *The World Viewed* (Cambridge, MA: Harvard University Press, 1979), 57–59.

64. I have developed this theme more extensively in "Where Are We when We Are beyond Good and Evil: Nietzsche and the Law," *Cardozo Law Review*, April 2003.

65. *Dawn of Day* 547, WKG V-1 p. 321: *Die Tyrannen des Geistes.* — Der Gang der Wissenschaft wird jetzt nicht mehr durch die zufällige Thatsache, dass der Mensch ungefähr siebenzig Jahre alt wird, gekreuzt, wie es allzulange der Fall war. Ehemals wollte Einer während dieses Zeitraumes an's Ende der Erkenntnis kommen und nach diesem allgemeinen Gelüste schätzte man die Methoden der Erkenntniss ab. Die kleinen einzelnen Fragen und Versuche galten als verächtlich, man wollte den kürzesten Weg, man glaubte, weil Alles in der Welt auf den Menschen hin eingerichtet schien, dass auch die Erkennbarkeit der Dinge auf ein menschliches Zeitmaass eingerichtet sei. Alles mit Einem Schlage, mit Einem Worte zu lösen, — das war der geheime Wunsch: unter dem Bilde des gordischen Knotens oder unter dem des Eies des Columbus dachte man sich die Aufgabe; man zweifelte nicht, dass es möglich sei, auch in der Erkenntniss nach Art des Alexander oder des Columbus zum Ziele zu kommen und alle Fragen mit Einer Antwort zu erledigen. "Ein Räthsel ist zu lösen": so trat das Lebensziel vor das Auge des Philosophen; zunächst war das Räthsel zu finden und das Problem der Welt in die einfachste Räthselform zusammenzudrängen. Der gränzenlose Ehrgeiz und Jubel, der "Enträthsler der Welt" zu sein, machte die Träume des Denkers aus: Nichts schien ihm der Mühe werth, wenn es nicht das Mittel war, Alles für ihn zu Ende zu bringen! So war Philosophie eine Art höchsten Ringens um die Tyrannenherrschaft des Geistes, — dass eine solche irgend einem Sehr-Glücklichen, Feinen, Erfindsamen, Kühnen, Gewaltigen vorbehalten und aufgespart sei, — einem Einzigen! — daran zweifelte Keiner, und Mehrere haben gewähnt, zuletzt noch Schopenhauer, dieser Einzige zu sein. — Daraus ergiebt sich, dass im Grossen und Ganzen die Wissenschaft bisher durch die moralische Beschränktheit ihrer Jünger zurückgeblieben ist und dass sie mit einer höheren und grossmüthigeren Grundempfindung fürderhin getrieben werden muss. "Was liegt an mir!" — steht über der Thür des künftigen Denkers.

SOURCES

Cavell, Stanley. 1979. *The World Viewed.* Cambridge: Harvard University Press.

———. 1984. *Themes Out of School.* Chicago: University of Chicago Press.

———. 1999. *The Claim of Reason: Wittgenstein, Skepticism, Morality, and Tragedy.* New ed. Oxford: Clarendon Press.

Derrida, Jacques. 1990. "Force of Law." *Cardozo Law Review* 11 (July–August, nos. 5–6): 919–1045.

Emerson, R. W. 1979. *Essays and Lectures.* New York: New American Library.

Euben, J. Peter. 1990. *The Tragedy of Political Theory: The Road Not Taken.* Princeton, NJ: Princeton University Press.

Heidegger, Martin. 1976. *Einführung in die Metaphysik.* Niemeyer, Tübingen.

Henrich, Dieter. 1992. *Aesthetic Judgment and the Moral Image of the World*. Stanford, CA: Stanford University Press.

Hobbes, Thomas. 1982. *Leviathan*. Cambridge: Cambridge University Press.

Kant, Immanuel. 1974. *Anthropology from a pragmatic point of view*. The Hague: Nijhoff.

———. 2001. *Critique of the Power of Judgment*. Cambridge: Cambridge UP.

McCormick, John P. 2001. "Derrida on Law: Or Poststructuralism Gets Serious. *Political Theory* (June): 395–423.

Moore, G. E., and T. Brobjer, eds. 2004. *Nietzsche and Science* London, Ashgate.

Nietzsche, Friedrich. 1979. *Gesammelte Briefe*. Berlin: Gruyter.

———. 1976. *Kritische Studienausgabe*. Berlin: Gruyter.

———. Ongoing. *Werke Kritische Gesamtausgabe*. Berlin: Gruyter.

Schmidt, Jochen. 1985. *Die Geschichte des Genie-Gedankens in der deutschen Literatur, Philosophie und Politik, 1750–1945*. 2 volumes Darmstadt: .

Strauss, Leo. 1991. *On Tyranny: Including the Strauss-Kojève Debate*, ed. Victor Gourevitch and Michael Roth. New York: The Free Press.

Strong, Tracy B. 1996. "Dimensions of the New Debate Around Carl Schmitt." In Carl Schmitt, *The Concept of the Political*. Chicago: University of Chicago Press.

———. 2001. *Friedrich Nietzsche and the Politics of Transfiguration*. 3rd ed. Champaign: University of Illinois Press.

———. 2003. "Where Are We when We Are beyond Good and Evil: Nietzsche and the Law." *Cardozo Law Review* (April).

———. Forthcoming. "The Sovereign and the Exception." Introduction to Carl Schmitt, *Political Theology*. Chicago: University of Chicago Press.

Weber, Max. 2003. "Politics as a Vocation." In *The Vocation Lectures*, ed. David Owen and Tracy B. Strong. Indianapolis, IN: Hackett.

Chapter 9

Tyranny from Plato to Locke

Nathan Tarcov

I should start by saying that I will not attempt a history of the term or concept "tyranny" during the immense and varied period implied by my title, let alone of the political phenomena it was meant to describe. I will instead speak briefly about some salient aspects of the analyses of tyranny by a handful of classical political philosophers, Xenophon, Plato, and Aristotle, and briefly compare them with the modern analyses of Machiavelli, Hobbes, and Locke to see how they might challenge some of our present-day notions.

Leo Strauss in the Introduction to his book *On Tyranny* wrote the following: "The analysis of tyranny that was made by the first political scientists was so clear, so comprehensive, and so unforgettably expressed that it was remembered and understood by generations which did not have any direct experience of actual tyranny. On the other hand, when we were brought face to face with tyranny—with a kind of tyranny that surpassed the boldest imaginations of the most powerful thinkers of the past—our political science failed to recognize it. It is not surprising then that many of our contemporaries, disappointed or repelled by present-day analyses of present-day tyranny, were relieved when they rediscovered the pages in which Plato and other classical thinkers seemed to have interpreted for them the horrors of the twentieth century."

Strauss, writing in 1948, was referring of course to the murderous tyrannies of Hitler in National Socialist Germany and of Stalin in Communist Russia. He explained further that "It is no accident that present-day political science has failed to grasp tyranny as what it really is. Our political science is haunted by the belief that 'value judgments' are inadmissible in scientific considerations, and to call a regime tyrannical clearly amounts to pronouncing a 'value judgment.' The political scientist who accepts this view of science will speak of the mass-state, of dictatorship, of totalitarianism, of authoritarianism, and so on, and as a citizen he may wholeheartedly condemn these things; but as a political scientist he is forced to reject the notion of tyranny as 'mythical.'"

We may add that the inability to recognize tyranny diagnosed by Strauss has not been confined to professional political scientists who eschew "value judgments." Intellectuals, journalists, and politicians who decry racism, militarism, and imperialism, even human rights activists, have sometimes been reluctant to speak of "tyranny." Those who do speak of tyrannies as evil regimes and of tyrants as evil men are often ridiculed and denounced at best as dangerously naive, and at worst as fanatical bigots who would impose their own absolute values on other cultures and societies. And quite apart from intellectuals, journalists, and politicians, two of the men whom Strauss considered among the greatest philosophers of the twentieth century, Martin Heidegger and Alexandre Kojève, defended, respectively, the "greatness and dignity" of National Socialism and the historical necessity of Communism.

Strauss devoted *On Tyranny* to Xenophon's dialogue *Hiero*, the only work of classical political philosophy on the theme of tyranny. It is a dialogue between Simonides, a poet and one of the proverbial seven wise men of Greece, and Hiero, the tyrant of Syracuse. In the first part, in response to Simonides' questions about the relative pleasures and pains of the tyrannical life and the private life, Hiero depicts the unhappiness of the tyrant, culminating in his assertions that the tyrant lives in continual fear of assassination even by his paid guards as one condemned by all human beings to die for his injustice, whose killers are magnificently honored by the cities, and that he might as well hang himself (4.5, 6.4, 6.11, 7.10–7.13). Simonides does not encourage Hiero to follow that counsel of despair, but instead in the second part advises Hiero as to how a beneficent tyrant could be the happiest of men (8–11). When Hiero asks Simonides whether he would advise him to do without his mercenary bodyguard, Simonides urges him to keep it but use it also to protect the citizenry (10). Thus Simonides refrains from urging Hiero to give up his tyranny, whether by returning to private life (one of the characteristics of a tyrant seems to be that he never willingly gives his rule), ending his life, or transforming his rule from one that leaves his citizens at the mercy of his security force to one that leaves him at the mercy of an armed citizenry. Altogether, this threatens to leave a reader with the shocking impression that Xenophon recommends the life of a beneficent tyrant as the happiest.

Although Xenophon's entrusting the praise of beneficent tyranny to a wise man and the indictment of ordinary tyranny to a tyrant seems to give the praise of beneficent tyranny greater weight than the indictment of ordinary tyranny, Strauss notes that Xenophon neither utters this praise in his own name nor entrusts it to his friend or teacher, the citizen-philosopher Socrates, but entrusts it to the supposedly wise but pleasure-loving poet Simonides, who himself does not publicly expound it but utters it only privately to a man already irretrievably committed to tyranny (Strauss 2000, 76–77). Strauss also brings out how even Simonides' praise of beneficent tyranny implies its defects: its lack of law, liberty, recourse against the possibility of oppression, public spirit, secure property rights, or equality of honor (Strauss 2000, 68–70). Strauss argues, furthermore, that Simonides' intention is to improve Hiero's tyrannical rule so as to benefit Hiero and perhaps himself as well as Hiero's subjects (Strauss 2000, 38). Strauss suggests that Simonides first praises the happiness of tyrants only to arouse the tyrant's fear that if the wise Simonides thinks tyrants are happy he might seek to become tyrant himself or advise a pupil or friend of his on how to become tyrant, so as to provoke Hiero to utter apparently disheartened lament over the unhappiness of tyranny so as to dissuade Simonides from any attempt at taking away his tyranny, but which opens the way for Simonides' advice as to how to rule more happily (Strauss 2000, 41–45, 52–55). Furthermore, to get Hiero to take his advice seriously, Simonides has to tacitly present himself as morally unscrupulous and argue for beneficent tyranny on the basis of its superior pleasure rather than its moral superiority to ordinary tyranny (Strauss 2000, 55–56, 61). The dialogue ends, however, without telling us of Hiero's reaction to Simonides' advice, compelling the reader to wonder whether Hiero, or indeed any tyrant, would take such advice (Strauss 2000, 34–64).

This puzzling and disturbing little dialogue may make us as modern democrats wonder whether a wise man or a philosopher, or as we would say an intellectual, ought to be advising a tyrant at all. If he finds himself in a situation where he can or must do so, we would be inclined to say he should do precisely what Simonides declines to do, that is, urge the tyrant if not to hang himself then to give up his tyranny or transform it into a constitutional order. We might be compelled to admit that such a course is likely to lead only to the speedy disappearance of the would-be adviser, whereas Simonides' course may not lead to any improvement of the tyrant's rule but at least leaves Simonides alive to try again another day or at least go on writing poetry. Such prudential considerations, however, do not seem adequate to explain Xenophon's focus on the question of just how much tyranny can be improved while still remaining tyranny. He did not have to write a dialogue portraying a wise man advising a tyrant; he could, for example, have stuck to portraying a wise man or philosopher urging a young man tempted by tyranny not to pursue that course (as Plato does in *The Republic*) or even have shown him urging the subjects of a tyrant to liberate themselves. Strauss argues that the dream of a beneficent tyranny may be presented to make clear by contrast the limits of law and legitimacy (Strauss 2000, 74–76).

In addition to the final praise of beneficent tyranny, what may seem strangest to us about Xenophon's dialogue on tyranny is its viewing tyranny almost totally from the perspective of the tyrant rather than his subjects, its concentration on the question of the happiness or misery of the tyrant rather than the happiness or misery of his subjects. This is a result of its being a dialogue with a tyrant, which is to say that it reveals that a tyrant is precisely a man who is not amenable to appeals on behalf of the good or happiness of others, the common good or justice. That consideration, however, seems again insufficient to explain Xenophon's concentration on the question of whether tyrants are happier or more miserable than private men. Perhaps not only for tyrants but for all of us, the fundamental question about tyranny must be whether it is good to be a tyrant, that it is not enough to know that tyranny is bad for others. Strauss suggests that the original question of the comparison or choice between the tyrannical life and the private life points to the question of the comparison and choice between the political life and the philosophic life, and concludes that the wise man alone is free, the superior or ruler of rulers, as self-sufficient as is humanly possible, and alone capable of justice in the highest, transpolitical sense (Strauss 2000, 78–91).

The choice between the tyrannical life and the philosophic life is also, of course, the ultimate theme of Plato's *Republic*. Already in Book I, Thrasymachus' claim that the just is the advantage of the stronger (338c–39a) turns into a praise of tyranny as perfect injustice and happiness (343d–44c), to which the rest of the work may be regarded as Socrates' response (368b). (Thus, whereas Xenophon's *Hiero* first presents the tyrant's condemnation of tyranny and then the wise man's praise of beneficent tyranny, Plato's *Republic* first presents Thrasymachus' praise of tyranny and then Socrates' condemnation of tyranny.) Glaucon's story of Gyges' ring suggests that every man would be a tyrant if he could (359d–360c). Similarly, Socrates himself asserts that the terrible, savage, and lawless form of desires at the root of tyranny is present in every man and becomes manifest in our dreams (571b–72b; see also *Laws* 687ac). And Socrates' final myth of Er suggests that even those who live in well-ordered regimes and participate in virtue habitually without philosophy would choose tyranny (619bd). We may be reminded of Nietzsche's claims that every Greek wanted to be a tyrant, a desire sublimated as lawgiving and philosophy (*Human, All Too Human* #261), and that the desire for tyranny and disbelief in justice was the dirty secret of every Greek aristocrat (*Daybreak*, no. 199).

For Thrasymachus, tyranny seems to differ from other regimes only in the number of rulers: each ruling group sets down laws for its own advantage and calls that justice alike in a democracy, an aristocracy, or a tyranny (338d–39a), though he later admits that this is not so where just, that is to say foolish, men rule (343de). Socrates in contrast sharply distinguishes tyranny from other regimes.

Socrates does not give a definition of tyranny, but he does give a vivid portrait of the genesis of tyranny out of democracy (562a–66d). The insatiable desire for freedom (as that which democracy defines as good) destroys democracy and leads to tyranny. Democratic citizens end up "paying no attention to the laws, written or unwritten, in order that they may avoid having any master at all." Extreme democracy is transformed into tyranny through conflict among its three classes: the rich who have become bankrupt and idle; the hard-working super rich; and the *demos* themselves, "who do their own work, don't meddle in affairs, and don't possess very much," the most numerous and most sovereign class in a democracy (564d–65a). Members of the first class usually become the leaders of the *demos*, confiscating the wealth of the second class to distribute some of it among the *demos* and keep the greatest part for themselves. As class conflict intensifies, the *demos* sets up one man as its leader who resorts to judicial murder of his enemies, promises cancellation of debts and economic redistribution, establishes a bodyguard to protect himself from his enemies, and, if not killed or exiled by his enemies, becomes tyrant, instigates continual wars, purges all the best elements in the city, and impoverishes, disarms, and enslaves the *demos* (565a–69c). Thus the failure to moderate the democratic desire for freedom leads to its opposite for the *demos*. The tyrant is the destroyer of a democracy and the enslaver of the *demos*.

In line with his general procedure in the *Republic*, Socrates sketches a parallel between a city under a tyranny and a tyrannical man, whether living as a criminal in a decent city or as the tyrant in a tyranny (571a–80a). Thus the primary question about tyranny, whether one should want to be a tyrant, is broadened into whether one should want to be a tyrannical man, one whose most decent part (his reason) is enslaved to his maddest part (his eros). The tyrannical man lives in fear, suffering, and misery, without a taste of freedom or true friendship. The assertion that the tyrant is dominated by eros establishes a certain connection between him and the philosopher dominated by eros for wisdom (cf. 474c–75b, 490b; see also 491d–92a, 495ab). The work culminates in a contrast between the philosopher and the tyrant or tyrannical man and, of course, a decision in favor of the superior pleasure and happiness of the philosopher (580c–92b). Thus Plato's Socrates condemns tyranny not only from the perspective of the tyrant's unhappy subjects but also, like Xenophon's Simonides, from that of the unhappy tyrant himself.

Plato's Socrates does not advise tyrants as to how to preserve their rule in *The Republic* as Xenophon's Simonides does in the *Hiero*, but he does something else that we may find even more disturbing: he attributes to the rule of his guardians means that we are inclined to describe as tyrannical. The guardians are supposed to censor poetry and the other arts (376c–402a); tell lies to the citizens for the benefit of the city (389bd, 414b–15e, 459cd); abolish privacy, private property, and private families at least for the guardian class (416a–17b, 457d–64e); and even expel all those over ten (541ab). (Similarly, in Plato's *Laws*, at 709d–12a, the Athenian Stranger makes his lawgiver pray more explicitly for a young virtuous tyrant so as to institute his regime most easily and quickly, though perhaps only as a myth showing how difficult it is for a city with good laws to come into being.) That last proposal, however, suggests that none of this is seriously expected to be implemented (Glaucon's agreement that Socrates has thereby shown how this city might be "most quickly and easily" established "if it ever would be" seems ironical: cf. 592ab). The city ruled absolutely by philosopher kings is proposed not with the expectation that it will be established, but as a blueprint for the proper order of the soul of the best individual or an analysis of the obstacles to justice or the elements of injustice within the city (368e–69a, 427d, 472be, 592ab).

A striking counterpart to the implicit attribution of tyrannical aspects to the hypothetical city of the philosopher kings in the *Republic* is its implicit attribution of tyrannical aspects to all actual cities, not only to those suffering under tyranny in the precise sense. Socrates says cities hate and kill those who tell them the truth about their regime and honor those who flatter it (426ac). They corrupt and turn toward tyranny the young with the best natures, and punish them with disfranchisement, fines, and even death if they fail to speak, act, and be like the rulers (490e–95b). The city is famously compared to a cave whose inhabitants are chained prisoners forced to take the shadows of artificial images and of themselves for the truth so that they resist their liberation and try to kill their would-be liberator (514a–17a, 539e)—what could be more tyrannical?

Indeed Strauss seems to consider the diagnosis of the attempt of every society to tyrannize thought the greatest contribution of classical political philosophy to the understanding of the problem of tyranny, along with its alternative, the idea of philosophy as liberation from such tyranny (Strauss 2000, 27). He argues further that what he calls "historicism," the doctrine associated with Hegel, Marx, and Nietzsche that all human thought is historical and hence collective, has become both the greatest obstacle to such liberation and the basis for the modern tyrannies that attempt in fact to collectivize humanity and human thought.

Although Plato's Socrates does not advise tyrants as Xenophon's Simonides advised the Syracusan tyrant Hiero, Plato himself notoriously advised the later Syracusan tyrants Dionysius the Elder and his son Dionysius the Younger, as recounted in the *Seventh Letter*. This was, however, far from an endorsement of beneficent tyranny on Plato's part, let alone an effort to establish the city described in his *Republic*. Plato opens the *Letter* (324ab; also 336a, 351c) by favorably invoking Dion's consistent opinion that the Syracusans should be free and be governed under the best laws (the opposite of tyranny). He then recounts his own youthful illusions about and disillusionment with the reign of the Thirty Tyrants in Athens, who not only failed to lead the city to a just way of life as the young Plato had hoped, but made the previous democracy look like a golden age (324c–25a). Plato then recalls that when he first came to Sicily he thought that the human race would have no respite from evils till those rightly and truly philosophizing should come to political office (326ab), reminding us of the absolute rule of philosopher kings in *The Republic*, but speedily endorses instead a just regime with equal laws (*isonomos*, 326d). By instructing Dion (Plato's pupil and Dionysius the Elder's brother-in-law and son-in-law), Plato says he unwittingly contrived Dion's future overthrow of the tyranny (327a). Plato recounts Dion's high hopes after the death of Dionysius the Elder for establishing a happy way of life in Syracuse through converting Dionysius the Younger to philosophy, but Plato himself does not seem to have shared these high hopes and returned to Syracuse and a tyranny ill-befitting his speeches and himself more from fear of betraying Dion in a time of danger (327c–29b; similarly he attributes his second visit to Dionysius to his desire not to betray Dion or his philosophical friends in Italy despite his doubts about Dionysius, 338b–39e, 347e). Although Plato vividly portrays Dionysius's passionate and tyrannically possessive devotion to Plato (330ab), the philosopher gives no sign of having had any particular attachment to the young tyrant. Instead, Plato explains that an intelligent man can only advise a regime moving in the right direction, not one going the wrong way, and that he should eschew attempting to overthrow a bad regime through killings and banishments (330d–31d). He therefore merely urged Dionysius to reform his own life, advice he conveyed only riddlingly since it would have been unsafe to do so directly (331d–33a). Plato's intention in Syracuse does not seem to have been either the establishment of the regime of *The Republic* through Dionysius' tyranny or the overthrow of that tyranny. Indeed Plato concludes his narrative of his first two visits by telling the associates of the since-assassinated Dion that his own reasoning (*logos*) is that neither Sicily nor any other city should be enslaved by human despots but by laws (334c), and that should they return to power they should above all avoid banishments and executions and subject themselves to laws equally pleasing to the vanquished and the victors to end the cycle of factional strife (336e–37d). Plato's Sicilian visits reveal him as neither an antityrannical revolutionary (though the teacher of one) nor a protyrannical utopian, but a sober advocate of moderation and the rule of law.

Although the theme of philosophy as the alternative to and cure for tyranny is far less prominent in Aristotle's *Politics* than in Plato's *Republic*, it does appear in his critique of Phaleas of Chalcedon's proposal to make an equal distribution of property so as to prevent crime and injustice. Aristotle argues that although having a modicum of property would indeed prevent crimes and injustices caused by need, the greatest crimes and injustices are not motivated by need: "men do not become tyrants so as not to shiver with cold." The greatest crimes and injustices, such as tyranny, are motivated instead by the desire for pure pleasure unmixed with pain, a desire that Aristotle says can be satisfied only by philosophy (1267a3–17).

Aristotle defines tyranny in the context of his typology of the basic kinds of regimes or constitutions (*politeiai*) in Book III of the *Politics*. The *politeia*, constitution, or regime of the *polis* or city is the organization of its ruling offices or its *politeuma* or ruling element (III 1278b9–12), and also its way of life (IV 1295b1). Aristotle's typology is emphatically normative: he distinguishes, first of all, between right constitutions (*orthai politeiai*) and perversions or deviations (*parekbaseis*), on the grounds that in right constitutions the rule is for the interest of the ruled or the common interest, whereas in perversions or deviations the rule is for the private interest of the rulers (III 1279a18–22). The perversions therefore are despotic rather than political in the sense that they resemble the rule of a master (*despotes*) over a slave, which is essentially for the sake of the interest of the master, and only incidentally for that of the slave insofar as the preservation of the slave is in the interest of the master, whereas political rule pertains to a polis, which is a community of the free (1278b32–38, 1279a21–22). By combining this distinction between right constitutions and perversions with that between rule by one, few, or many, Aristotle produces a sixfold typology of regimes: kingship (*basileia*) is political rule by one (*monarchia*) for the common interest, whereas tyranny is despotic rule by one for the private interest of the one ruling; aristocracy is political rule by a few for the common interest, whereas oligarchy is despotic rule by a few (the *oligoi*, or rich) for their own interest; and polity or constitutional government (*politeia*, the same term he uses for constitution or regime in general) is political rule by the many for the common interest, whereas democracy is despotic rule by the many (the *demos* or poor) for their own interest (III 1279a26–79b10). See table 9.1.

Aristotle's sixfold typology is not a simple dichotomy; there is more than one kind of right regime, in contrast to our common tendency to distinguish only between what we call democratic and undemocratic governments or

Table 9.1. Typology of Regimes

	Right	*Perversion*
One	Kingship	Tyranny
Few	Aristocracy	Oligarchy
Many	Polity	Democracy

regimes. We ought not to be confused by Aristotle's use of the term "democracy" to refer to the bad form of rule by the many, but we should note that for him rule by the many as such (approximating "democracy" in our sense) is neither sufficient nor necessary for a right constitution: the many can rule despotically in their own interest, oppressing the few, and one or a few can rule in the interest of the ruled (a full exploration of that view would have to be the subject of another paper). In particular, therefore, we should note that his condemnation of tyranny as a perversion, far from being a condemnation of all one-man rule, is precisely a condemnation of tyranny as a perversion of kingship, of right rule by one man. Indeed, Aristotle says tyranny is the worst perversion as the perversion of kingship as the "most divine" constitution (1289a38–b3).

Our typologies emphasize the *source* of government, in practice the presence or absence of accountability to the people (our representative democracy is not rule by the people in Aristotle's sense, but only accountability to the people) or, alternatively, limitations on the *power* or *scope* of government as in our contrasts between constitutional government and dictatorship, between liberalism and authoritarianism, or between pluralism and totalitarianism. Aristotle's sixfold typology, in contrast, emphasizes the *end* of government, whether it serves the interest of the ruled or that of the ruler.

Finally, we need to note that it would be a misleading simplification to reduce Aristotle's regime analysis to the sixfold typology of Book III; in Books IV through VI of the *Politics*, he elaborates subtypologies within each of these six kinds, as well as mixtures of them, blurring the lines not only between rule by one, few, and many, but also between right constitutions and perversions.

Aristotle complicates the distinction between kingship and tyranny in particular in his discussions of the different forms of kingship (1285a1–86a7) and of the different forms of tyranny (1295a1–24). He distinguishes among five forms of kingship. First, there is the *Spartan* form of kingship that rules according to law (*kata nomon*) and is sovereign (*kyrion*) not over all things but only over the conduct of war and matters concerning the gods, in effect a generalship/priesthood for life, whether hereditary or elective. Such a king does not constitute a distinct form of constitution but is instead compatible with any kind of constitution (accordingly, Aristotle describes the Spartan regime not as kingship but as a form of aristocracy [IV 1293b15–19] or as mixture of democracy and oligarchy [1294b19–35]). Second, there is the *barbarian* form of kingship, which is "near to tyrannies" in its power and even called a "despotic rule," but which rules according to law and is hereditary and therefore stable, and in which the king is guarded by armed citizens, rather than by hired foreigners, and rules over willing subjects, unlike tyrants, who rule over unwilling subjects.[1] Third, there is the *archaic Greek* form of kingship, which Aristotle calls an *elective tyranny*, which differs from the barbarian kind only in being elective for life, for a set term, or for a set task rather than being hereditary, but which also rules according to law and over willing subjects. This archaic form is despotic or tyrannical presumably in that its power extends over all things, but is kingly in that it rules according to law over willing subjects and is elective. Fourth, there is the even older form of kingship of the Greek kings of *heroic* times, who were hereditary, ruled over willing subjects and according to law, and were sovereign only over war and sacrifices and served as judges, a form that developed into later merely religious or military officials. Fifth, there is the *absolute* kingship (*pambasileia*), which is sovereign over all matters and rules over a city or tribe or tribes (*ethnoi*) as the head of a household (*oikonomos*) rules over a household according to the ruler's will rather than according to law.

In this discussion of the forms of kingship, Aristotle says nothing about rule in the interests of the ruled rather than that of the ruler, the distinction between kingship and tyranny he made in the sixfold typology, since presumably all of these forms of kingship, as forms of kingship as opposed to tyranny, involve rule in the common interest. Instead, here he implicitly introduces several additional criteria of distinction: (1) rule according to law as opposed to rule according to the ruler's will (see 1286b31–32, 1287a1–4, 10–11); (2) rule over all matters as opposed to rule limited to a few matters; (3) rule that is hereditary or elective, presumably as opposed to rule by force or fraud; and (4) rule over willing subjects as opposed to rule over unwilling subjects. We may call these criteria legality, limitation, legitimacy, and consent. Whereas tyranny is characterized by being rule without legality, limitation, legitimacy, or consent, kingship also can be rule without legality or limitation, but cannot be without legitimacy or consent. These criteria of legality, limitation, legitimacy, and consent are more easily determined than the one emphasized in the sixfold typology, whether the end of government is the common interest or the ruler's private interest, and they resemble more closely our usual criteria for distinguishing kinds of government. In practice, legal, limited, legitimate one-man rule by consent can serve as a proxy for rule in the common interest. It can be presumed that a ruler who rules according to law with limits on his power, a legitimate title of inheritance or election, and the consent of his subjects is a king who rules in their interest, whereas a ruler who rules according to his own will without limits on his power, a legitimate title, or the consent of his subjects can be presumed to be a tyrant who rules in his own private interest.

In Aristotle's analysis of the different forms of tyranny (1295a1–24), he says that what he previously distinguished as the barbarian and archaic forms of kingship, though they are forms of kingship insofar as they rule according to law and over willing subjects, are also forms of tyranny insofar as they rule despotically and according to the judgment of the ruler. He explains, however, that the form that is most especially tyranny (that is, not mixed with elements of kingship) and is the counterpart of absolute kingship is that in which one man rules without accountability over those who are his equals or betters for his own interest rather than theirs. Aristotle adds that such a tyrant rules over unwilling subjects since free men do not willingly submit to such rule. This indicates another distinction between tyranny and absolute (though not necessarily all kinds of) kingship: whether the ruler is superior or equal or inferior to the ruled (see also 1286b8–12, 1288a8–19). Like the criterion of whether rule is in the interest of the ruler or the ruled, this one involves what we would consider controversial value judgments; in addition, it offends our egalitarianism, our aversion to calling anyone superior or inferior to anyone else. Nevertheless, we are usually aware of the differences between rulers who are of unusual competence and decency, rulers who boast of their own mediocrity and resemblance to the average person, and rulers whose lack of decency and self-restraint would make them criminals were they not rulers. Furthermore, Aristotle's argument that free men do not submit to rule by their equals or inferiors that is unaccountable and for the interest of the rulers closely links the objective but controversial criterion of superiority/equality/inferiority to the subjective but more easily determinable criterion of consent, whether the ruled respect their rulers and submit to them willingly or despise and hate them and submit unwillingly. See table 9.2.

Although Aristotle reserves the term "tyranny" proper to describe the perversion of one-man rule, it is important to note especially for the later history of the term, such as Tocqueville's "tyranny of the majority," that Aristotle occasionally extends the term tyranny to describe the extreme forms of democracy and oligarchy. He says that the extreme form of democracy brought about by demagogues, in which popular decrees replace rule of law, is the analog to tyranny, and even that it is a tyranny (IV 1292a18, V 1312b6). Note that he says the demagogues are the analog not to the tyrant but to the flatterers in a tyranny; the *demos*, not the demagogue, is the analog to the tyrant so long as the regime

Table 9.2. Criterion of Consent

	Legality	*Limitation*	*Legitimacy*	*Consent*
Spartan	yes	yes	hereditary/elected	yes
Barbarian	yes	no	hereditary	yes
Archaic	yes	no	elected	yes
Heroic	yes	yes	hereditary	yes
Absolute	no	no	?	[yes]
Tyranny	[no]	[no]	[no]	no

remains a democracy. Correspondingly, he says that the extreme form of oligarchy, in which hereditary rulers rather than the law rule, is the counterpart of both tyranny and that extreme form of democracy (IV 1292b7–8, VI 1320b32–33). Both extreme oligarchy and extreme democracy, he says, are shared tyrannies (V 1312b37–38). Similarly, on the narrower level of specific institutions, he says that the Ephorate in the Spartan constitution was excessively powerful and equivalent to tyranny (*isotyrannon*, II 1270b14–15).

Aristotle's discussion of revolution and stability, the destruction and preservation of regimes, deepens and enriches his analysis of tyranny. In discussing revolutions in democracies, he reports that in archaic times when the same men were both demagogues and generals (rather than orators as in later times), they used hostility to the rich to win the people's trust and establish tyrannies (1305a7–28, 1310b15–17). But in contrast to the simplified scheme in *The Republic*, tyrannies can also arise out of oligarchies when they oppress the people and a popular leader makes himself tyrant, when through licentious living oligarchs squander their private means and such bankrupts establish a tyranny, or when out of distrust of the people oligarchs hire mercenaries whose leader makes himself tyrant (1305a37–42, b39–42, 1306a20–23). Tyrannies can also arise when kings or elected supreme magistrates aim at despotic power (1310b18–31).

I cannot do justice to the wealth of detail in Aristotle's discussion of revolutions in tyrannies but will discuss only three of its aspects.

First, Aristotle here elaborates the characteristics of tyranny as opposed to kingship. Whereas kings aim at the noble (*to kalon*) and seek honor, tyrants aim at the pleasant and seek money; whereas kings are guarded by citizens, tyrants hire foreign bodyguards (1311a5–7). Whereas kings protect both the rich from suffering injustice and the people from suffering outrage, tyrants openly or secretly kill or exile outstanding citizens and distrust, disarm, disadvantage, and even disperse the multitude (1311a1–2). Above all, whereas kings rule by consent and cease to rule when their subjects no longer wish it, tyrants rule by fraud or force when their subjects do not wish it (1313a5–15).

Second, Aristotle articulates the causes and motives of revolutions against tyrannies (following the lines of his more general account of the causes and motives of revolutions against all regimes, at 1302a16–1304b17). The fundamental cause of revolution against tyranny (as of revolution in general) is injustice, not so much the general injustice of a tyrant's ruling without superiority, legitimacy, or consent, but specific acts of injustice (or hubris) committed against individuals, especially sexual outrages, corporal punishments, insults, and sometimes deprivations of property (1311a25–b35). The motives for revolutions against tyrannies include the anger, resentment, and hatred stirred up by such injustices; fear of future action by the tyrant against oneself; contempt (especially on the part of their friends or generals) for tyrants who display weakness, softness, or luxury; desire to share in their wealth and honor; and ambition to gain fame for overthrowing the tyrant (1311b36–1312a39). Aristotle does not include the desire to liberate one's country as such. Discord among the families of tyrants can also lead to their overthrow, as can contempt for their self-indulgent heirs (1312b10–25; think of the sons of Milošević and Saddam Hussein).

Third, Aristotle contrasts two most opposite ways of preserving tyrannies. The first way involves destruction of outstanding men, abolition of communal and educational institutions and associations conducive to high spirit and trust, constant surveillance, instigation of divisions between friends and classes, impoverishment of the subjects through confiscatory taxation, sponsoring projects requiring labor without leisure, and favoring flatterers and foreign companions; all of these means are employed to promote pusillanimity, distrust, and impotence among the tyrant's subjects (1313a35–1314a29). Aristotle attempts to avoid being blamed for reporting on such nefarious means of preserving tyrannies, as Machiavelli is so often for the advice he gives in *The Prince*, by emphasizing that these means are already known to tyrants, having been handed down by their predecessors. The second way is almost the opposite, to make the tyrant more like a king ruling with the consent of the ruled except that he retains the power to rule without their consent (1314a31–38). This way requires him to be a careful steward of the public funds and to adorn the city as if he were its trustee; to avoid contempt by maintaining his dignity, cultivating at least military virtue, and being moderate in bodily enjoyments in public; and to appear serious about the gods, personally honor the good but leave punishments to other magistrates and courts, avoid all acts of hubris especially bodily punishments and sexual outrages, and associate with the notables and protect both rich and the poor from injustices by each other, especially keeping the stronger party on his side so as not to have to disarm them (1314b1–1315b5). Aristotle promises that as a result the tyrant's rule will be nobler and more enviable, since he will rule over better subjects, and more lasting since he will rule without constant hate and fear, and his own character will be half virtuous and only half wicked (1315b5–10). He thus addresses a tyrant presumed to be concerned not only with prolonging his rule but with ruling nobly, that is, with the good character of his subjects. This second way is only "almost" (*schedon*) the opposite of the first, both in that it preserves tyrannical power and in that it does not specifically eschew, let alone reverse, all of the means employed by the first way.

Whereas Aristotle's account of the first way of preserving tyranny may be only a report of what tyrants have traditionally done, his account of the second way is unmistakably advice to tyrants, thus similar in form though not always in content to that of Machiavelli in *The Prince*. Aristotle is paradoxically both more willing to condemn tyranny as a perversion than much of our political science, and more willing to give advice to tyrants as to how to preserve their power. This paradox reflects his general conception of the tasks of political science as determining not only the best regime simply and the best for the circumstances but also the means of preservation of a given regime (cf. 1314a35–39 to 1288b22–33). This paradoxical combination also reflects Aristotle's view that as injustice is the fundamental cause of the destruction of regimes, so the primary means of their preservation is their improvement, in this case bringing tyranny as close as possible to kingship while still leaving its tyrannical power. Doing so would approach the limit case of a ruler who ruled for the common interest and with consent but who for his own interest insisted on retaining the power to rule without consent. Whereas we tend simply to equate rule with consent with rule for the common interest, Aristotle distinguishes them at least hypothetically. Insofar as tyrants pursue pleasure rather than the noble, it is doubtful, however, that a tyrant would ever follow Aristotle's advice.

According to Aristotle, tyrannies, like extreme democracies, allow freedom to live as one likes (VI 1319b28–32). This contrasts sharply with the total regulation of private life we attribute to "totalitarian" regimes, but it may remind us of those contemporary regimes that allow social and economic freedom so as to preserve a total monopoly of political power on the part of the ruling party or dictator.

Aristotle's discussion of the destruction and preservation of tyrannies also has implications for foreign policy. Tyrants, to preserve their rule, stir up wars to keep the people busy and continuously in need of a leader, and their rule may be overthrown when stronger neighbors under democracies, kingships, or aristocracies seek to overthrow them, owing to the opposition between their regimes (1313b28–29, 1312b1–9; see also Plato *Republic*, 567a, 579a).

The modern phenomenon of philo-tyrannical intellectuals and even philosophers may remind us of some of the incidental portraits in Plutarch's *Lives*. Philistos, Plato's successful competitor at the court of Dionysius the Younger, is described in Plutarch's *Dion* as philo-tyrannical, which Plutarch links with his love of luxury and power (11–14, 19, 36). Anaxarchus (52–53) in Plutarch's *Alexander* seems to be philo-tyrannical and appears to be a flatterer, depending on whether one views Alexander as a tyrant as he was by Callisthenes, Anaxarchus' antityrannical philosophical competitor in the camp of Alexander (54–55), or instead as Plutarch describes him in *On the Fortune or the Virtue of Alexander* as a philosopher ruler who civilized Asia, realized Zeno's Republic, and conquered to make all mankind one people subject to one logos, one regime, one law, and one justice (328a–329c, 330de). The question of Alexander and his philosophical apologists corresponds to those of whether modern tyrants are practitioners of tyranny for the sake of implementing an ideological program rather than mere lovers of luxury, power, and praise, and whether modern philo-tyrannical intellectuals are sincere ("ideological") admirers of tyrants rather than mere flatterers and lovers of luxury and power. The distinction may be hard to make if the tyrants love to be admired by philosophers and praised for their wisdom like Dionysius the Younger (*Dion* 16, 18), though Dionysius seems to have been more interested in being praised for his philosophy than in putting philosophy into practice.

Machiavelli's *Discourses* appear at first to follow the classical analyses of tyranny. Book I, chapter 2 presents a version of the classical typology of forms of government (following Polybius VI), with three good forms, principality, aristocracy, and popular government; three bad ones, tyranny, oligarchy, and license; and mixed government, but with a few twists. Machiavelli radically diminishes the difference between the good and the bad forms: the good are "so easily corrupted that they too come to be pernicious" because of "the likeness that the virtue and the vice have in this case." The real alternative to tyranny seems to be not kingship or principality but mixed or republican government. Although his initial presentation of the cycle of regimes presents tyranny as the degeneration of kingship, Machiavelli is chiefly concerned with tyrants as the destroyers of republics (e.g., Caesar in I 10, 34.1, 37.2, 46, III 6.19, 24). Machiavelli argues for republican government over principality most emphatically on the grounds that "cities have never expanded either in dominion or in riches if they have not been in freedom," whereas under a prince or tyrant (used here interchangeably) they always decline, and if by fate a "virtuous tyrant" expands his dominion, he alone and not his fatherland profits from his acquisitions because he cannot honor the able and good or make his own city rich or powerful (II 2.1). Machiavelli avers that this can be confirmed with infinite reasons by reading Xenophon's treatise in *On Tyranny*, the *Hiero*. Presumably Machiavelli believed that no tyrant would follow Simonides' advice to Hiero to honor those who do best and enrich and augment his city (9.2, 11.13–15). Machiavelli adds (II 2.3) that in republics, wealth and population multiply because men know they can nourish the children they procreate, that their patrimonies will not be taken away, and that their children will be free and can through their virtue become "princes" (as he sometimes calls the leaders of republics). Machiavelli advocates republics over tyrannies or principalities not on the grounds that they promote virtue as dedication to the common good but on the grounds that they produce wealth and power achieved through virtue in the service of private goods protected by a protoliberal rule of law, as if he were arguing to what Plato would consider tyrannical men.

Book I, chapter 10 presents Machiavelli's equivalent of Socrates' contrast of the happiness of the just man and the tyrant in Book IX of Plato's *Republic*, lamenting that almost all are deceived by a false good and false glory and turn to tyranny instead when they could achieve perpetual honor and more security with satisfaction of mind and no less authority by making a republic or a kingdom. Machiavelli, however, appeals not to a love of justice or the common good or a concern for the state of one's soul but to a love of worldly glory, and argues for the superiority not of private life but of being the founder of a kingdom or republic or reorderer of a corrupt city as opposed to the creator of a tyranny (and thus the destroyer of a kingdom or republic).

Machiavelli's founder or reformer needs to rule alone and therefore may have to use violence to eliminate his rivals (I 9, III 30.1), and so may easily be mistaken for one who aspires to tyranny (I 9.4). A reorderer of a corrupt city can make it be "reborn" only with "many dangers and much blood" and by "the greatest extraordinary means" and by becoming prince of it so as to reorder it in his mode (I 17.3, 18.4, 55.4). Machiavelli thus articulates what we might call the problem of modern tyranny: the difficulty or impossibility of using bad means (violent one-man rule) for good ends (creating or maintaining a free state through eliminating corruption in the people and revolutionizing or equalizing the fundamental orders) (I 18.4). Machiavelli therefore distances himself from the classical distinction between kingship and tyranny. In Book I, chapter 25 of the *Discourses*, he announces that he will discuss in the next chapter the establishment of absolute power, which he says "is called tyranny by the authors," but in chapter 26 he never uses the terms "tyrant" or "tyranny" but writes instead only of "a new prince."

Accordingly, *The Prince*, with its focus on "the new prince," entirely avoids the terms "tyrant" and "tyranny." He distinguishes not between kingships and tyrannies but between republics, which alone are free, and principalities (I, V). Virtue is not the end or means of rule that distinguishes kings from tyrants but the means of acquisition employed by all successful princes. He distinguishes between princes who govern through ministers who are their slaves and those who govern through independent barons (IV), and between princes who command by themselves, which he calls an absolute order, and those who command by means of magistrates, which he calls a civil order (IX), but he does not call either of the first kinds tyrannies. The advice he gives princes may be said to combine the cruel tyranny Hiero condemns and the beneficent tyranny Simonides recommends, or Aristotle's two ways of preserving tyrannies: eliminating the envious (VI), using cruelty well (VII, VIII, XVII), attacking the great and preferring the pusillanimous to the ambitious (IX), and letting the soldiers injure the people (XIX) as in the first way; and winning over the people (IX), appearing virtuous (XVIII), abstaining from the subjects' property and women (XVII, XIX), and honoring the virtuous (XXI) as in the second way. But unlike both Simonides and Aristotle, Machiavelli recommends that the prince arm his subjects instead of hiring mercenaries, which together with his recommendation that the prince not trust in fortresses, leaves the prince at the mercy of the people rather than the people at the mercy of the prince. In this decisive sense, Machiavelli's prince may be said not to be a tyrant.

Hobbes followed the path Machiavelli blazed in *The Prince* of rejecting the distinction between tyranny and kingship. According to *Leviathan*, there are only three kinds of government, monarchy, aristocracy, or democracy, depending on whether the sovereign representative is one, more, or all (XIX). He explains that the other names of forms of government found in books of history and politics are not the names of other forms but only "the same forms misliked. For they that are discontented under *monarchy*, call it *tyranny*." He asserts that "the riches, power, and honor of a monarch arise only from the riches, strength, and reputation of his subjects," and "no king can be rich, nor glorious, nor secure whose subjects are either poor, or contemptible, or too weak through want or dissension to maintain a war against their enemies." He therefore expects and urges kings to promote the public interest as identical with their private interest. In particular, he says it is the duty of the sovereign to administer equal justice and impose equal taxes; to provide public charity and encourage commerce, agriculture, and manufactures; and to make only those laws necessary to prevent subjects from hurting themselves, leaving them as free as possible (XXX).

Locke, in contrast, pursued the *Discourses*' forthright advocacy of liberty against tyranny. He returns to the classical definition of tyranny as the ruler's exercise of power, "not for the good of those who are under it, but for his own private separate advantage" and making "not the law but his will the rule" (*Two Treatises* I 199). He defines the public good in the mode of modern liberalism as the preservation of their properties (understood as the lives, liberties, and estates of individuals; see also I 92, II 87, 88, 124, 134). But the violation of law and the pursuit of the ruler's private rather than the public interest can be presumed from the very existence of absolute arbitrary power, which is, as such, inconsistent with the existence of civil society at all (II 90–93). His dichotomy between lawful government, in which the legislative power is placed in collective bodies, and unlawful absolute arbitrary power (II 94) takes the decisive step toward our dichotomy between democracy and dictatorship. The lawful king differs from the tyrant first of all by his sharing the legislative power with a collective representative body. Locke, however, not only rules out formal and obvious absolutism, but urges vigilance on the part of the people's representatives against the efforts of those holding power to put their own wills in place of the laws, to take away the property of the people, and to reduce them to slavery under arbitrary power, and if necessary to lead resistance against those efforts before they result in full-fledged tyranny (II 202–243). The politics of liberty becomes constant vigilance against incipient tyranny.

Classical political philosophy is distinctive and remains instructive in that its paradoxical and nonpolemical combination of tyranny as regime without legality, legitimacy, limitation, or consent that rules in the private interest of the ruler and treats its subjects as slaves, together with advice to tyrants as to how to preserve their rule, reveals the tyrannical aspects of all societies, as it inquires into the character and motives of the tyrant and engages in a dialogue with the tyrant or would-be tyrant as to whether tyranny leads to happiness.

We might conclude that the modern tyrannies that, as Strauss wrote, "surpassed the boldest imagination of the most powerful thinkers of the past" and differed essentially from classical tyranny (Strauss 2000, 23), nonetheless can be said to have attempted to put into practice perverted versions of the advice that Xenophon's Simonides and Aristotle gave tyrants, and of the program that Plato's Socrates attributed to his philosopher kings, while retaining the most violent means, unlimited power, and unbridled passion of classical tyranny expanded by modern technology.

SOURCES

Aristotle. 1984. *The Politics.* Trans. Carnes Lord. Chicago: University of Chicago Press.

Hobbes, Thomas. 1985. *Leviathan.* London: Penguin.

Locke, John. 1965. *Two Treatises of Government.* New York: New American Library.

Machiavelli, Niccolò. 1996. *Discourses on Livy*, trans. Harvey C. Mansfield and Nathan Tarcov. Chicago: University of Chicago Press.

———.1998. *The Prince.* Translated by Harvey C. Mansfield. Chicago. University of Chicago Press

Nietzsche, Friedrich. 1997. *Daybreak: Thoughts on the Prejudices of Morality.* Cambridge: Cambridge University Press.

———. 1996. *Human, All Too Human: A Book for Free Spirits.* Cambridge: Cambridge University Press.

Plato. 1988. *The Laws of Plato.* Trans. Thomas L. Pangle

———. 1991. *Republic.* Trans. Allan Bloom. New York: Basic Books.

Plutarch. 1959. *Plutarch's Lives.* trans. Bernadotte Perrin. Cambridge: Harvard University Press.

———. 1969. "On the Fortune or the Virtue of Alexander." In *Moralia.* Cambridge: Harvard University Press.

Strauss, Leo. 2000. *On Tyranny.* Chicago: University Of Chicago Press.

Chapter 10

Is There an Ontology of Tyranny?

Waller R. Newell

In this essay, I explore the extent to which tyranny possesses an ontological basis, and how that basis shifts between ancient and modern thought. My premise is that, interesting and salutary as it may appear to do so, one cannot posit a single psychology of tyranny that explains its ancient and modern types. The theme of tyranny is intrinsically connected to the relationship between human beings and nature. As the meaning of tyranny alters, so does the relationship of reason, virtue, will, and technical prowess to nature—and the reverse is equally true. Tyranny thus emerges as a crucial avenue for thinking through the shift from classical political theory to that of modernity, crystallized as the conquest of nature.

I draw a contrast between the Platonic understanding of tyranny as a misguided longing for erotic satisfaction that can be corrected by the education of eros toward civic virtue and the modern identification of tyranny with terror. Although I do not discuss Hegel, the following reflections are very much informed by his analysis of the French Revolution in the *Phenomenology of Spirit* (Hegel 1977, nos. 582–95). Hegel locates a change in the meaning of tyranny in modern politics from the tyrant's pursuit of pleasure to an impersonal, self-abnegating, and therefore seemingly "idealistic" destruction of all premodern ties to family, class, and region in the name of a contentless vision of unified community or state. Thus, whereas Plato considered tyrants to be fundamentally venal, what has been so frightening about modern terroristic rulers like Robespierre, Stalin, Hitler, and Pol Pot is precisely their imperviousness to ordinary greed and pleasure in their rigorous dedication to a "historical mission" of destruction and reconstruction. Their savagery becomes a duty that cannot be "compromised" by their own self-interest or even love of glory, which arguably puts them outside of the Platonic starting point for the diagnosis and treatment of the tyrannical personality. Their eros cannot be rehabilitated because it is absent in the first place, rooted out by an exercise of will.

I argue that Machiavelli's formulation of the relation of princely *virtu* to *Fortuna* is at the origins of the ontological shift in the meaning of tyranny, transferring to the secular prince a transformative power of creation ex nihilo, formerly reserved for God. For Plato, tyranny is a misunderstanding of the true meaning of satisfaction whose cure is the sublimation of the passions in the pursuit of moral and intellectual virtues grounded in the natural order of the cosmos.[1] The Machiavellian prince, by contrast, stands radically apart from nature construed as a field of hostile happenstance, so as the more effectively to focus his will on attacking and subduing it. Mastering *Fortuna* includes the prince's mastering that part of his own nature—eros specifically—vulnerable to believing in the Platonic cosmology with (what Machiavelli takes to be) its unwarranted, delusory hopefulness about the success of nobility and reason in the world. The result is a new kind of power seeking that is at once passionately selfish and cold-bloodedly methodical—a mixture not accounted for in the Platonic psychology of tyranny. With Machiavelli, we encounter a new view of princely vigor according to which terror can be a catalyst for social and political reconstruction. For Plato and the ancients, the tyrant is a monster of desires who plunders and ravishes his subjects. Beginning with Machiavelli, the prince is envisioned as dispensing terror in a disciplined manner so as to purge society of its bloated desires and corrupt "humors" and thereby lay the foundations for a stable and productive social order.

I

Since I proceed at a certain level of abstraction, let me furnish some preliminary content by beginning with a specific set of contrasts between Machiavelli and his closest point of contact among the ancients, Xenophon.[2] The most important difference between them is the extent to which Xenophon's writings on princely rule (culminating in the *Cyropaedia*) explore a kind of high political hedonism. Cyrus' motivation in the *Cyropaedia* is not only the pursuit of honor, but the pursuit of pleasure from the successful arrangement of his life and tastes. More importantly, he is consumed by an eros to gratify "all men" (Xenophon 1968, 1.1.5) without their being in a position to gratify him in return. In this respect, Xenophon's presentation of his rise to empire is a riposte to the Aristotelian contention that magnanimity could be confined within the boundaries of the polis and republican self-government.

Xenophontic hedonism is also revealed by the fact that Cyrus' empire is the attempt to actualize the teaching about the Good explored by the Xenophontic Socrates, a teaching that (in contrast to Plato's *Republic*) is not only not necessarily connected to a polis, but in fact cannot be reconciled with republican government. Ruling on behalf of the Socratic Good, Cyrus builds a cosmopolitan multinational empire based on the division of labor (to this extent like the *Republic*) and the ability of individuals to actualize their respective capacities and enjoy the rewards of their merit.

Cyrus' own fulfillment as an individual at the peak of this vast multinational household crowns the ranked satisfactions available to the meritocracy that serves him. His rule is the working out of Aristotle's definition of monarchy strictly speaking in Book III of the *Politics* as the rule of a prudent man according to the proper art of household management and capable of extension over many cities and nations. In keeping with this teaching about political hedonism, which implies a rank ordering of respective human satisfactions, Xenophon—in contrast with Machiavelli—evinces serious reservations about man's capacity to interfere with or reshape the order of nature and the order of the soul's satisfactions. For example, Cyrus' father (a Socrates stand-in) warns the ambitious young conqueror that the variability of fortune (*tuch?*) sets limits on what we can impose on nature through art (*techn?*). To this we should add Xenophon's comparative assessment of Cyrus as a "good" man who practices the art of ruling vis à vis the gentleman or "beautiful" character pointed to by Iscomachus and the Spartan Lysander. These distinctions are also given in the order of the soul's natural satisfactions, and the possibility that even Cyrus' meritocratic empire cannot encompass all of them (particularly the *kalos kagathos*) reflects a natural limitation on the capacity of even the best regime to foster every form of human excellence (Xenophon 1968a, 1.6, 2.3.4; Xenophon 1968b, 11.8, 4.4–16, 4.17–25; Xenophon 1968b, 3.9.10–13).

From this perspective, Machiavelli's differences stand out starkly. The capacity to transform nature that Machiavelli attributes to the virtuous prince goes much further than anything entertained by Xenophon. Machiavelli has no teaching about political hedonism in the high sense of showing how the virtues of the statesman par excellence are also the key to happiness (that Machiavelli promotes the gratification of pedestrian desires in "the people" [*The Prince*, chap. 9] as a bond between them and the prince does not contradict this assertion). Machiavelli cannot have this teaching because he does not share Xenophon's view that there is an order of nature or the soul's satisfactions. The lack of a high political hedonism in Machiavelli's thought is connected to his view of the world as *Fortuna*, as clashing and hostile motions or "bodies." The radical elevation of motion over rest, reversing the priority of classical philosophy and political philosophy, is the source of a series of paradoxical assertions that stand the classical teachings (including Xenophon's) on their head—to wit, that "disunity" and "chance" were the source of Rome's greatness (Machiavelli 1996, 1:2, 4). By contrast, it is as true for Xenophon as it is for Plato or Aristotle that only unity or rest could be the source of the best regime or the art of ruling. For again, Cyrus' cosmopolitan empire is the proper art of household management writ large, a reflection of the natural order.

In this connection, we should note the continual privileging throughout *The Prince* of touch and sensation over sight ("everyone sees you, few touch what you are," chap. 18). The distrust of the visible phenomena of everyday politics, the preference for the hidden, the subterranean, the unproclaimed, goes together with the rejection of classical metaphysics (whose most famous Socratic metaphor is the eye of the soul, implying an initial trust in how the visible "looks" of political life present themselves to the eye and are clarified through logos). This is summed up in Machiavelli's maxim that it is better for the prince to be feared than loved (Machiavelli 1985, chap. 17). Love orients us to the world of the visible. The loving prince (for example, Scipio) believes he can trust his subjects' love for him as he stands revealed in his splendor for having successfully ascended the ladder from lower to higher virtues. He is in turn for them a visible object of erotic longing for the noble and good. Fear, by contrast, cuts underneath the world of the visible and touches us in our innermost passions, and for Machiavelli is therefore more reliable, since opinions about the noble can change, while our fear of death is constant. For Xenophon, by contrast, although Cyrus' status as a noble ruler and an object for his subjects' admiration is certainly open to suspicion and undercut by many of his own hidden actions, it is by no means a pure illusion or manipulation of appearances.

As Aristotle says in *Politics* Book I, there is room for the art of political construction and fabrication—what Machiavelli comprehends as the mastery of *Fortuna*—in statesmanship. But it must be severely circumscribed, or politics (whether republican or monarchical) would collapse into mastery, and the political realm would disappear. Hence, Aristotle says, we must believe that, just as nature provides us with a sufficient wherewithal for economic survival such that nature need not be radically transformed by *techné*, so is it also true that nature provides statesmanship with people whose natures possess a sufficient degree of virtue that they do not have to be "made" into citizens from scratch (Aristotle 1967, 1258a2030). For all the greater latitude that Xenophon gives to imperial politics, and notwithstanding his comparative diminution of the claims of republican government, he is in agreement with this argument of Aristotle's, and the limitation his political theory places on the constructivist dimension of statecraft is the fundamental philosophical difference between him and Machiavelli. A telling sign of this is that in the *Hiero*, the work of Xenophon's that is most candid about transforming a tyrant into a benevolent "leader," it is not a philosopher who dispenses the advice but a poet (literally, a "maker"). Evidently, Xenophon wishes to separate the philosopher from the teaching that suggests nature (in this case a human nature) can be transformed or refabricated. Machiavelli, by contrast, simply merges himself as philosopher with the poet, assuming the same transformative role with respect to the addressee of *The Prince* that Xenophon has Simonides assume with respect to Hiero.

Now, to be sure, Machiavelli also believes there are limits on our capacity to master *Fortuna*, providing a philosophical point of contact with the classics. Still, Machiavelli's optimism about the extent of our capacity to master *Fortuna* far exceeds anything to be found even in Xenophon, the classical thinker most open to a politics of imperialism, individualism, and acquisition. One need only mention the contention in chapter 6 of *The Prince*, that the most outstanding examples of virtue were able to "introduce into matter whatever form they pleased." This is a familiar scholastic formula for describing God's power to transform nature ex nihilo. That Machiavelli appears to transfer this capacity for open-ended transformation to a human ruler speaks for itself—its radicalism can hardly be exaggerated. It goes together with the assertion that *Fortuna* provides such men with nothing more than the "opportunity" to test themselves, in the form of dismally unpromising, obscure, dangerous, and hostile origins and circumstances. Think, by contrast, of how favored Xenophon's Cyrus was by nature and circumstance—his character and talents, the education he receives, his grandfather's preference for Cyrus as his heir to the throne of Lydia. For Machiavelli, by contrast, the only favor nature does us is to goad us to strike back and make a stand. Understanding *Fortuna* leads to radical alienation and dissociation from nature, an experience that equips us with the strength of will to turn back against nature and transform it.

In this connection, let me turn to Xenophon's *Hiero* and Machiavelli's rejoinder to it. Like Socrates in Book IX of the *Republic*, Simonides tries in part to convince Hiero that he will not only be more secure in his rule, but he will be a happier man, to the extent that eros gives way to friendship (*philia)* in his soul. Because neither his personal nor his public relations will be exploitive, he can trust the friendship others profess for him. Undoubtedly, Hiero is dissimulating about the degree to which he really wants friendship as opposed to the power to possess both the city and other people as a lover. Nevertheless, he is not *simply* lying, I think, when he says that he would prefer voluntary and trusting friends to minions who are afraid of him and secretly hate him. In other words, while Hiero may not be a promising candidate, it is plausible that the moderating of eros into *philia* both personally and politically is meant seriously as a possible way of reforming a tyrant (similar to the Platonic Socrates' argument to Callicles in the *Gorgias*).

For Machiavelli, by contrast, the problem is with the whole assumption that eros exists in the first place and can therefore at least be plausibly discussed as the basis for understanding tyranny and perhaps moderating it. Machiavelli is not simply saying: The ancients were naive to think that a tyrant will give up his erotic pleasures for the calmer pleasures of friendship. What he objects to is the whole characterization of the tyrant as erotic, the whole psychological category of eros, precisely because it *does* contain the possibility for reforming the tyrant however great the difficulties may be. It is the very belief in the existence of eros, of beauty and nobility, that corrupts—this is the problem with Scipio, who spoiled the soldiers with his love (Machiavelli 1985, chap. 17). This is why, again, properly understanding *Fortuna* jolts you into realizing that there are no objects in the world for your erotic longing, only alienation, dissociation, and the need to fight back. The ancients ask: Which way of life is erotically more satisfying, philosophy or tyranny? For Machiavelli, it is the very posing of the question in this way that obscures clear thinking. The methodical alternation within oneself of caution and impetuosity—of fox and lion—takes the place of the soul's openness to transcendence through the longing for the beautiful.

II

Having made these specific comparisons between Machiavelli and the classical thinker most congenial to his project as an initial way of disclosing what precisely is modern about Machiavelli's teaching on tyranny, I now want to broaden the argument into a general contrast between ancients and moderns. To this end, I suggest looking at politics as a tension between the primordial and transcendental, a tension revealed by the psychology of *thumos*. By primordial, I mean not only the idea that politics serves the passions, but the ontology that establishes the primacy of the passions: the sense that man is burdened with a consciousness of his finitude and individuality (an emphasis on anxiety stretching from Hobbes to Heidegger). In this view, origins are fundamental. By transcendental, I mean the view of politics as directed toward a common end that lifts man above his passions and orients him toward permanence and eternity. Whereas primordial politics has as its extreme the abstract heterogeneity of the passions (what Hobbes terms the "similitude of the passions" [Hobbes 1968, 82–83]),[3] the extreme of transcendental politics is the abstract homogeneity of pure self-identity and the One (exemplified by Socrates' argument in the *Republic* [420b–421c] that the citizens of the *kallipolis* should be united like the limbs of a single body). Tyranny emerges as the attempt to actualize as a political project these extremes of formal or genetic transcendence, corresponding respectively to the ancient and modern paradigms of tyrannical action.

In Plato, aggressiveness derives from the psychology of *thumos*—not psychology in the behavioral sense, but as an intimation of the link between the soul and the world. The spirited man is the revealer of the gods, whom he calls into being to lend his own suffering or frustration the significance of a cosmic opponent (as when Achilles challenges the river god [Plato 1968, 391a–b]). This man also invokes the gods as allies in punishing others, avenging himself for the deprivation he suffers. The spirited man can be subversive of the city when, like Leontius, he is drawn to dwell obsessively on the crimes and violence on which even lawful societies are founded [439e–440b]. Like Polus, he may feel he has to become a tyrant out of fear that he will otherwise be tyrannized over (Plato 1952, 469–470). What is common to these manifestations is that the disjunction between man's longings and their goal hurls him back on himself, with increased feelings of fear and vulnerability or anger and belligerence. *Thumos* is revealed in this tension (one of its etymologies relates it to rushing like the wind), calling on the gods from the depths of the soul not to forsake us. As the embodiment of *thumos* for Plato, Achilles is either a mad hero or a coward; in the *Laches*, the Athenians' *thumos* impels them either to attack madly or break and flee.

The complement of *thumos* is eros, the longing for completion through union with the beautiful or noble. Spiritedness comes to the fore when eros is thwarted. Callicles, who loves Demos and the Athenian *demos*, loses his temper when Socrates likens his position (both personally and politically) to a catamite. Before that, his mood is one of sublime confidence in his own capacities and of admiration for the even greater "natural master" who tramples over all convention (Plato 1952, 482–86). The most potent figure is the man whose *thumos* is absorbed into his eros, who sails above anxiety in his urge to consummate his union with the city, his "beloved." For Plato, the root psychological motivation behind tyranny is an erotic longing to possess the city in the same way that ordinary men would long to possess another human being. In such a deformed soul, the zeal and aggressiveness of *thumos* become the allies of the eros for possessing the city. The aim of Platonic civic pedagogy is to reorient eros toward the love of the Good glimpsed through philosophizing, so that *thumos* can act as the ally of wisdom and the civic virtues.

Much of Platonic and Aristotelian political psychology is concerned with elaborating this tyrannical longing to possess the city with a view to disarming it and converting the energies of tyrannical eros and *thumos* to the service of republican citizenship and, in the best instance, philosophy. But uncovering the treatment requires a certain hermeneutical attentiveness because as much is stated by silence as by assertion. The union of eros and *thumos* in the tyrannical longing to possess the city like a lover is treated with great circumspection, lest painting it too vividly might make it more appealing than its corrective therapy. This is most notable through the virtual disappearance of Alcibiades, who fully embodies the alliance of *thumos* with eros in tyrannical longing, after the early protreptic dialogues, interrupted only by the magnificently ambivalent portrait of him decades later buried deep within five layers of recollection in the *Symposium*. In the *Laws*, it is suggested that a man possessed of "an erotic love of the city" might be the one who could found a city in accordance with the mores being discussed by the Athenian stranger (709–12). Yet, although this hint of a Promethean human founder is by far the frankest discussion in the dialogues of the prospect of harnessing tyrannical eros to the achievement of a just regime, it is no more than a hint, rapidly submerged by a theological discussion of "the god" who is to be seen as the source of the city's belief in these laws after the founding. Similarly in Aristotle's *Politics*, a founder is mentioned briefly in connection with the admission that human nature does not "grow" into the city but requires a degree of "making" (*poiēsis*, 1253a29).

Most significantly, political eros is never adequately elaborated in the *Republic*. In Book IV, *thumos* is seen only as the master or slave of physical or (in the case of Leontius) morbid desires, and as distinct from calculation (*logismos*). Later on, when the education in philosophy is discussed, eros comes to the fore, but in a context largely abstracted from politics. The fullness of longing for and development toward the Good suggested by the analogy to the nourishing, warming qualities of the sun is an epistemological scheme. Politics, by contrast, is depicted as a cave where the sunlight does not penetrate, or only in a dim form. Life there is an imprisonment. The wall along which the masters of simulation walk recalls the wall that Leontius followed to the Piraeus. All this has the effect of depicting politics as a realm where eros cannot be satisfied, and where *thumos* is present only in its compulsive and anxious manifestations, unless it is educated to become the guardian of the laws. Only philosophy can channel eros toward its satisfaction. Hence, when the three parts of the soul are reinterpreted in Book IX as forms of desire, Glaucon has long since been ready to reject tyranny as a life of aimless, degrading pleasures. Only in the ostensibly more personal, less political milieu of the *Symposium* does Plato find it safe to present an eros for the city as being *on the route* to the satisfaction that philosophy more nearly approaches. But even in Diotima's sketch of a continuous ascent from lower to higher forms of eros entailing political virtue, the potential for clashing ambitions among the lovers of the city is largely suppressed. Alcibiades' belligerent entrance afterward provides, through the dramatic action of the dialogue, a tacit emendation of Diotima's untroubled assimilation of eros to civic virtue.

In Plato, the insufficiency of this presentation is evident to the attentive reader, which invites a dialectical rejoinder to the starting points. Socrates' attempt in the *Gorgias* to convert Callicles to moderate citizenship does not meet with evident success, while the cause of the best regime's downfall in the *Republic* is the rebellion of the warrior class, suggesting that *thumos* is an element of the soul that makes the reordering of political life "according to reason" highly problematic. Most muted of all, though, is a full elaboration of the man whose eros for the city could convert his thumotic energies to the creation of the conditions for transcendental politics. For to unleash this possibility would be to court the danger of a tyranny much worse than the sort of pleasure presented in *Republic* Book IX, a Napoleon or Stalin (to analogize somewhat broadly) who conquers on the basis of a universalistic conception of the state. Xenophon, by contrast, presents in full form the possibility that Plato suppresses: his idealized Cyrus is driven by an eros for the love of all human beings, and by placing his thumotic aggressiveness at the service of this motive, he creates a cosmopolis whose universality and meritocracy mirrors philosophic truth in as direct a manner as is possible for a regime, that is to say by dispensing altogether with the polis.

In Aristotle, the psychology of eros and *thumos* virtually disappears as politics is categorically divided from philosophy and, therefore, from the fullest human satisfaction. In Plato's dialogues, the life of philosophy is always present in the form of Socrates to surpass all political longings. At the same time, at least the possibility is sketched that, through the rule of philosopher kings, politics could bask directly in the light of the Good. Aristotle rigorously divides the two realms of life, endowing politics with greater stability and self-sufficiency by blanking out the superior competing alternative (philosophy). There cannot be a single apodictic "science" that would enable a monarch to grasp all political problems, as Plato had depicted in the *Statesman*. Instead, flesh-and-blood rulers and citizens must try to develop prudence in assessing how far particular events and variable circumstances can measure up to natural right. Although there is some question whether the great-souled man of the *Nicomachean Ethics* would really be satisfied with the austere aristocratic republic outlined in the last two books of the *Politics* (as opposed to becoming Cyrus), the contradiction is much less glaring than that between, for example, Callicles and the Auxiliaries of the *Republic*. *Thumos* becomes a mere subdivision (albeit the "most natural" form [Aristotle 1977, 1116a20–1117a10]) of courage, rather than (as for Plato) the part of the soul that is the source of this political virtue as well as of religious revelation and theology (the theology of Books II and III of the *Republic* is specifically fashioned for the thumotic part of the soul and city). Although there are cryptic references in Aristotle to a godlike ruler whose claim supersedes all others (*Politics*, 1288a25–30), the psychology of *thumos* and eros fades from view in the same measure as the politics of transcendence are conventionalized and fenced off from philosophy.

III

The overwhelming practical aim of classical political philosophy was, as it were, to make Coriolanus content with Rome. Plato is more revealing than Aristotle because he concedes that the longing for satisfaction from politics may be, in rare instances, guided directly by the longing to transcend human finitude altogether. Still, common to both is the conviction that philosophy is a superior life, both in dignity and pleasure, to any kind of politics. A useful way of taxonomizing subsequent political thought is to see how this assumption is challenged through a reinterpretation of the psychology of political ambition (eros and *thumos*). For Plato, the gods revealed by *thumos* are not a human project. They are an "enthusiasm" issuing *through us by way of thumos*, a revelation further clouded by the needs and passions men bring to their piety. Hence, the gods are not inventions, but both approximations and distortions of the divine *nous* that orders the world and is the source of wisdom. As Book X of the *Laws* shows, the spirited man's resentment and despair over the gods' indifference or malevolence toward the human situation can be an invaluable propaedeutic, if not to philosophy, at least to a philosophical theology that grounds republican citizenship (899–904). The same is true of eros—sexual passion is a low but real intimation of a beauty that objectively graces nature's most perfect beings.

The subsequent tradition, I would argue, is characterized by the ontological priority of *thumos* over eros. In other words, the time-bound, anxious, individualistic side of human longing is radicalized and separated from an openness to its objective satisfaction guided by eros—union with the beautiful. In keeping with this is the transformation of transcendental politics as the approximation by political life of the objective *nous* that orders the cosmos into a self-conscious human construct fashioned in opposition to a nature devoid of purpose. Looked at in Platonic terms, in other words, the rest of political philosophy is dominated by *thumos*: the thumotic man comes into his own virtually unchallenged—anxious, self-conscious, alternately fearful and arrogant, ready to storm the heavens in order to get three meals a day. What is more remarkable, however, is that precisely as *thumos* is liberated from its classical restraints, modern political psychology loses sight of *thumos* as a phenomenon about which it can give a reasonable and rounded account.

When everything is *thumos*, *thumos* disappears. Not being limited by anything, it cannot be defined and compared.

Of paramount significance to this change is the reinterpretation of political ambition effected by Christianity. In St. Augustine, for example, the happiness that Aristotle believed could only be achieved by the political community becomes the preserve of the City of God. Politics, the city of man, is separated and reduced from this happiness to the merely negative police function of restraining human sinfulness after the Fall so as to maintain order and the church as the City of God's earthly outpost. "Virtue," a term Plato and Aristotle use to describe various kinds of human excellence ranging from the statesmanship of Pericles to the talent of ordinary artisans, and not necessarily or exclusively synonymous with law-abidingness or self-restraint, is now narrowed to mean the suppression of worldly desires. Political virtues like pride and magnificence (fueled by an eros for honor) are denied to be virtues at all, and they are depicted as nothing but caricatures. Since all happiness has been banished to a spiritualized Beyond, political ambition is drained of its erotic character (the longing for happiness, immortality, the noble, and the good) and, thus deontologized, is depicted as a gray and compulsive drive toward "dominion," "power," and "vainglory." Whereas soul (*psyché*) had originally meant undifferentiated life, soul is now dichotomized as bodily *animo* versus spiritual *anima*. Christianity's diminution of nature to the corporeal and perishable helps explain the hardening of the two dimensions of primordial and transcendental politics into a metaphysical cleavage. St. Thomas tries to fill the chasm between the two worlds and preserve a place for human nature in its own right, to be filled with Aristotle's philosophy. But he, like Augustine, makes God the efficient cause, the creator who imposes final and formal causes on matter, thus elevating the lowest cause in the *Physics* to the highest. Nature can only hold up under the sustaining impact of God's will. For Aristotle, efficient cause had been, along with material cause, solicited to movement by the self-movement of substantive Being most clearly manifest in formal and final cause.

Machiavelli is the founder of modernity, but his transformation of political philosophy could not have taken place without Christianity. By viewing Machiavelli in light of the tension between the primordial and transcendental, the following emerges: Machiavelli accepts the Christian reduction of politics to "dominion" while rejecting the City of God. He urges the return to classical praxis (Rome) but the rejection of classical thought that he groups with Christianity (the "imagined republics" of Plato and St. Augustine). This means a new synthesis. In some sense, Machiavelli recovers the phenomenological richness that we find in Plato's and Aristotle's political theories, the full-blooded depictions of rule, virtue, and ambition. Yet he interprets these phenomena in post-Christian terms, as mediations and epiphenomena of *dominio*. In urging, for example, that man forsake the allegiance of his soul (*anima*) to the City of God so as to recover the commitment of his spirit (*animo*) to the earthly fatherland, Machiavelli, even in repudiating Christian otherworldliness, accepts its mundane interpretation of political virtue. Nowhere does Machiavelli account for political eros. His heroes have lusts that occasionally distract them from the frigid "glory" of mastery, but none of them are "lovers of the city."

Machiavelli accepts the primordialist view of politics as a field of passions and raises it to a metaphysical certainty, as had Christianity. While rejecting the Christian God, Machiavelli accepts the Christian view of nature as forces that issue out of a void and return to it. *Fortuna*, like God, is what/that it is. In this sense, God is assimilated by Being, or, put another way, nature is collapsed into existence subject to time. While for Christianity, nature so conceived was perishable and corrupt unless held up by God's supernatural will, for Machiavelli it is the source of all vitality, spontaneity, and energy. Whereas for the classics, *Fortuna* was a subsidiary dimension of the whole within its supervening beneficent orderliness, Machiavelli identifies it with Being *tout court*. By recognizing *Fortuna*, we recognize that nature does not support classical or Christian virtue and offers no prospect for peace and decency. This awful truth, however, liberates us to face the world without delusion and bend it to our will, making it as productive and livable as we can. This requires a politics in which acquisitiveness is liberated and served by the new art of government. The spontaneity and willfulness of *Fortuna* well up into each of us as our passions, the "lion" of human psychology. By releasing this chunk of *Fortuna* within ourselves, we adjust ourselves to *Fortuna* and anticipate her treacherous reversals. Being at home with our selfishness, we build dams to prevent the world from upsetting our plans. This requires, of course, that we purge ourselves ruthlessly of any lingering disposition to reify *Fortuna* as the objective support for our human longings for peace, order, and freedom—the "imagined republics." Paradoxically, the full release of the primordial in human nature requires the dispassionate mastery of the "fox"—the wary manipulator of his own and other people's passions to construct a self-consciously human transcendental project. *Fortuna* is so unreliable that she cannot be relied upon to be unreliable: dealing with her may equally require the impetuosity of "the young" or the caution of Fabius the Delayer. Neither principalities nor republics have a privileged place, though republics are more inclusive since they can accommodate princely natures in the appropriate camouflage of dictators and leaders of "the people." *Fortuna* generates "bodies," and republics and principalities are characteristic designations of how these bodies clash, repel, and coalesce. An expansionist republic whose masses are alternately unleashed and restrained as foreign and domestic conditions require by an elite enlightened as to the truth about *Fortuna* seems to anticipate all the possible manifestations of *Fortuna*, immanentizing them in a cosmopolitan empire composed of "men of many nations" that is progressively perfected by "chance" and "the aid of events" (*Discourses*, 1:11; *The Prince*, chap. 17). Since the cosmos is not ordered by *nous*, there can be no Aristotelian "middle way" in the destiny of regimes or in the moral life of individuals. Liberality, for instance, is not a mean between parsimony or extravagance. Exposed to the clashes and reversals of *Fortuna*, you must either be parsimonious so as to avoid financial ruin, or liberal with other peoples' possessions.

Thus, Machiavelli recaptures the phenomenological *range* of classical political philosophy but on post-Christian principles. *Thumos* becomes the chief trait of the soul because the primordialist view of politics entirely displaces the transcendental view oriented through eros, which is easier to get rid of because it has already been drained out of politics by Christianity—split into mere appetitive lust within the confines of nature and the incorporeal love of God. But precisely because the transcendental object of eros has disappeared, *thumos* is also occluded—it is no longer understood in the complexity of its relations with eros, philosophy, and the gods. It has become neutral "power," the engine for the reconstruction of nature. Even tyrannical eros, which Plato saw as the basis for the critique of the tyrant, is too moral for Machiavelli because it harbors the possibility of reformation: it is already a part of Plato's solution. What Machiavelli means by *gloria* is something colder, subjective, self-made, and containing no intimation of transcendence or immortality. It is *reputazione*, the ruler's external image based on the awe, fear, and gratitude of his subjects, stemming from his successful mastery of *Fortuna*. It is at most the nimbus, the surface sheen of eros, bereft of the immanent potentiality for development toward perfection. This begins the evasion of the classical starting point for understanding tyranny.

In rejecting the City of God, Machiavelli immerses himself in the City of Man in order to offer his own elaboration of the same phenomena that Plato and Aristotle explain. His synthesis of classicism and Christianity has the universal scope of both: the phenomenological richness of classicism freed of moral restraints and the creative, antinatural willpower of Christian revelation delivered from God, the chief artificer, into the hands of man. Machiavelli cannot be reduced to liberalism, though he offers a recipe for it. In light of the narrowing of Machiavelli's teaching effected by Hobbes and Locke, one can readily and even eagerly look behind them to Machiavelli for far more of the scope, substance, and historical variability of politics, including an awareness of the limits of what avarice alone can do for a sound political order. When

Burke, for example, counters the narrow appetitiveness promoted by certain strains of modernity as the chief aim of the social contract, with a historically more robust and rounded account of the traditional "powers" of the English constitution, his understanding owes more to Machiavelli's view of the equilibrium of powers in the Roman Republic as modalities of the self-originating motions of *Fortuna* than to Aristotle's discussion of the classification of regimes under the aspect of eternity.

IV

With Machiavelli, then, transcendental politics is reduced to an epiphenomenon of primordialist politics. *Thumos* comes to the fore but loses clarity because it is no longer limited, bounded by, and contrasted with eros. Future philosophy tries instead to clarify the ways in which freedom becomes conscious of itself through the opposition of nature. The outward manifestation of the pursuit of freedom is the will to reshape nature transferred from God to man. *Thumos*, stripped of its transcendental orientation by way of eros, reduces to an existential undertow of anxiety, alienation, and rage, fueling the will's negation of nature.

Beginning with Hobbes, liberalism can be seen as an attempt to curb the Promethean excess of Machiavelli by achieving an equilibrium between primordialist politics and the transcendental politics that man now constructs to serve the passions. Just as for Machiavelli, for Hobbes man's rationality is not given from an objectively rational world, but instead dawns on him as he struggles not to be destroyed by nature's purposeless chaos and the grip of that chaos on him through the passions. Hence, the criterion for rationality is what the passions require for their own safe and efficient pursuit. This symmetry between passion and rationality requires that the passions move even further in the direction of abstract heterogeneity than in Machiavelli. Starting as he did with the full range of political phenomena, the same broad canvas of war, peace, honor, and domestic faction surveyed by Aristotle, Machiavelli saw that glory could plausibly be more worth pursuing than self-preservation, and in a few rare spirits constitutes an independent source of human motivation (in effect preserving the distinction made by Xenophon's Simonides between the "real men" who aim for mastery [*andres*] and the common run of "humans" [*anthrópoi*] who are content with self-preservation [Strauss 1983, 2.1, 7.3]). Since, for Machiavelli, domestic politics are inevitably connected to foreign policy—indeed, a republic that does not wish to atrophy and die must have an expansionist dynamic—the pursuit of glory through conquest is an irreducible necessity for healthy political bodies. Because Hobbes confines himself to the internal ordering of the polity and begins with an a priori method—the "similitude of the passions"—even these approximations of eros (as glory) fade away, replaced by the abstract and contentless *summum malum* of nonexistence.

Since the "objects" of the passions—what we want from, and how we relate to, the political community and the world—are too diverse and changeable (as are we ourselves) for us ever to be able to agree on what they are and whether they are good or bad (and even if we agreed for a time, we would change and no longer agree with our own selves), we should turn away from the world to the "similitude" of the passions themselves (*Leviathan*, 82–83). Severed from their objects in the world (and opinions about them), the passions of every individual are universally reducible to such simple modes of self-preservation as fear and desire. Aristotle had argued that humans fulfill their natures by living in a polis and offering reasoned opinions about the just and the unjust, the noble and the base, and the advantageous and the disadvantageous. These reasoned opinions correspond to what Hobbes terms the "objects" of the passions. By denying that these opinions possess any rank order or even stability, Hobbes in effect demolishes the Aristotelian understanding of the common good. Every man becomes a pedestrian tyrant motivated by the desire to stay alive and avoid violent death. By orienting ourselves by the similitude of the passions rather than their objects, we also deny from the outset intrinsic natural differences of virtue, "wit," and prudence, as well as the classical assumption that there is an independent capacity in the souls of some men to seek honor for its own sake, as opposed to mere self-preservation. Every one who introspects and understands his true motive will realize that he seeks power to remain alive. In Xenophontic language, there are no "real men," only "humans." And this is the fatal flaw in Hobbes' theory.

Why? Let us reiterate that the similitude of the passions stripped of their objects is a rationality of the origins, not of the end. Like the Cartesian ego, it is an abstraction of the conditions for pure self-hood from all mediating traditions and social practices. Machiavelli's delicate interplay between *Fortuna* and man, embodied in the cycles of history and the rise and decline of republics, becomes in Hobbes a frozen dichotomy between nature as a field of random happenstance and the anthropocentric power to refashion it to maximize survival. The great puzzle that Hobbes cannot explain is, Why would anyone want to become the Sovereign? Since the toils and dangers of attempting to rise to supreme power are by definition an insane goal for every human qua human—since we are compelled by nature to seek survival and avoid danger—how does the Sovereign achieve power in the first place? Hobbes seems to assume that these tyrants emerge like spontaneous natural forces. He envisions them as supplying the institutionalized terror that, by simulating the terror of the state of nature where the absence of government exposes us all to the daily danger of violent death, will remind every subject that no advantage to be gained from breaking the contract and attempting to tyrannize could possibly outweigh the dangers involved (Hobbes 1968, 202). At least one "real man" is needed to keep the "human beings" in line. But Hobbes' theory cannot account for the possibility of such a man.

Clearly this tyrant will be a man of *thumos*. In a tacit revision of Plato's three states of the soul and city, Hobbes says that it is not the highest part, the "head" and the seat of "counsel" that will rule, but the middle part—which Plato identifies as *thumos*, and which Hobbes identifies altogether with the "soul" and the seat of "will" and "command" in contrast with "counsel," thus joining Machiavelli in preferring *animo* to *anima* (Hobbes 1972, no. 19). But he cannot elaborate this psychology on his own principles. It is apparent only through the most cryptic inferences—for example, Hobbes' claim that although Sovereignty by institution (consent) can be distinguished from Sovereignty by acquisition (conquest), "the (Sovereign's) rights are the same in both," because both are based on fear (Hobbes 1968, 252–53). The lacuna is further illustrated by the famous conundrum as to whether Hobbes believed that man's natural power seeking is limitless in everyone or only in the "vainglorious" few. If it is limitless by nature in everyone, then politics as a universally applicable, deductively rigorous science is impossible, since no one can be relied upon (even when terrorized) to prefer safety to vainglory. If (as Hobbes mostly seems to suggest) it is limitless by nature only in a troublesome few ("young men mad on war"), however, this would suggest that the majority of human beings are by nature intrinsically capable of moderating their desires for the sake of peace—that is, in the state of nature, prior to the construction of the compact. This conclusion would undermine what Hobbes argues is the self-evidently necessary transition from the state of nature to the compact and its conflation with the Sovereign, preferably a monarchy, because it would be possible in principle for men to reach a peace treaty among themselves in the state of nature prior to coercion.

I think there is no consistent answer to this question on Hobbes' terms. Whether and how often these Sovereign natures would arise is literally a matter of accident: they would emerge spontaneously from *Fortuna*. Reason, being an anthropocentric faculty with no intrinsic connection to the world, can supply no account of these unfathomable upsurges, no psychology of statesmanship in which ambition is understood (as in Plato) as a mode of the longing for union with the immortally Beautiful and Good. The link between the anthropocentric ratiocination that demonstrates the necessity of the Sovereign and the spontaneous appearance of such natures is, at bottom, fated. This is a corollary of the larger and central ambiguity of Hobbes' philosophy. Humans are able to make sense of nature by assigning it causality, and to remedy its deficiencies by reconstructing it (the compact, for example, supplies an artificial supplement and improvement to humans' natural inability to pursue their rights without degenerating into the war of all against all, contradicting their ability to pursue their rights). But this human capacity is at bottom unfathomable, since nature itself is not objectively ordered so as to render itself intelligible to human reason. Accordingly, the possibility of Sovereign natures emerging can only be inferred from the primordialist undertow of Hobbesian methodology, the self-emergence of *Fortuna* as what/that it is. Because of Locke's bourgeois-democratic emendation of Hobbes, and through the historical evolution of liberalism in practice, this theoretical lacuna has not been glaringly evident in the world of events. Indeed, within the liberal democracies, the taming of eros and *thumos* is one of the most striking indications that Hobbes may have been right to believe that these traits, the psychological core of classical statecraft, could be ignored, suppressed, or gradually bourgeoisified by the promulgation of a psychology of pedestrian hedonism and appetitive self-interest "in the universities," successfully actualized through the rise of commercial economies (Hobbes 1968, 728).

However, looking at the pace of modernization in the non-Western world (Mao, Pol Pot) or in Western regimes hostile to the West (Stalin, Hitler), one may wonder whether the Hobbesian Sovereign has not in fact haunted the modern project all along. In these cases, terror has been used all too literally to reduce people to the "similitude of the passions" and strip them of all religious, family, and national traditions so as to convert them into human integers who are interchangeable with one another as units of a unified and contentless compact. Perhaps nowhere is the poverty of the liberal psychology of pedestrian power seeking more apparent than here. When a tyrant is needed to reshape human nature through terror to make it conform to a psychology that by definition dismisses such tyrannical natures as impossible or absurd from the outset, then one invites the emergence of a tyrannical project that exceeds the worst prognostications of the classics while at the same time sacrificing the classics' capacity for identifying the tyrannical nature as a deformed version of the erotic longing for immortality by contrasting it with the healthy pursuit of civic honor and an ambition to serve the common good.

When everything is *thumos*, *thumos* disappears, becoming the ghost in the machine of modernization.

NOTES

1. For an elaboration of this theme, see Waller R. Newell, *Ruling Passion: The Erotics of Statecraft in Platonic Political Philosophy* (Lanham, MD: Rowman & Littlefield, 2000).

2. The trailblazer here, of course, is Leo Strauss. See *On Tyranny* (Ithaca, NY: Cornell University Press, 1968); *Xenophon's Socratic Discourse: An Interpretation of the 'Oeconomicus'* (Ithaca, NY: Cornell University Press, 1970). See also Waller R. Newell, "Machiavelli and Xenophon on Princely Rule: A Double-Edged Encounter," *The Journal of Politics* 50 (1988); "Tyranny and the Science of Ruling in Xenophon's *Education of Cyrus*," *The Journal of Politics* 45 (1983); "How Original Is Machiavelli? A Consideration of Skinner's Interpretation of Virtue and Fortune," *Political Theory*, November 1987; "Superlative Virtue and the Problem of Monarchy in Aristotle's *Politics*," *The Western Political Quarterly* (March 1987).

3. Thomas Hobbes, *Leviathan*, ed. C. B. Macpherson (New York: Penguin, 1968).

SOURCES

Aristotle. 1967. *Politics*. Trans. Rackham. London: Loeb Classical Library.

———. 1977. *Nicomachean Ethics*. Trans. Rackham. London: Loeb Classical Library.

Hegel, G. W. F. 1977. *Phenomenology of Spirit*. Trans. Miller. Oxford: Oxford University Press.

Hobbes, Thomas. 1968. *Leviathan*. Ed. Macpherson. London: Penguin.

———. 1972. *The Citizen: Philosophical Rudiments Concerning Government and Society*. In *Man and Citizen*, ed. Gert. Garden City, NY: Anchor Books.

Machiavelli, Niccolò. 1985. *The Prince*. Trans. Mansfield. Chicago: University of Chicago Press.

———. 1996. *Discourses on Livy*. Trans. Mansfield and Tarcov. Chicago: University of Chicago Press.

Newell, Waller R. 1983. "Tyranny and the Science of Ruling in Xenophon's *Education of Cyrus*." *The Journal of Politics* 45.

———. 1987a. "How Original is Machiavelli? A Consideration of Skinner's Interpretation of Virtue and Fortune." *Political Theory* (November).

———. 1987b. "Superlative Virtue and the Problem of Monarchy in Aristotle's *Politics*." *The Western Political Quarterly* (March).

———. 1988. "Machiavelli and Xenophon on Princely Rule: A Double-Edged Encounter." *The Journal of Politics* 50.

———. 2000. *Ruling Passion: The Erotics of Statecraft in Platonic Political Philosophy*. Lanham, MD: Rowman & Littlefield.

Plato. 1952. *Gorgias*. Trans. Helmbold. New York: Bobbs-Merrill.

———. 1968. *The Republic of Plato*. Trans. Bloom. New York: Basic Books.

———. 1980. *The Laws of Plato*. Trans. Pangle. New York: Basic Books.

———. 1989. *The Symposium*. Trans. Nehemas and Woodruff. Indianapolis, IN: Hackett.

Strauss, Leo. 1970. *Xenophon's Socratic Discourse: An Interpretation of the Oeconomicus*. Ithaca, NY: Cornell University Press.

———. 1983. *On Tyranny*. With a translation of Xenophon's *Hiero* by Marvin Kendrick. Ithaca, NY: Cornell University Press.

Xenophon. 1968a. *Cyropaedia*. 2 vols. Trans. Miller. London: Loeb Classical Library.

———. 1968b. *Memorabilia, Oeconomicus, Symposium, Apology*. Trans. Marchant and Todd. London: Loeb Classical Library.

Chapter 11

Tyranny and the Womanish Soul

Leah Bradshaw

Tyranny is both a political phenomenon and a disposition of the soul, or the psyche. This is something we learn from Plato in the *Republic*, where Socrates explores the affinities between dispositions of the soul and types of regimes. This chapter focuses on the psychology of tyranny, and in that respect, it looks at the permanent characteristics of tyranny as a human proclivity. When we think of tyrants, we conjure images of brutality, excess, appetitive excesses, immoderation, and shamelessness. Tyrants rule without law in their regimes, and they rule without order in their own psyches. What should prompt this degeneration is a matter of some puzzlement, even to the greatest minds in the Western tradition who have pondered the matter. It has been suggested that tyranny, both in the soul and in politics, is the extreme degeneration of politics, something that can be resisted only by elaborate structures of artifice.[1] That is a disturbing thought, as it means that tyranny is somehow "natural" to human beings and must always be countered through great efforts of will and reason. Another account holds that tyranny is the absence of good (even of what is "human"), in which case the evil of tyranny is unfathomable, merely a void of substantive good.[2]

Although I have no new definitive account of tyranny to offer, I am interested in the associations between the "womanish" soul and the tyrannical soul, as they have been explored by some of the philosophers in the Western tradition. There are some similarities between the two in these accounts, notably, preoccupation with the body, incapacity to rule the emotions, and an absence of shame. Moreover, there are suggestions that the openness of democracies encourages these traits, is friendly to woman and tyrants alike, and that the febrile laxness of democracy and its cultivation of feminine characteristics may embolden tyrants and lead to the corruption of democracy. First, let us look at the characteristic features of the tyrannical soul as they are depicted by Plato, and compare them to some of the characteristic features ascribed to the female soul throughout the tradition of political thought.

In Plato's *Republic*, we are given, as far as I know, the best account in the tradition of the affinities between the tyrannical soul and the tyrannical regime. Importantly, the tyrannical soul grows out the degeneration of democracy. *The Republic* chronicles the decay of regimes from the standpoint of philosophy, the love of truth. Since the rule of philosophers is neither practical nor possible—people would not willingly accept the rule of the philosopher, nor would the philosopher have any good reason to seek rule, since he is a pursuer of truth, not rule—Socrates looks at four types of practical political organization. They are, in descending order of virtue, the rule of the honor seekers (timocracy) the rule of the money makers (oligarchy), the rule of the freedom seekers (democracy), and the rule of the power mongers (tyranny).

Each of the four kinds of regime depicted in the *Republic* fosters a particular kind of rule and cultivates a certain sort of person. Timocracies are places of masculine vigor, warlike ethos, and high discipline. The contrast that Socrates draws between the timocratic type and his philosophic "father" is striking. In the story of decline of souls paralleling that of regimes, Socrates describes how the timocratic son emerges from the union of his philosophic father and his mother. The philosopher is a man who does not care about money, who does not "fight and insult people for its sake in private actions in courts and in public but takes everything of the sort in an easygoing way" (549d). The philosophic father has a wife who finds it vexing that her husband always "turns his mind to himself and neither honors nor dishonors her very much" (549d). The philosopher husband is indifferent in fact to his wife, possibly to any attachments in the world, because his attention is riveted on truth and divine matters.[3] Out of resentment, the wife of the philosopher father cultivates a different ethos in her son. She complains to her sons about the father's lack of courage and his lack of concern for establishing a reputation in the community. The father's indifference appears to others in the city as cowardice and meekness. "She complains about all this and says that his father is lacking in courage and too slack, and, of course, chants all other refrains such as women are likely to do in cases of this sort" (549d).

The wife has allies in the servants of the household, who see that the philosopher father does not exact what is due to him and seems to passively accept injustices committed against him and his household, and they too urge the sons "to be more of a man than his father" (549e). Torn by the conflicting demands of his father, and those of his mother and the household servants, the son sets out to prove his virility. He becomes an honor lover so that he will be praised. And so we have the decline of regimes set in motion by the pressures of women and the resentment of slaves. The kind of citizen one finds in a timocracy is a "haughty minded man who loves honour" (550b).

Timocracies are the best sorts of practical regime, in one sense, because of the high degree of cohesiveness in the community, and because the dedication to country elevates people's sentiments beyond the more immediate concerns of household and acquisition. The love of one's country and the desire to be esteemed by one's peers in the public arena is nobler than the love of one's own, even one's family. The timocracy is a regime that leans toward spirited but simple men, men who are more inclined toward war than peace, and whose principal motivation is the love of honor and victory.[4] There is no question that the timocracy is a place that fosters the most masculine of virtues. A timocratic man will be brutal to slaves but will be open and conciliatory to freemen, whom he respects. "He is a lover of ruling and honour, not basing his claim to rule on speaking or anything of the sort, but on warlike deeds and everything connected with war; he is a lover of gymnastic and the hunt" (549a). It is not stated explicitly in the *Republic*, but we can infer from Socrates' comments that the timocratic man is also a lover of women. After all, in the story of the decline, the admonitions of the mother are absolutely key to the direction of the timocratic man. It is the female who divides the son from his philosophic father and who shames the son with tales of courage and honor.

Timocracies are fragile regimes, perhaps because once fallen from grace, the honor-loving son is destined to fall even further. While honor and victory in war are appealing things to women, so too is money. The timocratic man loses his edge and his virility as his life becomes soft with acquisition and luxury. The mother figure described by Socrates in the story of the decline of regimes is not only concerned about the lack of courage in her son, but she is covetous of the wealth of others. Governed by opinion, it seems, she cares mostly for how she will be seen in relation to the status of other women. "Her husband is not one of the rulers and as a result she is at a disadvantage among the other women" (549c). What ultimately destroys the timocratic man is "the treasure house full of gold, which each man has" (550d). As wealth becomes more abundant and more coveted, the more masculine virtues of courage dissipate. Poverty becomes shameful, and the lean asceticism of the warrior is disdained. Again, the wives are invoked as central in this drama. "First, the men seek out extravagances for themselves, and begin to bend the laws so as to benefit themselves. They and their wives are willing to disobey the laws so as to increase their own wealth and status" (550d). It is at this point in the dialogue that Socrates begins to talk about the appearance of "drones," those who grow up like a disease in a hive. There is no other transformation so quick and so sure, Socrates tells us, as that from a young man who loves honor to one who loves money (553d).

The decay of timocracy, and the culpability of women in its demise, is noted by Aristotle as well. Aristotle identifies "laxness toward women" as one of the key elements in the decline of Sparta, that ancient Greek city-state most often cited as the exemplary timocratic regime (*Politics*, 1269b10). In a city where legislation is poorly handled for women, says Aristotle, one might as well consider that half the population is not ruled. This is what happened in Sparta, where the women "live licentiously in every respect and in luxury" (1269b20). A community that is "fond of soldiering and war" seems to be one that degenerates into an excessive fondness for wealth and licentiousness, except, Aristotle says, for the Celts who managed to avoid this decline because they openly honored sexual relations among males (1269b25). Too much license to women, and too much love of women, we find again, seems to be central to political decline.

The Spartans made the mistake of according some ruling functions to women, and Aristotle castigates them for this. "What difference is there between women ruling and rulers who are ruled by women? For the result is the same. Boldness is something useful in war (if then) rather than in everyday matters, but the Spartan women have been harmful even in this respect. This became clear in the Theban invasion; they were not only wholly useless, like women in other cities, but they created more uproar than the enemy" (1269b39).

Aristotle gives some account of the causes of the infection of Spartan masculine virtue by women. First, the men were away at war too much and did not pay enough attention to states of affairs at home. When women are not governed properly, they tend toward greed (127010). Because much property and wealth was in the hands of women in Sparta (Aristotle claims it was two-fifths), they could bequeath it to whomever they wished. The women did not distribute their wealth in a way that could sustain the fifteen hundred cavalrymen and thirty thousand heavily armed troops that were required to sustain Sparta's military presence. The implication of course is that the covetousness and greed of women prevented them from attending to the greater good of the regime. Women may want their men to be brave and honored, according to Plato and Aristotle, but they may love money and luxury even more.

Here, too, I cannot help but think of the famous passage in Machiavelli's *Prince*, where he exhorts the aspiring prince, the man of masculine *virtu*, to control fortune as if she were a woman, and that is by force. The glory-seeking prince, arguably a timocratic type in its pure form, without the residual conscience induced by the philosophic "father," needs both the commanding, hypermasculine force of his own will, plus the winds of good fortune, to accomplish his acts of singular founding. What is most likely to bring him down is the unpredictable force of *Fortuna*, described by Machiavelli as a woman. "It is better to be impetuous than cautious," writes Machiavelli, "because fortune is a woman; and it is necessary, if one wants to hold her down, to beat her and strike her down. And one sees that she lets herself be won more by the impetuous than by those who proceed coldly. And so always, like a woman, she is the friend of the young, because they are less cautious, more ferocious, and command her with more audacity" (Machiavelli 1985, 101).

What are the messages here from these canonical texts in political philosophy? The best kind of politics is spirited, warlike, masculine, disciplined, and frugal. For Plato, the timocratic regime is the second best, but only to the utopian rule of philosophers. Nevertheless, timocracy is afflicted by the conscience of philosophy, and is a reaction, propagated by woman, against the perceived effeminacy, cowardice, and passivity of philosophy. It is women initially who encourage the masculine virtues of honor, war, and victory. Yet it appears that it is primarily women who are responsible for the degeneration of the timocracy they encourage. For women are also lovers of luxury and licentiousness. They encourage the coveting of riches, and they aspire to rule over men. When they are successful, the masculine traits that are critical for timocracies begin to dissolve. The lean, mean warrior turns into the soft, cautious, and indulgent oligarch. The more that men turn to satisfy the desires of women, both materially and sexually (if we take Aristotle's remark seriously about the Celts), the more the regime erodes. The more power accorded to women, the more lax the state.[5]

Democracies, one tier down from oligarchies, are even more hospitable to the wiles of women, for in democracies, there is no "governing" principle, neither the pursuit of honor nor the pursuit of wealth. Democracies welcome all ways of life, affording equality to equals and unequals, which is to say, there are no distinctions qualitatively between differing types of activities. Every individual in a democracy is free to choose his internal regime, and the city is "full of freedom and free speech" with "license to do whatever one wants." Many people, Socrates says "like boys and women looking at many-coloured things, would judge this to be the fairest of regimes" (557c). Boys and women have in common the fact that they may be the love-objects of men, and the fact that they are passive rather than active participants in citizenship. They are not honor lovers. In fact, of all activities possible in a democracy, it seems that the only one that is actively discouraged is the pursuit of honor, that activity appropriate to the timocratic soul. The absence of any compulsion to rule in the democratic city, even if one is competent to do so, and the possibility of avoiding being ruled altogether, is one of the sweet attractions of democracy. The regime has "gentleness toward the condemned," an equality of treatment toward all, and contempt for anything deemed noble. In such a regime, all the timocratic virtues are inverted, and there is praise for a new kind of man. The drones of the democracy "name shame simplicity, they push it out with dishonour, a fugitive; calling moderation cowardliness and spattering it with mud, they banish it; persuading that measure and orderly expenditure are rustic and illiberal, they join with many useless desires in driving them over the frontier" (560c–d). The restraint, frugality, and courage of the timocratic man are eroded completely, so that anarchy replaces freedom, wastefulness replaces magnificence, and shamelessness becomes the new courage. The new democratic man is open to the unleashing of "unnecessary and useless pleasures"; he becomes a hedonist with no other goal than satiating his immediate desires.

Such a state declines easily into tyranny, Socrates tells us, for it is "pretty plain that it [tyranny] is transformed out of democracy" (562a). Under the conditions of tyranny, things get even more chaotic. Relations between the young and the old, between the student and the teacher, deteriorate so that all are fawning on the young. But the "ultimate in the freedom of the multitude," Socrates says, "occurs in such a city when the purchased slaves, male and female, are no less free than those who have bought them. And we almost forgot to mention the extent of the law of equality and of freedom in the relations of women with men and men with women" (563b).

Aristotle says, "everything that happens in connection with democracy of the extreme sort is characteristic of tyranny—dominance of women in the household, so that they may report on their husbands, and laxness toward slaves for the same reasons. Slaves and women do not conspire against tyrants, and as they prosper [under such circumstances] they necessarily have a benevolent view both of tyrannies and democracies (for, indeed, the people want to be a monarch)" (Aristotle 1984, 1313b, 30–40). Other characteristic features of tyranny, according to Aristotle, are the culture of suspicion (no one trusts anyone else), the welcoming of foreigners into the city "as companions for dining and entertainment" (1314a10), and the encouragement of flatterers and sycophants.

A question at this point may be, What is it specifically about women that incline them to favor democracies and tyrannies? Why should they draw men toward the pursuit of recognition (separating the son from his philosophic father), and wealth, and finally, toward power? Is there such a thing as the womanish soul, and does it incline toward tyranny? Apart from the brief but scathing remarks made by Socrates in the *Republic*, we have no other discussion of this matter. We do have of course the construction of the city in speech in Book V of the *Republic*, in which it is suggested that in this city women could participate equally with men in rule if they were severed from the rearing of their children and stripped of any monogamous relations with men. Much has been written about this project, and interpretations vary from the embracing of the city in speech as a model for reform in politics, to characterizing it as a warning against ideals that are contrary to conventional inclinations.[6] However one interprets Book V, though, we are still left with the view that in the practical world of possible and actual regimes, barring any radical transformation in human relations, women are lovers of those things that lead to political degeneration, and they have a deleterious effect on men if they are improperly ruled.

Aristotle tells us something about the distinctive souls of women. Women have the capacity for deliberation (or reason) just as do men, according to him (Aristotle 1984, 1260a). Yet we know from his discussion of the household in the *Politics* that he thinks that men should rule women, albeit in a "political" fashion, that is, the manner appropriate to equals. So women are equals in some sense to men, yet ought to be permanently ruled by men. The only reason apparent in Aristotle's texts for this is that while women have the capacity for reason, they lack self-restraint. They are incapable of ruling their emotions, therefore incapable of the ruling virtue of prudence; they have the deliberative element but "lack authority" (Aristotle 1984, 1260a10). They also seem for Aristotle to be more tied to the demands and sensations of the body, and have a weakness and softness of the flesh that is opposite to the masculine vigor required for the timocratic man. It is disdainful for a man to give in to physical pain or suffering, Aristotle says, and we tend to think that these kinds of effeminate men are diseased or the unfortunate victims of some innate tendency. As examples of weakness, Aristotle cites the "hereditary effeminacy of the royal family of Scythia, and the inferior endurance of the female sex as compared with the male" (Aristotle 1926, 1150).[7]

What we can surmise from the account of decline of regimes in Plato, and from Aristotle's scattered remarks on women, is nonetheless a pretty clear picture of the fact that when men allow themselves to be ruled by women, things go badly. Laxness, disorder, the collapse of authority, the taste for luxury and excess, the excessive concern for the opinions of others—all these characteristic features of democracies and tyrannies are features that have a decidedly feminine cast.

There are other figures in the tradition of political thought who give more explicit treatment to the "womanish soul" and its rootedness in sexuality. Rousseau tells us that the only thing we can know with certainty about the sexes is that what they have in common belongs to the species, and the ways in which they differ pertains to their different sex. Rousseau suggests that, by nature, women's sexuality is all-encompassing and insatiable (Rousseau 1979, 406). By contrast, men's sexuality is intermittent. If this sexuality that is natural to women were not constrained by law and the decorum of modesty, women's sexuality would lead to the ruination of both sexes. If women acted on the basis of their natural impulses, Rousseau admonishes, "men would be tyrannized by women" and would see themselves "dragged to their death without even being able to defend themselves" (Rousseau 1979, 358–59). It is the invariable law of nature, Rousseau tells us, that women have more facility to excite desire than men have the capacity to satisfy it.

What reigns in the natural tyrannical impulses of women, according to Rousseau, is an elaborate artifice of law, custom, and habit that converts female shamelessness and audacity into modesty. Woman ought to be made to please man "to make herself agreeable to him instead of arousing him" (Rousseau 1979, 358). The subjugation of women to men, according to Rousseau, is not the work of nature but the work of *amour proper* attached to desire (358). The *moral* differences between men and women do not accord with their *natural* differences, but rather, are directly contrary to them. In the story of *Emile*, Rousseau's discourse on the education of one man, Emile's ideal partner, Sophie, is instructed from a young age by her mother to quell her natural disposition in preparation for her life with Emile. Sophie, like all girls, Rousseau says, tends by nature toward an excess of freedom, so she must be educated to repress this natural inclination. Rousseau cautions in the education of girls, "Do not allow for a single instant in their lives that they no longer know any restraint" (370). Sophie is to be trained to be an obedient wife and to uphold the ethos of the state. She must learn the art of adornment, careful to make herself pleasing but not dazzling. A beautiful woman is a plague to her husband. She must learn to speak pleasing thoughts rather than truthful ones, to become proficient in taste rather than in knowledge, and to accept the yoke of religion and to value industriousness and cleanliness above all things. If the project of "educating" Sophie is successful, "Sophie has a mind that is agreeable without being brilliant, and solid without being profound—a mind about which people do not say anything, because they never find in it either more or less than what they find in their own minds" (396). Sophie is to be governed by opinion.

If Sophie is not ruled properly, Rousseau suggests, havoc will ensue for both her husband and the state. Since her nature inclines toward the tyrannizing of men, her nature must always be constrained. Is this akin to Aristotle's recommendation for the *political* rule of women? I am reminded of the drama between Petruchio and Kate in Shakespeare's *Taming of the Shrew*. As Petruchio begins his forcible confinement of Kate, an unruly and headstrong woman whom he is determined to subdue and marry, he announces, "thus have I politicly begun my reign, and 'tis my hope to end successfully. My falcon now is sharp and passing empty; And, till she stoop, she must not be full-gorged, for then she never looks upon her lure (Shakespeare 1938, IV.I, 147–183). The "lusty wench" to whom Petruchio is so attracted is tamed into her moral role. Petruchio had sworn to Kate, "Thou must be married to no man but me; for I am born he to tame you Kate, and bring you from a wild Kate to a Kate conformable as other household Kates" (II.I, 260–308).

Shakespeare's play ends with Kate's speech about how she has learned well her proper role. "Thy husband is thy lord, thy life, thy keeper, thy head, thy sovereign; one that cares for thee, and for thy maintenance commits his body, to painful labour both by sea and land, to watch the night in storms, the day in cold, whilst thou livest at home, secure and safe, and craves no other tribute at thy hands but love, fair looks and true obedience. Too little payment for so great a debt, such duty as the subject owes the prince, even such a woman oweth to her husband" (Shakespeare 1938, V.II, 155–190).

The tradition is full of such references, the need to quell women lest they overreach their place and tyrannize over men and states. Control over women seems to work better through force than through persuasion, because women are not constrained by the power of reason, even though they are capable of deliberation. Women and tyrants are not moved by reason, but by desire, and a soul governed by desire cannot moderate itself by reason.

Now we move back to Plato's *Republic* to look at the psychological portrait of the tyrant and his uncanny resemblance to the psychological portrait of women in their natural sexuality. The tyrannical soul, as depicted by Socrates, is one wracked by eros. A tyrannical soul is one that "dares to do everything as though it were released from, and rid of, shame and prudence" (Plato 1968, 571c). A man who has a healthy and moderate relationship to himself "awakens his calculating part and feasts it on fair arguments and considerations, coming to an understanding with himself," and rules his desires. Even though "surely some terrible, savage and lawless form of desires is in every man," the prudent man controls these (572b). The tyrannical "son," Socrates tells us, is born from the democratic father, a man who "lives a life that is neither illiberal nor hostile to law, a man of the people come from the oligarchic man" (572d). Without sufficient guidance from the father, and with enticement by complete freedom, the son is "stung to frenzy." It is understandable, Socrates says, that "love from old has been called a tyrant," and "a man who is deranged undertakes and expects to rule not only over human beings but gods too" (573). A tyrannical man is drunken, erotic, and melancholic, someone who revels in parties, feasts, prostitutes, and all manner of excessive desires. Such a man will willingly throw over any loyalty to his parents or to the law "for the sake of a newly-found lady-friend and unnecessary concubine" or a "newly found and unnecessary boyfriend" (574). All constraints are stripped away, both externally in the regime and internally in the order of the soul, and in such a man "love lives like a tyrant in all anarchy and lawlessness" (575). The soul that is governed by love of this sort is one that is slave rather than free. Maddened by love, Socrates argues that the tyrant actually is the most miserable of men.

The images of corporality and sensuality in Socrates' accounts of tyranny are striking. Those who live with "no experience of prudence and virtue" are always brought down "after the fashion of cattle" to the gratification of the senses, "fattening themselves and copulating" (Plato 1968, 586). In one telling passage, Socrates says that the pleasure pursued by the tyrannical souls are always mixed with pains. "Each takes its color by contrast with the others, so that they look vivid and give birth to frenzied lovers of themselves in the foolish and are fought over, like the phantom of Helen that Stesichorus says the men at Troy fought over out of ignorance of the truth" (586c). The face that launched a thousand ships is thus cited as a catalyst for tyrannical desire. The spirited part of the soul—that which is aimed at honor and victory—is enslaved to desire when it is not instructed by the more "calculating part" of the soul. Inclining toward tyranny, men turn their ambitions and their energies toward the gratification of desires.

Apart from the reference to Helen, there are no other references specifically to women in Socrates' account of the degeneration of the tyrannical soul to women. But we can draw some obvious parallels from the references we have drawn from other parts of the text, and from other philosophers. The "womanish soul" is one that is covetous, disdainful of the prudence and virtue of the philosophic "father," prone to celebrate honor, but easily led from true honor to the worship of opinion and flattery. Women love democracies and tyrannies because they have more freedom under them. Women are physically weak and inclined toward the indulgence of the body. The love of women by men is a cause of political degeneration and of deviation from the highest callings of philosophy and prudence. Is woman not the embodiment of the tyrannical psyche in some manner? Is to love women to incline toward tyranny because in fact to love women is to become more like them?

The most compelling characterization of this that I know of is in the portrait of Alcibiades, that most arresting and dynamic of Greek rulers, whose love of the *demos* and of women is well documented.[8] We know from Socrates' admission in the *Gorgias* that Alcibiades was the only love in his life that could rival his love of truth. Famously, in the last speech of Plato's *Symposium*, Alcibiades unsuccessfully attempts to seduce Socrates, and Socrates responds to these advances by saying, "I shudder at his madness and his passion for love" (213d6). My reading of Alcibiades is profoundly influenced by the account given by Martha Nussbaum in *The Fragility of*

Goodness, which is among the most arresting pieces of political philosophy that I have ever read. Nussbaum begins her portrait of Alcibiades with this depiction.

He was, to begin with, beautiful. He was endowed with a physical grace and splendor that captivated the entire city. They did not decline as he grew, but flourished at each stage with new authority and power. He was always highly conscious of his body, vain about its influence. He would speak of his beauty as his "amazing good fortune" and his "windfall from the gods" (Nussbaum 1996, 217a), but this was not the limit of his natural gifts. Energy and intellectual power had made him one of the best commanders and strategists Athens had known, one of the most skillful orators ever to enchant her people. In both careers, his genius was his keen eye for the situation—the way he could discern the salient features of the particular case and boldly select appropriate action. About all these gifts he was equally vain—yet almost morbidly concerned with criticism and gossip. He loved to be loved. He hated to be observed, skinned, or discovered. His heart, generous and volatile, was rapidly moved to both love and anger, at once changeable and tenacious (165).

The way in which Nussbaum describes Alcibiades vividly arouses for us the picture of the successful demagogue, a man whose flamboyance and splendor captivates the people. He was shameless, except before Socrates. He was profoundly democratic, and as Nussbaum remarks, "those who hated democratic disorder hated him as its inspiration" (Nussbaum 1996, 165). As Allan Bloom says, "Alcibiades is distinctly not a good man, but is certainly a splendid one" (Bloom 1993, 506). While in one respect, Alcibiades appears to us as the most glorious and impetuous of men—waging battles, smashing the faces and genitals of Greek statues in a rage, walking off with an unprecedented number of victories in the chariot competition at Olympia—he lacks the moderation of the timocratic man. He is excessive in every way, and according to Nussbaum, "his story is, in the end, a story of waste and loss, of the failure of practical reason to shape a life" (Nussbaum 1996, 166).

There are other characteristic features of Alcibiades, which Nussbaum describes, that can be identified with the "womanish" elements of his soul. Alcibiades in his pursuit of Socrates, according to Nussbaum, seems to take on the role of the *erastes* (the sexually active partner), while Socrates is the *eromenos* ("a beautiful creature without needs of his own").[9] This makes Alcibiades the needy one, one who, according to Nussbaum, is both open and has a desire to open up the other. "Alcibiades reminds us," says Nussbaum, "that the urge to open things up, to get at and explore the inside concealed by the outside, is one of our earliest and strongest desires, a desire in which sexual and epistemological need are joined and, apparently, inseparable" (Nussbaum 1996, 190).

But perhaps they are inseparable only for those who are "womanish," that is, those who have all the characteristics ascribed to Alcibiades. Alcibiades may have loved Socrates, but in his life, he was a great lover *mostly* of women, and he exhibited many of the traits ascribed to women by philosophers in the tradition: lack of moderation and restraint, a taste for luxury and license, and incapacity to rule himself.[10] Plutarch records the exploits of Alcibiades, many of which have to do with bold conquest, but many also concerning the conquest of women. At one time, Alcibiades "selected for himself one of the captive Melian women, and had a son by her, whom he took care to educate." The Athenians forgave Alcibiades this indiscretion, Plutarch writes (as they forgave him many), since he nobly took upon himself publicly the acknowledgment and education of his son, yet it was Alcibiades himself who was the instigator of the slaughter of all the young men of Melos. In another example, Plutarch writes that Alcibiades had the artist Aristophon render a portrait of him reclining in the arms of a prostitute, and displayed it in public. "The multitudes seemed pleased with the piece, and thronged to see it, but older people disliked it and disrelished it and looked on these things as enormities, and movements toward tyranny" (Plutarch 1992, 269). Alcibiades appears in his drunken and erotic state at the symposium, crowned with a wreath of ivy and violets, a sign of Aphrodite, and suggestive, as Nussbaum notes, of "the strange fact that this aggressively masculine figure sees himself as a female divinity" (Nussbaum 1996, 193). The violet crown stands also for the city of Athens, "the delicate, growing sign of the flourishing of this strange and fragile democracy, now, in the time of Alcibiades, in its greatest danger" (Nussbaum 1996, 193). We know, from Plutarch, that the night before he died, Alcibiades dreamed of himself garbed in women's clothes. Alcibiades was trapped and killed while he was secluded with a courtesan, and after the arrow had killed him, "the courtesan Timandra 'Honour-the-Man,' wrapped his bitten body and his soul of flesh in her own clothes and buried him sumptuously in the earth" (Nussbaum 1996, 199).

Could it be that the most "masculine" of men, as depicted in Alcibiades, those unrestrained by the tempering effects of philosophy (think back to the decline of regimes in Book VIII of the *Republic*) are those drawn to the love of women, and to the things that women love, and hence to degeneration and ultimately toward tyranny? What appears to be hypermasculinity may not be the opposite of what is womanish; it may in fact be an aspect of what is womanish, because it is enthralled by womanish things. The alternative to Alcibiades given us in the *Symposium* is Diotima, the female goddess, who shows us the way of abandoning particular loves for the love of the good in itself. Nussbaum describes this life as one that is attached to an "immortal object," rather than to mortal flesh, "instead of painful yearning for a single body and spirit, a blissful contemplative completeness" (Nussbaum 1996, 183). The model for this kind of life is Socrates, the man who appears to have no needs, a man who can drink without ever getting drunk, who is not sexually tempted, who cares nothing for luxury, or even apparently for ordinary sustenance, who certainly cares nothing for the reputation of others. This is the picture of the "philosophic father" whom we encounter at the beginning of the decline of regimes in *Republic*, Book VIII. This is the man whom women disdain as being indifferent to their charms, and indifferent to the positions and honors accorded by the city. This is a man who is not seducible by women or men. This is a man whose eros is categorically different from that of most people. Here is Nussbaum on this difference: "We are not allowed to have the cozy thought that the transformed person will be just like us, only happier. Socrates is weird. He is in fact 'not similar to any human being.' We feel, as we look at him, both awestruck and queasy, timidly homesick for ourselves. We feel that we must look back at what we currently are, our loves and our ways of seeing, the problems these cause for practical reason. We need to see ourselves more clearly before we can say whether we would like to become this other sort of person, excellent and deaf" (Nussbaum 1996, 184).

I have quoted Martha Nussbaum at length because I think she captures so well the dissonance between Alcibiades and Socrates, though she does not draw the explicit parallels that I am attempting between the tyrannical and the "womanish" soul. Nussbaum's reading of the *Symposium* raises important questions about the pursuit of philosophy, and its relationship to the political world, but it may, by inference, raise also some important questions about the relationship between the love of philosophy and the love of women, and the relationship of *both* of these loves to the political world.

Here are some of the questions. Can one love both truth and women? If one tries to do this, is this in fact the prototype of the timocratic man? Is the timocratic project a tragic project necessarily, because the love of women (and the things they love) will put in motion an inevitable decline from pursuit of honor, to the pursuit of money, to the pursuit of power? Is it the case that the love of women makes men incline toward a "womanish soul," a soul that becomes more and more wed to the desire of desire itself? Socrates says in the *Republic* that a man who has a healthy and moderate relationship to himself, who feasts his soul on fair argument and considerations, who "soothes the spirited part," who sets the prudent part of his soul in motion, is one who "most lays hold of the truth and at this time the sights that are hostile to law show up least in his dreams" (*Republic*, 572ab). The contrast would indeed seem to be the man who is not self-contained, the man who gives in to the enticements of women, boys and slaves, those who water "the desiring and spirited parts" of the soul (Plato 1977, 550b).

The most radical conclusion is that the political world is a world in which women and the desires of women play an absolutely paramount role. If we take our understanding from Plato, we know that one is shaped by the things one loves. To love the truth is to become more *like it*. And so too to love women is to become more *like them*. If women are, as Aristotle suggests, incapable of moderating their emotions (even though they have the capacity for deliberation), and if we add on to that Rousseau's suggestion that the sexuality of women is devouring, insatiable, and "tyrannizing," and we further add the many references from Plato that associate women with the promotion of honor in their men, and their own acquisitiveness, then the picture is striking of the womanish elements of political deterioration. To be "manly" is, paradoxically, to be ruled by women, and is to develop a "womanish soul." We can understand how it is that Alcibiades, that most manly of men, ends his life dreaming of himself painted by a courtesan, and dressed in the robes of women.

Perhaps, too, we can understand much about democracies and tyrannies in general from making these associations between sexual identity and politics. In her profile of Madonna, whom she regards as "pornographic," "decadent," and "avant-garde," and as "alternatively a cross-dressing dominatrix and a slave of male desire," Camille Paglia calls Madonna "the true feminist" of the modern democratic world (Paglia 1998, 4). "Madonna loves real men," Paglia says. "She sees the beauty of masculinity in all its rough vigor and sweaty athletic perfection. She also admires the men who actually are like women: transsexuals and flamboyant drag queens" (Paglia 1998, 5). The "many coloured coat" of democracy, as Socrates warns us, appeals to women and young boys. The spectacle of Madonna reminds me, in overblown form, of the cabaret phenomenon of Berlin in the last breaths of the Weimar Republic. The flirtatious interface of democracy, fluid sexuality, and tyranny is captured brilliantly in the 1972 film *Cabaret*. Alex de Jonge writes that "cabaret was in many ways the supreme form of Weimar Berlin. Not only did it inspire works like *The Blue Angel* and *The Three Penny Opera*, it had a kind of ironic quality and informal looseness and cheekiness, a sense of political awareness that combined to make it capture the spirit of its age" (Jonge 1978, 160). The author characterizes cabaret star Anita Berber, whose "urgent dancing seemed to contemporaries to express the feverish urgency of their age" (162). "She was to be seen at boxing matches, six-day bicycle races, and in nightclubs keeping dubious company. She loved men but probably preferred women, and was fond of brandy, morphine and cocaine. . . . She was myth as much as, if not more than, artist—rather like the image of Isadora Duncan, filtered through the movies, a German version of the beautiful and the damned." As one commentator put it, "she personified the feverish twenties in Berlin, in public, as no one else" (162). So many images of Weimar and the decline into Nazism are images of this sort, including beautiful but doomed women, ambiguous sexuality, brownshirts and big boots, drugs, revelry, and decadence.

Waller Newell, in his book *What Is a Man?*, a fascinating compendium of fragments on being male, starts his introduction by announcing that "as America heads into the twenty-first century, there is an increasing widespread feeling that we have forgotten the meaning of manliness" (Newell 2000, xvii). According to Newell, in his chronicling of the manly virtues throughout the Western tradition, there is remarkable consistency in the identification of what the manly virtues are: "honour tempered by prudence, ambition tempered by compassion for the suffering and the oppressed, love restrained by delicacy and honour toward the beloved." According to the sources examined in this chapter, none of these manly virtues is conferred by the association with women, in fact, quite the opposite. Women lack prudence (Aristotle), they are ambitious for their sons in a way that detracts from real honor (Plato), and they by nature have a sexuality that is avaricious (Rousseau). Newell calls for a "return to the highest fulfillment of which all people are capable—moral and intellectual virtues that are the same for men and women at their peaks—while recognizing the diverse qualities that men and women contribute to the common endeavor for excellence" (xix). In the conclusion of his book, Newell invokes Diotima from Plato's *Symposium*. "Diotima' s ladder ranks the objects of erotic longing in a hierarchy, ascending from bodily love upward through family life, the civic virtues and, on the highest rung, philosophical contemplation. Properly explored, and articulated, our erotic attachment to another leads us in and of itself to cultivate the virtues of character—moderation, honesty, gratitude, compassion and honour" (784).

All of this is true of Diotima's account, as far as I understand it, but it does not necessarily make sense to invoke Diotima's account as a resolution to the problem of manly virtue, at least insofar as that virtue is seen in relation to women. Diotima's account does indeed draw one away from bodily love, and from the love of particular human beings, and almost certainly from the love of women. We are drawn back to the harrowing account of Alcibiades in Martha Nussbaum. It is Alcibiades who loved women, and women loved him. He was neither moderate, nor compassionate, nor grateful, nor honorable in any conventional way. We are drawn back also to consider Shakespeare's comical account of the taming of Kate in the *Shrew*, and to Machiavelli's powerful but not-often-cited remarks about the subduing of fortune and women, and women's love of the impetuous, the reckless, and the brave. Newell closes his book by telling us that "love perfects," but it is difficult to see from the canon of Western philosophy how love perfects manliness, except in the way that one might see it in Diotima's account.

There is another message in Diotima's speech in Plato's *Symposium* that may support the argument in this chapter regarding the association of tyranny with the "womanish soul." Eros, Diotima tells us, is a son born of his mother, poverty, and his father, resource. Poverty "formed the plan of relieving her lack of resource by having a child by Resource; she slept with him and became pregnant with Love" (203c). Love (eros) resembles both his mother and his father, as children are wont to do: from his mother "he's always poor; far from being sensitive and beautiful, as is commonly supposed, he's tough. . . . Sharing his mother's nature, he is always in a state of need." Insofar as he resembles his father, "he schemes to get hold of beautiful and good things" (203d). "He desires knowledge and is resourceful in getting it; a lifelong lover of wisdom; clever at using magic, danger and sophistry" (203e).

Eros is between wisdom and ignorance, Diotima says, as between his father who is "wise and resourceful" and his mother "who has neither quality" (204b). From this in-between state, born of woman and man, Eros can fulfill his proper end only when he moves toward the father, toward a greater share in wisdom and resource. To embrace the mother, Poverty, is to embrace ignorance, which Diotima tells us is to behave in some fashion as if one were a god. The ignorant have in common with the gods a lack of love of wisdom, and a lack of the desire to become wise. We may be able now to understand Nietzsche's infamous statement that "Truth is a woman." This is so only in a world in which the pursuit of wisdom is eclipsed, and Resource is trumped by Poverty. To follow the ways of the mother, to *love* the neediness of women, is to cultivate a "womanish soul" and, inevitably, to fall into tyranny. Love perfects when it goes beyond the love of women. Love destroys and corrupts when it is enthralled by women. Love perfects when it is love of the good. Love destroys when it is the love of love itself (the Socratic definition of tyranny).

NOTES

1. This is the view of Leo Strauss. Strauss holds that tyrannical rule is the extreme case of political rule in general. "The difference between the tyrant and the non-tyrannical ruler is ultimately not a simple opposition but rather that in the case of the tyrant certain elements of the character of the ruler are more strongly developed or less easily hidden than in the case of the non-tyrannical ruler." Leo Strauss, *On Tyranny*, 94. For Strauss, all forms of political rule incline toward tyranny. Only philosophy resists this inclination.

2. This is the view of Hannah Arendt. Arendt ascribes this view to Plato (though Strauss may have disagreed with Arendt's attribution). "Classical political theory used to rule the tyrant out of mankind altogether," writes Arendt, "and to call him a 'wolf in human shape'" (Plato). "What Is Authority," *Between Past and Future*, 99.

3. Allan Bloom writes in *Love and Friendship* of this divide between the philosophic temperament and all others. "If they [men] really wanted to pursue the good simply, they would have to give up their cities, their homes, those who by habit they call friends, and even perhaps themselves. This is what Socrates actually does. He lives in Athens but is not really of it; he is married and has children but pays little attention to them" (508).

4. Leon Craig in his book *The War Lover* analyzes at length the timocratic man, and Craig draws a clear distinction between honor loving and victory seeking. Timocrats can be further divided, Craig claims, between those who seek the acclaim of others (honor seekers) and those whose ambitions are more singularly directed at victory. The latter are the spiritual types open to the possibility of philosophy, argues Craig, because they are by disposition immune to the judgment of the many. The lover of victory "enjoys a kind of self-sufficiency insofar as he is the judge of his own accomplishments. . . . The good he seeks does not necessarily wed him to the crowd." It is from the ranks of this victory-loving nature, Craig claims, "that the most promising prospects for the philosophic life are to be found" (78). Craig makes a persuasive argument, but in this paper I am looking at the timocratic soul as one "fallen from grace" from the standpoint of philosophy. I am not looking at the potential rescue of timocrats by philosophy, but at their degeneration through political decline.

5. A contemporary, cranky turn on this is provided by Camille Paglia. She writes that male homosexuality in the contemporary world is a reassertion of the spirited, masculine, world-forging characteristics of the Greek pagan timocrat. "Male lust . . . is the energizing factor in culture. Men are the reality principle. They created the world we live in and the luxuries we enjoy. . . . Maleness at its hormonal extreme is an angry, ruthless density of self, motivated by a principle of 'attack.' . . . There is nothing deviant or effeminate in this kind of homosexuality. On the contrary, I view the modern gay male as occupying the ultimate point on a track of intensifying masculinity shooting away from the mother, who begins every life story. Gay men and straight men have much more in common than do gay men with lesbians or straight men with straight women." Camille Paglia, "Homosexuality at the Fin-de-Siecle," *Sex, Art and American Culture*, 22–25.

6. For the former, see Susan Okin, *Women in Western Political Thought*, where she identifies the city in speech as still the strongest and clearest model in Western political thought for the equality of men and women. For the latter, see Allan Bloom, "Interpretive Essay," where he argues that "Socrates has elaborated a regime in which no citizen has a family and thus no one can be unreasonable in the name of the family. Socrates' demand that the city be unified is identical to the demand that the body and its extensions—property and the family—be perfectly mastered. If that mastery is impossible, so is the city. We would learn from this fact that philosophy is essentially a private activity and that the city must always be ruled by prejudices" (*The Republic of Plato*, 387).

7. I have written elsewhere at length about Aristotle on women. "Political Rule, Prudence and the Woman Question in Aristotle," *Canadian Journal of Political Science* 24: 3.

8. I would like to thank the Liberty Fund, and especially Professor Charlotte Thomas of Mercer University, who invited me to a conference in December 2003 on "Alcibiades and the Democratic Soul." It was out of that conference, and the extremely interesting conversations there, that I first conceived the ideas for this chapter.

9. Nussbaum takes this from Kenneth Dover's study *Greek Homosexuality*.

10. In the dialogue *Alcibiades*, Socrates tried to persuade Alcibiades to take the road of justice, and that the appropriate course for a free man is a life of virtue. Alcibiades pledges to "attend" on Socrates and to have him as his constant companion, and to "start to cultivate justice in myself." Socrates responds skeptically: "I should like to believe that will persevere, but I'm afraid—not because I distrust your nature, but because I know how powerful the city is—I'm afraid it might get the better of both you and me" (135e). In Plato's *Symposium*, Alcibiades claims that Socrates is the only person who has ever made him feel shame, "I'm well aware that I can't argue against him and that I should do what he tells me; but when I leave him I am carried away by the people's admiration" (216b).

SOURCES

Arendt, Hannah. 1954. *Between Past and Future*. New York: Viking Press.

Aristotle. 1926. *Nicomachean Ethics*. Trans. Harris Rackman. London: Loeb Classical Library.

———. 1984. *Politics*. Trans. Carnes Lord. Chicago and London: University of Chicago Press.

Bloom, Allan. 1993. *Love and Friendship*. New York: Simon & Schuster.

Bradshaw, Leah. 1991. "Political Rule, Prudence and the Woman Question in Aristotle." *Canadian Journal of Political Science* 24: 3.

Craig, Leon. 1994. *The War Lover*. Toronto: University of Toronto Press.

Dover, Kenneth. 1978. *Greek Homosexuality*. Cambridge, MA: Cambridge University Press.

Jonge, Alexis de. 1978. *The Weimar Chronicle: Prelude to Hitler*. Toronto and New York: New American Library.

Machiavelli, Niccolò. 1985. *The Prince*. Trans. Harvey C. Mansfield. Chicago and London: University of Chicago Press.

Newell, Waller. 2000. *What Is a Man? 3,000 Years of Wisdom on the Art of Manly Virtue*. New York: Harper Collins.

Nussbaum, Martha. 1996. *The Fragility of Goodness*. Cambridge, MA: Cambridge University Press.

Okin, Susan. 1979. *Women in Western Political Thought*. Princeton, NJ: Princeton University Press.

Paglia, Camille. 1998. *Sex, Art and American Culture*. New York: Vintage Books.
Plato. 1968. *Republic*. Trans. Allan Bloom. New York: Basic Books.
———. 1977. *Alcibiades*. The Complete Works of Plato. Ed. John M. Cooper. Indianapolis, IN: Hackett.
———. 1999. *Symposium*. Trans. Christopher Gill. New York: Penguin.
Plutarch. 1992. *The Lives of the Noble Grecians and Romans*. Dryden Translation. Vol. 1. New York: Modern Library.
Rousseau, Jean-Jacques. 1979. *Emile*. Trans. Allan Bloom. New York: Basic Books.
Shakespeare, William. 1938. *The Taming of the Shrew*. In *The Works of William Shakespeare*. New York: Oxford University Press, 1938.
Strauss, Leo. 1963. *On Tyranny*. Ithaca, NY: Cornell University Press.

Chapter 12

The Soul of the Tyrant, and the Souls of You and Me: Plato's Understanding of Tyranny

Ronald Beiner

On the face of it, it would be rather odd for any of us to put much energy into worrying about Saddam Hussein's soul. We want him in custody, we want him put on trial, we want civil rights for the Iraqis he oppressed, and we want security for neighboring states. But should we worry about the state of his soul? Yet concern about Saddam's soul, about the soul of the tyrant, is precisely what should interest us if we pursue a Platonic approach to the analysis of tyranny. And Plato's purpose in steering us toward radical reflection on the nature of the tyrant's soul, it turns out, is to get us to reflect simultaneously on the nature of *our own* souls. To what extent do we want what the tyrant wants? To what extent are the tyrant's temptations also our temptations? What is the radical problem in the soul (in the human soul per se) to which philosophy is meant to be a response (i.e., *the* authoritative response)?

What I want to suggest in this essay is that tyranny occupies the fundamental place that it does in Plato's *Republic* not because Plato is preoccupied with tyranny as a type of regime but because he's preoccupied with tyranny as a type of soul. What Plato tells us in his preoccupation with tyranny is that politics is fundamentally about the soul, and that the decisive political alternatives are defined by, on the one side, the well-ordered soul, and on the other side, the corrupted soul. According to this interpretation, one has to see the central importance of the fact that tyranny is present in the drama of *The Republic* not just in the explicit analysis of regimes in Books VIII and IX, but right from the beginning of the dialogue. The sophistic soul is a tyrannic soul (like the "drones with stings" discussed in Book VIII: 564b–e); therefore Thrasymachus, as a representative of the sophistic type, also represents the tyrannic type. And Glaucon and Adeimantus, insofar as they feel moved to express Thrasymachean temptations in their own arguments with Socrates, also give expression to the tyrannic temptation within their own souls. One might extrapolate from this to say that *all* human beings who don't already enjoy a philosophic or Socratic ordering of their souls are vulnerable to the tyrannic temptation, and therefore political philosophy must address as its central concern this impulse in all nonphilosophic types to swing to the Thrasymachean pole rather than to the Socratic pole. Tyranny lies close to the center of Plato's theoretical universe because Plato's politics is a politics of the soul.

Socrates, at the beginning of Book VIII, refers to the preceding analysis of the best regime as a "detour" (543c) to remind us that the real question of the dialogue remains: "which man is [absolutely] best and which [absolutely] worst" and whether it's true that "the best man is happiest and the worst man most wretched" (544a). In this sense, the whole of *The Republic* presents itself as a complicated set of detours, for all the discussion of the ideal regime and all the discussion of inferior regimes never changes the fact that the contest between the best/most just man and the worst/least just man with respect to happiness and wretchedness remains the undisplaceable center of the dialogue, and the unalterable center of Plato's reflection on politics. As Plato puts it at 545a, the account of the tyrannic man is privileged in relation to the other bad regimes because only by "seeing the most unjust man [can we] set him in opposition to the most just man," and thereby address the original and still central issue of the dialogue: "how pure justice is related to pure injustice with respect to the happiness and wretchedness of the men possessing them," such that "we may be persuaded either by Thrasymachus and pursue injustice, or by the argument that is now coming to light and pursue justice" (545a–b). That is, what is truly at stake in moral and political life is only comprehensible in the light of the two ultimate extremities of that life (namely, human life as such). If the tyrant is a happy man, then both justice and philosophy are refuted. But if the tyrant is a wretched man, and his life, the most wretched life, then justice and philosophy are vindicated, and political philosophy has accomplished its purpose. In that sense, the ends of human life (as apprehended by philosophy) hang on the happiness or wretchedness of the tyrant.

If we attempt to read the regime analysis in Books VIII and IX as a serious and methodical political science, we will surely experience the same frustration with it that Aristotle expressed (Aristotle 1984, bk. 5, chap. 12). But notwithstanding Aristotle's objections from the point of view of political science proper, Plato makes sufficiently clear what his real purpose is. As Socrates very significantly emphasizes at 548c–d, one can content oneself with a mere *outline* of the various regimes precisely because the true purpose of the catalog of regimes is only to clarify the relationship between "the justest man and the unjustest one," and from this point of view it wouldn't be worth the bother "to go through all regimes and all dispositions and leave nothing out." In other words, political science for the sake of political science is not the purpose here. The purpose is to stage an all-or-nothing confrontation between absolute justice and absolute injustice and to see which wins with respect to a life of happiness versus a life of wretchedness. The survey of regimes is conducted in the shadow of the problem posed by the story of the ring of Gyges in Book II. (The ring of Gyges confers invisibility upon its wearer, allowing one to commit the most unspeakable crimes without suffering the least harm to one's public reputation; it thereby provides the most exacting test of one's love of justice in the face of the temptations of injustice: 358b–362c; cf. 612b.) The challenge posed by the supposed happiness of a life of unlimited injustice (i.e., the tyrant's life) constitutes *the* problem of the dialogue, and hence Socrates sketches the various regimes only to the point where the ultimate challenge of the ring of Gyges story can be addressed.

Even the least bad of the four bad regimes, namely timocracy (the honor-loving regime), which Socrates presents as a "middle between aristocracy and oligarchy" (547c), actually already contains much that is latently tyrannical: for instance, Plato highlights the fact that the timocrat is "brutal" in his dealings with slaves, not just contemptuous toward them (549a). In general, Plato's purpose is to highlight the *vices* of this regime, not its virtues: "pushed on by desire, [the timocratic men] will love to spend other people's money. . . . They will harvest pleasures stealthily, running away from the law like boys from a father" (548b). Even to the extent that the timocratic regime may display certain virtues (at least relative to subsequent regimes), it's unable to sustain these virtues in the next generation. Central to this analysis of timocracy, as it's central to the other analyses in Book VIII, is the idea that whatever virtues may be present in the fathers of this regime unavoidably dissolve in their sons (549c–550b; cf., for instance, 553a–e, 560a–b, 568e–569b, 572c–e, 574a–c). This is supposed to be Plato's account of the highly disciplined Cretan-Spartan regime, "praised by the many" for its superior civic spirit, yet judging by this description, it doesn't sound very different from the democratic regime that Plato sees as a short step away from tyranny. Far from being exemplars of civic virtue, even citizens of the Cretan-Spartan regime will be carousing boys stealing pleasures behind the backs of their fathers. If timocracy is the least tyrannical of the four bad regimes, it's hard to escape the conclusion that we've already crossed the threshold into tyranny (or virtual tyranny) as soon as the aristocratic/kingly regime has been undone by the miscalculation of the nuptial number.[1]

The timocratic man's love of honor doesn't prevent him from turning into a "money-lover" (549a–b), thus anticipating the characteristic vice of the second bad regime. The very fact that there's so much emphasis on money loving within the analysis of timocracy makes it a bit hard to see why oligarchy is a worse regime than timocracy. Indeed, much of the discussion of oligarchy is anticipated in the discussion of timocracy (as also applies to the relationship between democracy and oligarchy). One can say, however, that in the analysis of oligarchy, we are given a sharper account of virtue and moneymaking as contradictory ends: the more we love wealth, the less we love virtue—like a balancing scale that can only tip in one direction or the other (550e). The oligarchic man "puts the desiring and money-loving part [of the soul] on the throne and makes it the great king within himself" (553c). That is to say, the oligarchical type has a soul ruled in the manner of a Persian despot, with the other parts of the soul turned into slaves that are at desire's disposal (553d).

If the oligarchic man has a soul that is ruled by a despot, the democratic man has a soul that is ruled by the mob. Anticipating Hobbes' claim that Thucydides gives us the most compelling indictment of democracy ("Life of Thomas Hobbes of Malmesbury," 2), Plato renarrates the Thucydidean narrative of the *stasis* (civil discord) in Corcyra (*History of the Peloponnesian War*, III 82) as a narrative of anarchy within the soul (560c–561a). What Plato describes under the rubric of democracy in fact captures much that we would associate with a liberal society. It is not a form of social life that offers much attraction to Plato—yet he makes the colossal concession to the democratic regime that it is a form of society that's uniquely conducive to living a Socratic life (557d).

Just as the seed of oligarchy (love of money) is, according to Plato, already planted in timocracy, so the seed of democracy (license, or licentiousness) is already planted in oligarchy (555c–d). Each bad regime is already developing the vices of worse regimes. Hence it's hardly surprising that the tyrannic dispositions are much in evidence in Plato's depiction of democracy. Again anticipating Hobbes, Plato presents democracy as rule by demagogues (564d–e; cf. 572e: "dread enchanters and tyrant-makers"; Hobbes 1840, 141; cf. Hobbes 1996, 132; Hobbes 1998, 120, 122–25; Hobbes 1843, xvi–xvii). Aristotle, in *The Politics*, 1292a, allows for this demagogic or tyrannical democracy as one possible variety of democracy (cf. 1296a, 1305a, 1312b, 1313b), but then states that it's really a *perversion* of democracy, not a proper democracy qua regime.

Democracy is a kind of prototyranny just as oligarchy is a kind of protodemocracy (and timocracy is a kind of proto-oligarchy): "tyranny [comes] from democracy in about the same manner as democracy from oligarchy" (562a–b). "The same disease . . . as that which arose in the oligarchy and destroyed it, arises also in this regime—but bigger and stronger as a result of the license" (563e). Just as the stingy money lovers of the oligarchical regime breed sons who are licentious spendthrifts (555b–c), so the excessively freedom-loving character of democracy breeds contempt for law and therefore, eventually, absolute slavery (563d–e, 564a, 569c). Sons react against the characteristic traits of their fathers; hence the graspingness of oligarchic fathers turns their sons into licentious democrats. By the same logic, these licentious democrats undergo a reversal whereby they or their sons aren't averse to putting all their liberty into the hands of tyranny-oriented populist leaders (565c–d). The gravitational pull of tyranny upon the three bad but nontyrannical regimes is unstoppable, and of course it becomes more inexorable with every transformation of regime; by the time we arrive at democracy, it has become a full-blown free fall into outright tyranny. Because the evolution of regimes is governed ultimately by the natural gravitational pull exercised by tyranny, the change from one regime to another can only go in one direction (hence Aristotle's complaint that Plato presents the succession of regimes as unidirectional, whereas in reality the transition between regimes is multidirectional: Aristotle 1984, 1316a). Plato's whole regime analysis leads inexorably toward the conclusion that there are really only two human possibilities: Socratic justice, and one or another mode of tyranny. The teaching of Book VIII is that honor, wealth, and freedom are all tyrannic temptations, and hence each of the first three bad regimes is an anticipation of the fourth. It follows that if *tyranny* is condemned, then *all* political (i.e., nonphilosophical) regimes are condemned.

Sure enough, the main features of tyranny as a regime are those that have already been anticipated in the account of other bad regimes: for instance, tyranny, like oligarchy, is characterized by bleeding dry established properties (573d–574a). Tyranny is also associated with the "money-loving" and "gain-loving" part of the soul (580e–581a) that looms so large in the other three bad regimes. Most significantly, the father-son motif that pervades the analysis of the other regimes is also applied to the sketch of tyranny: 568e–569b. Democracy is the "father" of the tyrant, and gets abused by its "son" just as all the other regimes fall into corruption through a collapse of generational discipline. Notwithstanding Plato's hostility to democracy, at 572c–d he concedes that there is the possibility of a certain kind of moderation in democracy, but all it takes is one more father-son succession to implant the "great winged drone" in the thoroughly tyrannic soul (572d–e).

There is a common disease that "grow[s] naturally in oligarchy and democracy alike" (564a–b). What is the common disease that grows naturally in both (all?) regimes? It's the general human incapacity for fathers to inoculate their sons against tyrannic desire. Timocratic fathers can't control their money-loving (and therefore virtue-averse) sons. Oligarchic fathers can't control their licentious sons. Democratic fathers can't control their tyrannical sons. The evolution of regimes thus repeatedly replicates the pattern inscribed in the succession of Socrates's first three interlocutors in Book I: father-son-tyrant. This continual replication of the logic of tyranny can be broken only by instituting a new pattern: father-son-philosopher (namely, the pattern inscribed in Aristophanes' *The Clouds*, although this pattern appeared to Aristophanes himself as merely another instance of father-son-tyrant). What ties together the whole of the regime analysis in Books VIII and 9IX, and connects this in turn with the beginning of the dialogue in Book I, is precisely the motif of fathers, sons, and tyrants. The common thread that runs through all the transitions of regime is the incapacity of the father, without philosophy (and in the case of aristocracy, even *with* it!), to prevent the wayward son from being seduced by tyrannic desire. This dynamic is what drives the moral decline of *all* the regimes, which suggests that tyranny as a force of seduction is present in *all* souls (democratic, oligarchic, timocratic, and even aristocratic).[2] All regimes, and therefore all souls, are united by their vulnerability to "the idle desires" stoked up by the "tyrant-makers" (572e). Hence Book IX begins with an account of the human psyche as revealed in dream-life in order to suggest that dreams prove to us that "some terrible, savage, and lawless form of desires is in every man, even in some of us who seem to be ever so measured" (572b; cf. 574e). The tyrant is the one who "has the biggest and most extreme tyrant within his own soul" (575c–d), but if the testimony of dream-life is to be believed, there is a tyrant—perhaps not so large or so extreme—within the souls of each of us.

What we get at the end of Book VIII (562a–569c) is a sketch of tyranny as a *regime*, whereas what we get in Book IX is what fundamentally concerns Plato: an account of the tyrannic *soul*. The challenges put to Socrates by Glaucon and Adeimantus in Book II raised the question of whether the most unjust man can live a happy or even the most happy life, and the account of the tyrannic soul in Book IX promises finally to answer this long-postponed challenge, namely, "how [the tyrannic man] lives, wretchedly or blessedly" (571a). Following the project initially laid out in Book II (368e–369b) of employing patterns of justice and injustice in the city as a guide to justice and injustice in the soul, the state of the tyrannic city instructs us in the state of the tyrannic soul. In the city ruled by a tyrant, the populace, including those in it who are decent human beings, are in a state of absolute slavery (577c–d), and are reduced to poverty, fear, and misery (577e–578a). The wretchedness of life in the tyrannic city is proof of the wretchedness of the tyrannic soul (576d–e). The life of tyranny is essentially *a life without friendship*, for the tyrant always stands in relation to others as either flatterer (slave) or master. Tyrannic natures "live their whole life without ever being friends of anyone"; the "tyrannic nature never has a taste of . . . true friendship" (576a). What the tyrant aims at is boundless freedom in the satisfaction of his desires, but what results from tyranny is the opposite of freedom for the tyrant himself. Because he is essentially and necessarily friendless (cf. Xenophon 1991, 10, 13), his life is dominated by fear, and hence he becomes a prisoner in his own house, unable to "go anywhere abroad or see all the things the other free men desire to see" (579b). The tyrant learns the hard way that without friendship there can be no freedom (hence the connection between freedom and true friendship at 576a), and tyranny is the destruction of friendship (just as philosophy is the best foundation for true friendship).

Socrates presents Glaucon with three arguments for rejecting the tyrannic life as a happy life. According to the first argument (575e–580c), *even if we unproblematically accept at face value* what are taken by most human beings as the goods of life (satisfying conventional desires, obtaining honor from fellow citizens, living freely according to a conventional conception of freedom), these goods are unavailable to the tyrant because he is utterly imprisoned by his condition of being friendless, of being unable to trust anyone but himself. We can call this the "Xenophontic" argument against tyranny since it basically replicates the arguments presented in Xenophon's *Hiero* by the tyrant himself in order to demonstrate that the life of the tyrant is one that is wretched rather than blessed. By implication, the fact that Plato goes on to present more ambitious arguments against tyranny shows that he wants to carry the argument against tyranny to a philosophically deeper level than that upon which Xenophon conducts his critique.

The second argument (580c–583a) is what we can call the argument from asymmetry of experience. Since acquaintance with the goods associated with a life devoted to pleasure loving and a life devoted to honor loving is easily available to all, the lover of wisdom is familiar with the kinds of pleasure that those kinds of life supply. But since the joys associated with the life of wisdom are rare, and therefore *not* available to the pleasure lover and the honor lover, the latter two are poorly positioned, relative to the wisdom lover, to judge which kind of human satisfaction is truly pleasurable.[3]

The third and most important argument (583b–588a) is a kind of radicalization of the second argument. We can call it the argument from the ontological status of human goods. Various goods present themselves as good not in themselves but in relation to the range of goods along the whole spectrum of human experience. If one has a truncated experience of the full spectrum, one will misperceive or have a distorted perception of the good in question—for instance, respite from pain will be experienced as a substantial pleasure not because it really *is* a substantial pleasure but simply because the experience of it will be determined by its relation to states of being that are *less* pleasurable (583c–584c). It follows that one can only properly assess the fulfillment conferred by a state of being through a correct apprehension of its place within the full range of experiential possibilities. And since only the wisdom-loving man, or the wisdom-loving part of the soul, *aspires* to an apprehension of the whole, only this man, or this part of the soul, has the possibility of apprehending goods as they truly are (as they are "immortally" and not merely contingently: 585c). One can summarize this argument by saying that true pleasure attaches to fullness of being (see 585d–e), and fullness of being can be experienced only by a kind of soul dedicated to its intellectual apprehension (the wisdom-loving or philosophic soul).

The first argument is the most straightforward (but least philosophical): it draws upon familiar features of tyrannical regimes, including such regimes as they continue to present themselves in contemporary political life (the tyrant as ever fearful, always on the lookout for the next conspiracy against his rule, absolutely isolated by his hatefulness and ugliness of soul, alternatively flattering or servile and domineering, catering to populist caprice and enslaving the populace to his own capricious desires).[4] This argument clearly applies directly to tyranny proper. But—and this is important for the interpretation developed throughout this essay—the two more philosophically sophisticated arguments impugn not only tyranny as a form of life, but *all* experience of human goods that fall short of a fully philosophical mode of life. If the latter two arguments are correct, not just tyranny as a kind of human life but *all* nonphilosophical forms of life involve misperceptions or distorted perceptions of pleasure and the good, are caught up in mere contingency rather than what is immortal, and fall decisively short of an experience of the fullness of being. The philosopher alone is properly inoculated against tyranny because only the philosopher has a proper apprehension of the full spectrum of human goods. The second and third arguments aim at doing more than merely displaying the ultimate wretchedness of what the tyrant wants; they are meant to make a case for the illusory character of what is desired by all non-wisdom-loving souls. Although Socrates's first argument suggests that the tyrant's life is wretched because the tyrannic life can't deliver the pleasure, honor, and freedom it promises, the deeper subsequent arguments contend that the tyrannic life cannot be a satisfying one because it operates according to a conventional conception of human good that it *shares* with other nontyrannic types, and the goods postulated by this conventional conception are not real goods. When Socrates states that the philosophic part of the soul is the part that "cares least for money and opinion" (581a), he makes clear that the uniquely nontyrannical character of the philosophic experience of life is founded on the philosopher's immense distance from the ordinary goods and aspirations of ordinary human life. Kant beautifully captures Plato's view of the resolutely nontyrannic character of the Socratic soul when he writes, "reason, matured by experience into wisdom, serenely speaks through the mouth of *Socrates*, who, surrounded by the wares of a market-fair, remarked: *How many are the things of which I have no need!*" (Kant 1992, 355). Naturally, Kant is indirectly descended from the Socratic line through his theoretical debt to the Stoic tradition (namely, the idea of self-dependence as a central moral conception), so in that sense one could speak of Kant as himself in a significant way a descendant of the Socratic tradition.

In fact, there's a final argument put to Glaucon concerning the unattractiveness of the tyrannic life (588b–591d) that deals precisely with "autonomy" in the sense of proper rule over one's own soul. (In order to highlight the Platonic pedigree of this idea as developed in the Stoics and in Kant, we can call this fourth argument the autonomy argument.) The tyrant (and all human beings to the extent that tyrannic forces rule in their souls) has a bad soul, a soul that is unhealthy, because it is ruled by the bestial elements in the soul. This finally explains why Gyges gorging his desires with impunity is not happy or living a good life: to be sure, his ring exempts him from outward punishment inflicted by his society, but he suffers inward punishment by virtue of living with a soul that is disordered, "unmusical," and hence unfree. As Kant was later to argue, Plato, too, argues that the unjust soul is therefore more free, and profits better, if it is punished than if it evades punishment (591a–b).[5] The truly free human being is one who is *not* ruled by beasts within, and no quantity of outward goods or outward honors can compensate for forgoing the health or musicalness of soul that goes with rule of the bestial parts of the soul by the intelligent parts of the soul. The ephemeral goods of the world are trivial in comparison with the true good associated with freely ruling one's soul.

There are two important criticisms that one can make of Plato's understanding of tyranny as I have presented it. First, as undeniably harsh as is his account of tyranny proper, the fact that he draws the true boundary between nontyranny and tyranny at the miscalculation of the nuptial number has the consequence that tyranny proper appears not as some extraordinary evil at the extremities of the human condition, but rather virtually as the norm, or at least as an extension of the norm, of human life as we generally experience it. One can interpret this as the suggestion that there's a bit of Saddam Hussein in all of us, which is not exactly a flattering or hopeful way to think of the human situation. Second, for the same reason (namely, the miscalculation of the nuptial number as the essential boundary between nontyranny and tyranny), the prospects for decent political life in nonphilosophic regimes are made to look extremely grim. The purpose here is to present philosophy as the necessary condition for good politics, but it has the effect of making all nonphilosophical regimes appear as semityrannical or latently tyrannical. It's true that Plato structures his political science in such a way that all regimes other than kingship ruled by a philosopher/aristocracy ruled by philosophers are characterized from the outset as bad regimes, but Plato goes well beyond this when he specifies the badness of the bad regimes as culminating naturally in tyranny. The whole range of ordinary political life from Spartan timocracy to Athenian democracy, and the whole range of ordinary moral life corresponding to these regimes, are in effect reduced to various modes of virtual tyranny.

In what follows, I'll focus on Plato's minimalization of the prospects of decent political life (apart from the philosophic regime) through a juxtaposition with Aristotle. Although there is a vast affinity between the political philosophies of Plato and Aristotle (i.e., Aristotle's debt to Plato is obviously huge), in light of Aristotle's vindication of moral life in the *Ethics* and his vindication of political life in the *Politics*, one could plausibly view Plato's account of the relation between the tyrannical soul and the ordinary non-Socratic soul as a slander against moral life and a slander against political life. One might even hypothesize that Aristotle undertook to vindicate moral life and political life in these two works *because* he understood that Plato's teaching on tyranny has the effect of doing the opposite. There's space for ordinary politics in Aristotle that there isn't in Plato precisely because Aristotle doesn't see the stark encounter between the philosopher and the tyrant that Plato depicts as the central problem of *The Republic*.

The fact that Plato devotes an entire book of *The Republic* to tyranny (Book IX), whereas the political-psychological analysis of the three intermediate regimes are almost absurdly compressed into one book (Book VIII) constitutes an essential key for interpreting the dialogue. One way of formulating this interpretation is to say that Plato is only interested in timocracy, oligarchy, and democracy to the extent that they culminate in tyranny and thus set the stage for the final reckoning between philosophic kingship/aristocracy and tyranny; only *two* regimes matter to Plato because only they shed light on the happiness/wretchedness of the just and unjust souls that defines the core problem of *The Republic*.[6] A more blunt way of formulating the interpretation is to say that Plato's view of politics, precisely insofar as it gives excessive emphasis to the problem of tyranny, is bound to result in a distorted account of political life. Aristotle, by contrast, gives much more serious attention to democracy and oligarchy as distinct regimes in their own right—not just as barely distinguishable anticipations of tyranny—and thereby restores tyranny to its rightly marginal status within political life. Or conversely, Aristotle, in what is likely intended as a deliberate rejection of Platonic politics, restores the middle regimes, the regimes that are neither philosophic nor tyrannic, with both their vices and virtues, to their rightful place at the center of political life.[7]

The analysis of (existing) regimes in *The Politics* extends from Book III, chapter 6 until the end of Book VI, and throughout this whole core of the book, apart from passing references, only one brief chapter (Book IV, chapter 10) is devoted to tyranny as a regime per se; in addition, the three last chapters of Book V (chapters 10–12) are devoted to transitions among tyranny and other regimes, including an explicit criticism in the final chapter of Book V of the account of regimes in *The Republic*. If, as we've suggested throughout this interpretation, Plato's true purpose in his catalogue of regimes is simply to steer us toward a psychological-philosophical encounter between the soul of the tyrant and the soul of the philosopher, it can hardly be a big surprise that his categories of regime analysis strike one as more caricaturish and mythologized than serious and literal. (When Plato says, introducing his discussion of the original fall from the best regime, "the Muses . . . speak to us with high tragic talk as though they were speaking seriously, playing and jesting with us like children" [545d–e], the thought naturally occurs to us, as it perhaps occurred to Aristotle, that this description applies not just to Socrates' presentation of the nuptial number [546a–547a], but to the whole of his "political science.") Responding to Aristotle's criticisms in Book V, chapter 12, one could say that Plato's typology looks like "amateur political science," certainly relative to Aristotle's more complicated, more nuanced, more "professional" regime analysis, mainly because it wasn't really *intended* as political science at all. Rather, what it was meant to supply was an illumination of the human condition in relation to an analysis of possibilities of order/disorder in the soul—that is, an analysis geared toward the two decisive extremities of psychic ordering: the Socratic or just soul, and the tyrannical, unjust soul.

In Books VIII and IX of *The Republic*, tyranny looms enormously large, and the ordinary regimes that define the preponderant political experience of human beings are given short shrift because Plato's "science of regimes," insofar as he can be said to offer one, is dominated by the continuing challenge of how to respond to the ring of Gyges story told by Glaucon in Book II (hence Plato makes a point of reminding us in Book X that the ring of Gyges is still the most powerful encapsulation of the question whether "justice by itself is best for soul itself": 612b). The point of the story is that *anyone* (with the exception of those with specially equipped Socratic souls) can feel the compulsion of tyrannic desire.[8] Not just the tyrant but the common person will ask, If I can have all my desires (wealth, power, living entirely as I please) unjustly but with impunity fulfilled, why shouldn't I? I'd be a fool not to! It says something astounding about Plato's view of the souls of ordinary people that he thinks only living a Socratic life offers a proper remedy to the tyrannic temptations encapsulated in the ring of Gyges story. The life of philosophy occupies the enormous place that it does in Plato's scheme of human life precisely because tyranny is seen to be the *completion* of desires in the souls of you and me. When Plato says that the timocratic man has a soul that is not properly ordered because he's been abandoned by his supreme guardian, the savior of his virtue, namely "argument mixed with music" (549b; cf. 560b), what he's saying is that philosophy, and philosophy alone, is the answer to the tyrant in all of us.[9] But again, if tyranny is as it were the "default position" of the soul, for which the Socratic life ("argument mixed with music") provides the only possible fully reliable remedy, then this implies an extremely grim assessment of the possibilities of political life, for Socratic politics—turning all citizens into Socratic types—is an impossible project.

According to Hobbes, the ancient political philosophers take their bearings by the *summum bonum*, whereas he, more appropriately, takes his bearings by the *summum malum* (Hobbes 1998, chap. 11). There is an important sense in which this isn't quite true. Plato's *Republic* takes its bearings as much from the *summum malum* as from the *summum bonum*. But of course the *summum malum* that decisively concerns Plato is not an evil in the world or in the public relationships between human beings but an evil in the interiority of the private soul. This is why he concludes Book IX by saying that the man with a truly musical soul "looks fixedly at the regime within him" (591d–e), that it's his soul that constitutes "his own *polis*" (592a), and that what matters is the polis he has "[founded] within himself," for "he would mind the things of this city alone, and of no other" (592b). Contrary to what Hobbes suggests, Platonic politics is not simply preoccupied with virtue as "the Good," the positive telos of human existence, but just as much preoccupied with honor, money, and the desire for ruleless living as corrupted ends. The tyrant, precisely by developing these ends to a state of absolute corruption, clarifies their nature *as* corrupt. In this sense, philosophy and tyranny stand in a symmetrical relationship. It's not just that philosophy enlightens us by revealing what's "wretched" about the soul of the tyrant. It's also the case that tyranny, by exposing the illusory character of everyday human ends, illuminates philosophy as a positive good.

What guidance can Plato give us in dealing with contemporary tyrants? First of all, Plato would tell us that we should not be surprised that tyrannical politics, with all its brutality, ruthlessness, and its subordination of whole societies to the whims of the tyrant, are still on the scene. As long as human beings in general are still in the grip of desires less sublime than the eros for eternal wisdom—that is, as long as human beings are human beings (and not gods)—we have to expect that certain individuals will be gripped by base desires with far greater ferocity and criminality than the rest of us. This is the fundamental source of tyrannical politics. If we are surprised by this, it shows that we have not yet reflected on human nature with the seriousness that political philosophy requires. As Mark Lilla has helpfully argued in "The New Age of Tyranny," we moderns have been too quick to flatter ourselves that the politics of tyranny belongs to the premodern past. Plato would suggest that we look on this as another symptom of modern hubris.

Philosophically speaking, the prior question, of course, is whether tyranny actually exists as something real in the world of political experience. One cannot simply assume that this is the case, or assume that it will be theoretically uncontested. Hobbes, famously, denied the reality of tyranny (*Leviathan*, chap. 19; cf. *Leviathan*, "A Review, and Conclusion," p. 486),[10] and Hobbes certainly has followers in this respect among contemporary students of politics. In that sense, Plato's assertion of the reality of tyranny as a political category and as a category of the soul is a substantive philosophical claim, in intellectual competition with philosophical claims to the contrary (such as that of Hobbes). Even if it were the case, as we've argued in this essay, that Plato gives exaggerated attention to tyranny within his table of regimes, this certainly doesn't prove that Plato was wrong to include tyranny as a distinct regime, nor does it give us reason to think that tyranny as a regime is limited to the ancient world. On the contrary, Plato and the other ancient political philosophers would find it very easy to identify twentieth- or twenty-first-century tyrannic regimes whose rulers have the soul of a tyrant.

What *is* tyranny? A philosophical investigation into tyranny begins with the awareness that it's in no way obvious what the phenomenon is (or indeed whether it exists). According to a Platonic view, tyranny is a disorder in the soul where the lower part of the soul rules and enslaves the higher part of the soul. All human beings suffer this psychic disorder to some extent, but in the tyrant, the disorder is enflamed to the point where it not only enslaves the tyrant's own soul, but also enslaves all other members of the society. The reality of tyranny therefore flows from the reality of an objective structure in the soul. People who are skeptical about the idea of a natural ordering of the soul will also, from this point of view, be skeptical about tyranny as a natural type in the world that philosophy confronts and analyzes. There are, of course, other ways in which to recognize tyranny as a political phenomenon, or to accept it as a legitimate category of social analysis. But Plato gives us an especially robust philosophical basis for affirming the reality of tyranny.

Above all, Plato will insist to us that "the soul" is not a dispensable category in arriving at political understanding, and therefore his doctrine of the inextricable connection of soul and regime, if it applies to anything in the world of political experience, certainly applies to our understanding of contemporary tyrannies. Comprehending the full range of political possibilities (emphatically including the absolutely worst regimes) requires an understanding of the lower desires of the soul in the light of the higher or highest desires of the soul. The spectrum of human possibilities as Plato would see it is bounded at one extremity by the lust, murder, and sadism[11] of Saddam and his sons, and bounded at the other extremity by the simple desire for understanding on the part of Socrates and his successors within the philosophical tradition (especially the Stoics, for whom the soul is also the main site of politics). Politics fundamentally concerns "the just," and the nature of justice will not be fully visible to us until we appreciate that certain bestial regimes, ruled by bestial souls, embody perfect injustice.

The problem of tyranny as Plato understands it is a problem implanted in human nature. The problem is that human beings are fundamentally oriented toward the things that are mutable rather than toward the things that are of everlasting being. If we could somehow reorient human beings toward that which is of everlasting being, then we could create a polis that would be more Spartan than Sparta—perhaps a polis infinitely more Spartan than Sparta, the "perfection" of Sparta as it were, a city of perfect citizenship. But of course this can't be done. Why not? Because the tyrant is in all of us.

NOTES

1. Barry Strauss, in his chapter in this book, makes the Rousseauian argument that among the Greek city-states, Sparta was uniquely free from the tyrannic temptation. By implication, that was not Plato's view in his account of timocracy in Book 8.

2. Cf. Nathan Tarcov's chapter in this book: "[the *Republic*'s] implicit attribution of tyrannical aspects to all actual cities"; and: "Classical political philosophy . . . reveals the tyrannical aspects of all societies." One might well ask: If the city in speech is such a perfect regime, why does it, too, degenerate in the direction of tyranny? (And the fact that there is already much that is latently tyrannic in timocracy suggests a shockingly quick jump from philosophic aristocracy or kingship to de facto tyranny.) The inescapable answer seems to be that while for Plato certain souls can be secured in a stable way against tyranny, regimes (even the best) never can be.

3. This line of argument is a direct inversion of what Simonides the poet says to Hiero the tyrant at the start of their dialogue in the *Hiero*: "Since you have experienced both [the private life and the life of a tyrant], you also know better . . . how the tyrannical and the private life differ in human joys and pains" (Xenophon 1991, 3).

4. In "The New Age of Tyranny," Mark Lilla makes the interesting argument that the epic theorists of modernity from Hegel to Weber regarded political tyranny as a thing of the past; as a result, modern political theory has been poorly equipped to reflect on tyrannic regimes as a continuing presence in political life. It's possible that Plato's characterizations of tyranny are still quite relevant to contemporary experience precisely because he focused his account of tyranny so emphatically on the nature of the soul. One might argue that even if certain forms of political life fade away

while others rise into prominence, the things of the soul remain more or less the same. In that sense, it's not surprising that Plato's descriptions remain true to the phenomenon of tyranny as we encounter it today. Although Waller R. Newell is skeptical that the Platonic psychology of tyranny suffices as an account of modern tyranny, the Platonic characterization as summarized by Newell ("a monster of desires who plunders and ravishes his subjects") still works pretty well as a description of modern tyrants like Saddam.

5. In the *Hiero* (Xenophon 1991, 15), the tyrant argues that he dare not cease his life of tyranny, however wretched, because he will then be subject to punishment for his crimes. Plato's response is that it is in the tyrant's own interest to be punished for his injustice.

6. Bloom (*The Republic of Plato*, 425): "In the *Republic* Socrates has included both god and beast in the city, and this accounts for the difference between his political science and Aristotle's." What my interpretation has tried to highlight is not simply that Plato has *included* the regimes corresponding to god and beast, but that he has *privileged* them to the extent that the three commonplace (merely human) regimes nearly cease to be theoretically significant.

7. Cf. Bloom (*The Republic of Plato*, 415): Aristotle "turned [Socrates' sketch] into a true political science by adjusting his standard to the possibilities of political life."

8. Bloom, in his commentary on Books 8 and 9 (*The Republic of Plato*, 412–26), makes the important point that one should distinguish between Book 8 as a discussion whose main addressee is Adeimantus, and Book 9 as a discussion whose main addressee is Glaucon. According to Bloom, Books 8 and 9 aim at transforming the interlocutors such that "Adeimantus must no longer see philosophy as an enemy of the city, and Glaucon must no longer be tempted by tyranny" (415). It would follow from Bloom's interpretation that the vindication of justice in Book 9 is not a response to the *general* human vulnerability to tyrannic temptation, but more specifically a response to the distinctively erotic type represented in Glaucon (as opposed to the more civic-minded type represented in Adeimantus). Running counter to Bloom's reading is Socrates' suggestion at the beginning of Book 9 that it's "plain in dreams" that "the lawless form of desires is in every man" (572b). Bloom's attention to the dramatic interplay between Socrates and his specific interlocutors is a good and useful corrective to interpretations of *The Republic* that are over hasty in ascribing various doctrines to Plato; but here it leads Bloom to discount any universal doctrine whatever (apart from the doctrine of the superiority of the philosophic life). In particular, it leads Bloom to question Plato's commitment to the doctrine of the intrinsic goodness of justice as instantiated in the just soul (411). This is an interesting interpretation of Book 9, but it would seem to take too far the hermeneutical policy of interpreting *The Republic* strictly as a set of responses to the souls of particular interlocutors.

9. Cf. Gadamer (1980, 62n9) for a nice encapsulation of how, for Plato, philosophy is *indispensable* for resisting the tyrannic corruption of the polis.

10. See Tarcov's observation concerning the more subtle way in which Machiavelli drops the concept of tyranny. However, unlike Hobbes, Machiavelli—as Tarcov also notes—does use the term "tyranny" pejoratively and even endorses the ancient critique of tyranny in *Discourses on Livy* (bk. 2, chap. 2).

11. Sadism is a pretty reliable indicator of having a tyrannical soul (and of course the Saddam Hussein family easily qualifies). The relevant attribute is nicely captured by Gershom Scholem in the following phrase (referring to the Nazis): "The gentlemen enjoyed their evil" (Scholem 2002, 402).

SOURCES

Aristotle. 1984. *The Politics*. Trans. Carnes Lord. Chicago: University of Chicago Press.

Gadamer, Hans-Georg. 1980. "Plato and the Poets." In *Dialogue and Dialectic: Eight Hermeneutical Studies on Plato*, ed. P. Christopher Smith, 39–72. New Haven, CT: Yale University Press.

Hobbes, Thomas. 1840. "De Corpore Politico." In *The English Works of Thomas Hobbes*, ed. Sir William Molesworth, vol. 4. London: John Bohn.

———. 1843. "Of the Life and History of Thucydides." In *The English Works of Thomas Hobbes*, ed. Sir William Molesworth, vol. 8. London: John Bohn.

———. 1982. "The Life of Thomas Hobbes of Malmesbury." Trans. J. E. Parsons and Whitney Blair. *Interpretation* 10 (January, no. 1): 1–7.

———. 1996. *Leviathan*. Ed. Richard Tuck. Cambridge: Cambridge University Press.

———. 1998. *On the Citizen*. Ed. Richard Tuck and Michael Silverthorne. Cambridge: Cambridge University Press.

Kant, Immanuel. 1992. "Dreams of a Spirit-Seer Elucidated by Dreams of Metaphysics." In *Theoretical Philosophy, 1755–1770*, ed. David Walford in collaboration with Ralk Meerbote. Cambridge: Cambridge University Press.

Lilla, Mark. 2002. "The New Age of Tyranny." *New York Review of Books* 49 (October 24, no. 16).

Machiavelli, Niccolò. 1996. *Discourses on Livy*. Trans. Harvey G. Mansfield and Nathan Tarcov. Chicago: University of Chicago Press.

Plato. 1968. *The Republic of Plato*. Trans. Allan Bloom. New York: Basic Books.

Scholem, Gershom. 2002. *A Life in Letters, 1914–1982*. Ed. Anthony David Skinner. Cambridge, MA: Harvard University Press.

Thucydides. 1972. *History of the Peloponnesian War*. Trans. Rex Warner. Harmondsworth, UK: Penguin.

Xenophon. 1991. "Hiero or Tyrannicus." In Leo Strauss, *On Tyranny*, ed. Victor Gourevitch and Michael S. Roth. New York: The Free Press.

Chapter 13

The Education of a Tyrant

Toivo Koivukoski

The purpose here is to speak out from the great texts of political philosophy and address the world as we experience it, not merely to run errands of application or to indulge in antiquarianism, but to speak to the phenomenon of tyranny. For tyranny is evident in the world now as always, and the word is increasingly and appropriately finding its way into our political discourse, which could be informed through the study of classical political philosophy. I would like to see what can be learned specifically from Plato's attempt to moderate the tyrant Dionysius through a philosophical education, the story of which is told in Plato's letters,[1] the theory of which we see in the *Republic*, first in order to understand the nature of tyranny, and second to consider how we should go about confronting it.

Though we may not find direct applications from classical political philosophy to contemporary politics, we can adopt its principles as standards of justice and its virtues as guides for good living and reform. I will get to virtue later in this essay when I look at the story of Plato and Dionysius, but we should start with what is simplest. One of the guiding principles that Plato teaches is that tyranny is bad, that it is the "most miserable" (Plato 1999, 575c) of regimes because a person cannot live a free and happy life under it, even if one is the tyrant himself. Tyrant and subject alike are compelled by insatiable lusts, nervous agitations, and an impossible quest for absolute security. A tyrant is free from fear only when he is locked in his bedroom, and then he has his lovers to worry about. It is also hard to be a virtuous citizen in a tyranny, because tyrants call upon their subjects to do vicious things. Indeed it requires a rare courage to speak out against a regime armed and ready for insurrection, under threat to property, life, and family.[2]

These may seem like unremarkable statements in line with common sense, but this is more than modern political science can say. Machiavelli for one admits the usefulness of tyranny and the necessity of evil in politics. He advises rulers to learn how not to be good when it is necessary to preserve the security of the state (Machiavelli 1977, XV). Hobbes, too, drops the distinction between just and unjust regimes, and so for him tyranny falls from usage as a term of analysis (Machiavelli 1977, XIX). In modern political science, there are no true tyrannies in the classical sense of deviant, essentially bad regimes; rather there are states more or less capable of maintaining social order. This is not to say that there is no distinguishing between good and bad forms of government for modern political science, but rather that the bar is lowered from the high standards set by Plato and Aristotle, so that the kind of regime that the classics abhorred as incompatible with the good life is accepted for its instrumental value. The use of tyrannical means may even be compatible with some form of republicanism, as Rousseau suggests in his deconstructive reading of Machiavelli (Rousseau 1967, III.vi), which has Machiavelli revealing the tyranny inherent in statecraft, even as he advises the prince to act as a tyrant. My own sense is that Machiavelli does have the people's good in mind when he advises the prince to dispense cruelty quickly rather than over a protracted time, and when he recommends slaughtering a city to save it: better one generation of oppression and murder than many if the founding and security of a state require brutal measures. This ruthless republicanism promoting dictatorial power as necessary for the security of the state and safety of the people is consistent between *The Prince* and *The Discourses*: in the latter Machiavelli recommends that tyrants secure their power backed by the masses (I.40); he insists that exceedingly cruel and morally repugnant means are sometimes necessary for security, especially during the founding of new states (I.26); and he advises collective punishment and racial profiling in times of crisis to preserve freedom within a multicultural republic (III.49). Rousseau likewise promotes the necessity of dictatorship in times of crisis—silencing the laws and rising above the democratic basis of sovereignty in consent of the governed to ensure the security of the state (Rousseau 1967, IV.vi).[3]

Such openness to tyranny as a means to an end has contributed to the terrible excesses of modernity, from the terror of the French revolution, to the dictatorship of the proletariat in the Russian revolution, to China's cultural revolution. In such times of revolutionary crisis, tyrannical means are considered necessary for the good of the people. In light of our horrible experiences with tyrannies in the twentieth century, a return to classical political philosophy and the unequivocal condemnation of tyranny is in order. However, to this moral note we must add their practical realization that tyranny is a danger coeval with politics, along with the observation that attempts to make a perfect world and drive out tyranny once and for all may paradoxically and unintentionally require tyrannical means.

After the early modern assault on tyranny as a moral term for political science, a final purge was executed by Max Weber, as questions of good and bad—which the term "tyranny" necessarily implies—were separated from facts, considered the proper domain of an objective social science. Tyranny became a subjective, emotive, and rhetorical term. With that change in meaning, social science lost a standard based in reason by which to judge good and bad in politics. For to call a regime a tyranny is to include a value judgment within the terms of one's analysis, and therefore to fail the standard of objectivity that such a science sets out. An objective social scientist can express value judgments, but such judgments must remain separate from statements of facts. According to this view, judgment on the essential goodness of any one regime over another could not be included in one's terms of analysis, which would consist rather of "systems" and "structures" or, more objectively yet, cold, hard statistical data. On this leveled landscape, talk of tyranny, revived and sustained through the twentieth century largely by Leo Strauss and Hannah Arendt, seems inflated, rhetorical, un-Enlightened, and hopelessly old-fashioned.[4]

Now, however, the possibility and desirability of a purely neutral social science are in serious doubt; for given strict neutrality the social scientist becomes a mere instrument for measuring public opinion and a tool for social engineering, and citizens lose their capacity for making rational judgments about political affairs. Such tendencies of course make recognizing and confronting tyranny that much more difficult. Yet against the tide of objectification in social science and society, tyranny has reentered political discourse to inform political action. We can see this most clearly in an American foreign policy articulated in the language of good and evil and directed toward confronting tyrannies. This direction was declared when American President Ronald Reagan cast the Cold War in theological terms and called the Soviet Union an "evil empire."[5] It continues with the American-led war in Iraq, most recently justified as a war against an evil tyrant and his oppressive regime—not at all the terms of neutral statecraft. David Frum borrowed from Reagan's lexicon when he penned the "Axis of Evil" speech in which President George W. Bush put all tyrannies on watch, effectively marking them for regime change.[6] A world-historic mission to battle evil and pit freedom against terror and tyranny is front and center in the 2002 U.S. National Security Strategy, which makes preventative wars against tyrannies into a centerpiece of American foreign policy.[7] We may doubt the sanity of religion-inspired millenarianism in geopolitics, and disagree whether preventative wars against tyrannies are practically necessary and prudent courses of action for democratic states, but in any case it is clear that judgment concerning tyranny has a renewed importance in the debates around global politics.

We use the term "tyranny"—with all its moralistic baggage—in the first instance to keep close to the phenomenon studied, to give voice to the commonsense revulsion toward tyranny felt by all those who enjoy their freedom and see it threatened. As academics and political thinkers, we of course enjoy our freedom, too, it being a necessary condition for our liberal studies. Therefore, when we speak about tyranny we should also in some manner speak out against it, so that our analysis of what tyranny is includes some guidance on what to do about it.

Of course, the particulars of action depend upon changing circumstances, and beyond articulating general principles and goals and recognizing tyranny as the worst kind of regime, political philosophy can do little to direct action except to keep it within proper limits and in accordance with virtue. Plato's letters to a tyrant and to reformers are a good place to look for such guidance in forgotten virtues. The letters are the only instance in which Plato attempts to establish a clear connection between his thoughts on politics and actual political reform, where he and his friends set out to "take-in-hand and bring-to-an-end our thoughts on laws and politics" (Plato 1999, VII.328c). There is one immediately practicable limit and lesson to be found in the letters: Plato summarily and emphatically rejects assassination as a way to deal with tyrants in the "Sicilian fashion" (Plato 1999, VII.336c), what we might call the Mafioso school of diplomacy. Virtuous statesmen must "detest the methods of assassins who would do anything" to remove a tyrant (Plato 1999, VII.336d). Reformers should instead be patient and demonstrate worthy example and self-restraint for the tyrant to imitate, however unlikely that may be. One cannot trust a tyrant, it is true, but one cannot trust an assassin either; both kinds of treachery undermine the faith that is necessary for future good relations, and instead give rise to unintended consequences and cycles of reciprocal, escalating violence.[8]

Plato also vigorously discourages revolution as an answer to tyranny. He writes that one "must not apply force to change his fatherland; whenever exiling and slaughter are necessary for reform," one should wait instead of act (Plato 1999, VII.331d). As with assassination, the remedy is worse than the evil, since revolutions have unpredictable outcomes, and their violence tends to beget violence—perhaps even yet another tyranny. According to Plato there are no final solutions to the problem of tyranny: it is coeval with politics, and cannot be eliminated. The effort to decisively eradicate tyranny through assassination or revolution is as delusional as the tyrant's paranoid compulsion to violently suppress all forms of dissent. In both cases, violent means do not pacify; rather they produce, in Plato's words, "a state of terror" (Plato 1999, VII.333a).

Tyranny, whether it is just one man and his private army, or if it is represented by a totalitarian state with a shadowy bureaucracy and secret police, is sustained by terror. The substance of tyrannical rule is enforced consent and obedience through terror. Tyranny is rule without law, that is rule with its basis in the raw fear of the masses. In tyrannies there can be no trust, either in the government or in the future, except in periodic indiscriminate violence toward subjects and neighbors, if we can call that trust.

At a deeper level, Plato provides us with a psychology of the tyrant that extends from an analysis of the psyche of the tyrant as overflowing with frantic desires and anxious fears to the mass psychology that sustains tyrannical regimes.[9] Plato's tyrant is the personification and radicalization of the compulsive, terrorized social psyche of the masses. For tyranny is not only in the person of the tyrant and his troubled mind, but has its own culture that permeates into the masses, that is, a culture of terror. Tyranny is in the minds of the subjects of tyranny as much as it is in their oppressors. In tyrannies, people live in fear of the secret police knocking on their doors; they live in fear that their neighbors could be spies, that spies are everywhere, and these fears morph into terror—not knowing where danger will come from next, and so seeing it everywhere. The amorphous fear of plots and uprisings that keeps the tyrant awake at night translates into a general terror and an impossible security dilemma—the quest for absolute security, undertaken through the frantic violence of a strong-arm state.

Liberating the oppressed from tyranny has to involve more than lashing out against tyrannical regimes and deposing tyrants; it must address the culture of terror that sustains tyrannical rule and that infects the minds of subjects under tyranny. This lesson is now being learned at great cost in Iraq, where simple decapitation of a tyrannical regime has not truly liberated the Iraqi people from fear, and where tyranny echoes with every gunshot, haunting the Iraqis and their would-be liberators.[10]

Plato's social psychology of tyranny has also significance closer to home, and indicates a present danger. Not that Americans are subjects to a tyranny—certainly they are not—but that their democratic society is agitated by compulsive consumption, anxious paranoia, and lack of trust between citizens—shades of Plato's scatterbrained *demos*—that could make them potential willing subjects to a tyrannical government offering personal indulgence and corporate security. Given the possibility of more terrorist attacks on American soil, with states of emergency resulting, democracy could be moved in the direction of tyranny, with democratic freedoms fatally compromised. Guilt by association, restrictions on public gatherings, surveillance of private communications, secret detentions without charges laid or access to legal counsel, and torture are all fixtures of tyrannical rule, and are now being called upon as means to secure state and society in our time of crisis. This is a warning, not a prediction, though if we follow Plato's account of the succession of regimes in the *Republic*—from democracy to tyranny—we at least see this possibility opened up, so as to guard against it. However, what we might experience in a tyranny equipped with contemporary technology would be beyond Plato's imagination, a more efficient tyranny capable of sorting out potential subversives from passive subjects, and with far greater powers of propaganda for the passive and policing for the resistant. We put too much trust in Hobbes' machinelike state if we believe that we have progressed beyond the possibility of tyranny, that mechanical checks and balances make watchful, virtuous civic involvement unnecessary. What we can trust is Plato's principle that no human being can live a happy life under tyranny, and that whatever security dilemma it may be called upon to resolve is not worth the suffering of its subjects. We should guard the protection of liberty by law and do our best to preserve the "sweet regime" (Plato 1991, 558c) that we now enjoy against emergency dictatorial powers and the slide from democracy to tyranny.

Tyranny does give the false promise of usefulness in emergency situations: it is a quick and dirty way to impose order within a state and to marshal a state's powers of war for the purposes of defense and conquest. It is for such security concerns that Machiavelli recommends tyrannical methods to Lorenzo de Medici—to protect against barbarous invaders and defend Italian nationhood—and it was under similar circumstances that the tyrant of Syracuse, Dionysius I, came to power. Plato notes that the Syracusan tyranny was originally established to protect colonies in Sicily against the Carthaginians and local barbarians and to extend Hellenic civilization to the island (Plato 1999, VIII.353a–b). Dionysius I was at first elected into office and later, as a war measure, was given the office of *strategos autokratôr*, supreme commander in war, a position for which he was annually reelected by the Syracusan assembly. Tyrannies concentrate the military and policing powers of the state in one person for the sake of efficiency, to rise above the petty quarreling of democratic politics for the higher purposes of security in times of crisis. Dionysius I billed his accession to autocratic power as necessary for the safety of the democracy that preexisted his tyranny, though only the superficial institutions of democracy survived his rule, while true freedom did not.[11]

Dictatorship may seem to be a necessary evil for dire circumstances and a useful defense against the enemies of a threatened civilization. Plato gives a powerful rejoinder against both the instrumental use of tyranny and violent countermeasures against it—in general the "ends justify the means" attitude—when he writes to those who would reform tyranny that,

> the end of evils is never reached, but the apparent ending of the old is always bound together with the budding of a new beginning, a dangerous circle that threatens to utterly destroy the people along with the tyrant (Plato 1999, VIII.353d).

Tyrannies do not produce political stability, but their violent means beget violent reactions from the populace, which in turn prompt ever more desperate attempts at the imposition of order.

Rather than using violent means to do away with tyranny, Plato undertook to educate and reform tyrants. Plato made three visits to Sicily, taking counsel first with Dionysius I, then educating the son Dionysius II when the tyranny was passed on. However, Plato's efforts to tame these father-son tyrants had less to do with making philosopher kings out of them than with moderating their violence by encouraging them to observe conventions and tradition. The letters from philosopher to tyrant only occasionally betray hints of Plato's philosophical teachings, which are preserved even in their presentation as esoteric wisdom (Plato 1999, II.312d, 314c). Rather, in the thirteenth letter, for instance, Plato dwells on such practical concerns as the provision of dowries for grand nieces, the construction of a tomb for Plato's mother, and equipping a chorus, all along advising Dionysius to repay his debts and to observe the conventions of his city and civilization (Plato 1999, XIII.361c–362e). Outwardly, this is a request for payment for Plato's services as a philosophical advisor, while implicitly it is encouragement to Dionysius to think of public reputation, both at home in Syracuse and abroad in Athens. Concern with reputation is a key pedagogical hook that Plato uses in trying to persuade Dionysius to moderate his behavior, raising the tyrant's sights above his own personal pleasures to more enduring and universal goods—honors over appetites. Plato urges Dionysius to think of how he looks to others in his own city and abroad. A similar approach is used today when the international community expresses its revulsion at tyrants who abuse their populations and threaten their neighbors; true, these are only expressions of indignation not enforceable through arms, but they carry with them the force of moral suasion and the incentive of public honor. The tyrant's appetite for aggrandizement is close to honor seeking, and he could be rehabilitated through this fascination with reputation.

In terms of explicit advice, Plato counsels Dionysius to watch carefully over the financial affairs of his city and to practice fiscal conservatism, not wasting public funds on monuments and expansionist wars,[12] and not appropriating private property for his own purposes. Plato does not ask Dionysius to make a radical conversion to philosophy; though he encourages the tyrant to lead a philosophic life (Plato 1999, XIII.363c), philosophy properly so-called is not reducible to the good habits of moderate living. Retiring early from the banquets and orgies that were common in the courts of Syracuse would be a necessary condition for living the life of a philosopher, but doing so would not make Dionysius a philosopher king; it would only make him perhaps less dangerous, less indulgent of his appetites, and hopefully by consequence less excessive in his indiscriminate violence and thievery. Plato simply asks Dionysius to keep still for a moment: "Be always the same" is how he signs off the thirteenth letter.

That introductory letter deals mainly with practical business and lays out the preconditions for a friendship between Plato and Dionysius. The issue of friendship is the central focus of the second letter and a recurring theme in Plato's letters as a whole. If Plato's rudimentary purpose is to moderate the tyrant through fiscal conservatism, adherence to tradition, and the cultivation of good reputation, his most ambitious purpose is to bring about a friendship between philosophy and political power. However, this does not mean a fusion of wisdom and power in one person, or even a permanent position for Plato as advisor to the king. Rather, an intermediary is involved: Plato attempts to warm Dionysius up to his friend and student, Dion, who would act as a liaison between the philosopher and the tyrant, and a friend to both (Plato 1999, III.316e). But making Dionysius capable of friendship would prove no easy task for Plato, since the tyrant sees friendly reformers as potential usurpers. Although Dionysius was enamored of Plato's reputation of wisdom, he did not fully trust the intentions of his advisor and detained Plato as his songbird sage when it was rumored that the philosopher's pupil was fomenting dissent.

There was of course some substance to Dionysius' concerns. Beyond gossipy paranoia, it would seem that the tyrant who takes advice from the philosopher does, in a sense, become his disciple and subordinate. In fact, Plato's letters to Dion and the friends of Dion betray some cause for Dionysius' wariness. In the last letter to Dionysius after their falling out over his preventative detention, Plato cheekily describes his role as philosophical advisor to the tyrant as that of "supreme commander" ("*autokratôr*," Plato 1999, I.309b). Indeed, Plato had a fairly active role in the shaping of the Syracusan regime, drafting a prelude to its laws that would anchor the government in a written constitution of sorts, through which Plato took a guiding hand in Syracusan politics and attempted to reign in Dionysius.

As the great teacher of philosophy represented a challenge to the tyrant's absolute rule by subordinating him to law and philosophical tutelage, so did

Plato's students pose real threats to Dionysius' dictatorship. According to Plato, Dion "believed in liberty for the Syracusans under the guidance of the best system of laws" (Plato 1999, XII.324b). To realize this political creed in Syracuse under Dionysius would have amounted to revolutionary regime change; and indeed Dion would go on—against Plato's vigorous insistence—to remove the tyrant using arms, unleashing nearly twenty years of civil war for Sicily. And whatever Plato's explicit arguments against the use of force in reforming tyranny, in the tyrant's eyes Plato would be guilty of subversion, too, just because he was Dion's friend and teacher—guilt by association being a fixture of "justice" under tyranny. However, it would not be right to paint Plato as a tutor of revolutionaries. As Plato tells the friends of Dion, his own initial enthusiasm for revolution in Athens was deflated by his experience with the Thirty Tyrants that the revolution vomited up. Under the Thirty and in the reinstated government of exiles that replaced them there was no ground for trust between friends, and politics was reduced to reciprocal exchanges of retributive violence between factions, a downward spiral that would eventually lead to the death of Socrates (Plato 1999, VII.324b–325c), much as factional violence in Sicily would eventually lead to Dion's death.

Plato's disillusionment with revolution in Athens and reform in Syracuse led him to believe that philosophy is best practiced from a vantage over and above the mess of politics. Along with this elevated attitude goes Plato's tragic commentary that,

> evil will not cease for mankind until either those who are right and true philosophers come to sole political authority or those who have political power, by some divine fate, are really philosophic (Plato 1999, VII.326b).

Bearing witness to both his failures to educate tyrants and the vicious degeneration of revolution into tyranny, Plato's judgment on the possibility of eradicating tyranny and of progress in politics is not encouraging. In the end, after his aspirations for applying ideals to reality were exhausted, Plato gives up on the possibility of an end to evil, calling it a matter of "some divine fate," that is, beyond human powers to effect. We find an almost identical passage in Book V of the *Republic* (473d), which we can take as a warning, along with the letters, that efforts to engineer the best of all possible worlds require the same tyrannical means that they are intended to remove.[13]

The religious aspect of Plato's counsel is telling. Plato's letters are, in a sense, advice for angels, that is, for those removed from the exigencies of political power. Those concerned with acquiring political power (like Dion) or keeping it (like Dionysius) cannot really afford the kind of purity that Plato recommends. Dionysius had likely cause to be suspicious of his advisors and to violently suppress dissenters, and Dion had every incentive to take up arms against the ruthless tyrant. At least, that's the sort of thing that usually happens (Plato 1991, 566b). But in the face of realistic assessment, we should remember that the realities of power do not make such courses of action just, only predictable. And predictably also, neither cruel oppression nor violent revolution produced a lasting, lawful peace for Syracuse. By calling us toward a pure peace and a lawful order over and above the reciprocal exchanges of belligerence that characterize power politics, Plato moves us to a vantage outside of that violent circle. Certainly, the principle repeated here—that tyrannies are bad—cannot act as a charm to ward off the evils of the world, but it can allow us to see those evils with perspective, so that we are not ourselves compelled to blindly follow the exigencies of the moment, driven by mad fear on a frenzied quest for an elusive, absolute security, so that we do not become tyrannical in our response to tyranny.

While Plato doubts the likelihood of reconciliation between wisdom and power and the eradication of tyranny, he did carry on after his failed experiment with Dionysius to encourage friendship among the students of philosophy. In his sixth letter to Hermias, Erastus, and Coriscus, Plato sets out to encourage friendship between these friends of Dion, telling them to make their friendship secure, guard against the evils of men, read his letters aloud, practice philosophy together, and pray. What Plato demonstrates in his letters to the tyrant and those friends of philosophy subject to tyrannical rule is not only the difficulty of fostering a friendship between wisdom and power, but also the difficulty of friendship as such in a tyrannical regime, where rumor and paranoia crowd out reasonable discourse and mutual trust (Plato 1999, VII.329b–c). Friendship and faith are the bases of political community, and one of the effects of tyranny is to make friendship difficult by terrorizing citizens so that they trust neither state nor neighbor. Tyrants, too, have their own fears. Tyrants fear free association and prosecute enemies of the state based upon guilt by association, so that all political friendships become suspect. In the culture of terror endemic to tyranny, living the good life becomes difficult, limited to private nooks sheltered from the storms of power politics gone berserk.

Judging from the practical success of Plato's missions to Syracuse, the friendship of philosopher and tyrant and the reform of tyranny are unlikely possibilities. For although the philosopher is attracted to the tyrant's reputation for power, and the tyrant attracted to the philosopher's reputation for wisdom, it is not clear that the two can be friends, or that the philosopher is suited to educating the tyrant. Both are proud types, and the philosopher would no sooner stoop to flattery than the tyrant would subjugate himself as a compliant student. And it may be better that way, with wisdom kept separate from power. For the tyrant's excessiveness could be dangerously increased by a superficial education and a half-cooked notion of philosophy. Abstract universals brutally applied liberate tyrannical violence from natural constraints, as the history of ideological tyranny in the twentieth century clearly shows. Instead of seeing the city as an extended, prosthetic stomach for the satisfaction of personal desires, the tyrant set loose by an incomplete philosophic education—in modern terms, by ideology—could imagine grander designs for conquest. A tyrant with a full belly in his fortress is less a hazard to his subjects and neighbors than a tyrant with stars in his eyes. Hence a prudential reluctance to represent philosophy as a doctrine, expressed in Plato's intriguing, repeated claims in his letters never to have written his philosophy down (Plato 1999 II.314c, VII.341c).

This would make it difficult to find application for Plato's philosophy to contemporary politics, or to the realities of power at all, Plato's time included. Indeed, Plato's working advice to tyrant and reformers seems more conventional than critical, more conservative than radical, and more religious than rational, that is, not properly philosophical in character.

So, aside from religious prohibitions and beyond Plato's judgment on tyranny as the worst of all regimes in which none can be truly happy, what should we take from Plato's encounter with tyranny? We should take note of his social psychology of tyranny, which links the paranoid psyche of the tyrant to the terrorized subjects he oppresses. Tyranny is not limited to the person of the tyrant himself, but gains its impetus from a collective paranoia, a perceived security dilemma according to which all are seen as potential enemies. Within this environment of mutual distrust, the superficial strong-arm security that the tyrant promises starts to seem preferable to a life spent in terror. At least then fear has a definite source. But what is lost when terror is promoted as the glue that binds a state together are the capacities for political friendship and communal faith.

Given this social psychology of tyranny, and as we now see in Iraq, simple decapitation of a regime cannot be expected to bring about reform when tyranny so deeply affects the minds of its subjects and propagates its own culture of terror. In the words of Major General James M. Marks, who served as the chief intelligence officer during the invasion of Iraq, "We did not appreciate the 'fear factor' and the grip that the regime had on the people."[14] It is curious to suppose that a war would relieve this terror, as if a few well-aimed missiles and midnight house-to-house raids could be the instruments of liberation. Enlightened nations should not conduct themselves in the manner of paranoid tin-pot tyrants lashing out against shadowy threats, nor should liberal democracies adopt the political culture of anxiety and terror endemic to tyrannies. And yet, the mind-set of the tyrant seems to approximate today's *Weltenshauung*, cueing in as it does to a terror instinct that is as powerful as it is base. This is precisely why tyranny is a recurrent and a present danger, and something that we should be on constant guard against, because it takes as its animus our basest fears and desires, turning them back on themselves, making a continuous feedback circuit of desire after desire and terror after terror. To the end of stepping out of this paranoid, compulsive, and oppressive circle, Plato's encounter with tyranny serves better as a cautionary tale than as a program for revolutionary change, as a warning rather than a remedy.

NOTES

1. I accept Plato's letters, whether authentic or not, as instructive narratives: not windows into Plato's private mind, but illustrations of the philosopher's sojourn in public life. The claim that some or all of the letters are spurious is based in a preconceived notion of who the real Plato was. Apparently to some, the rhetorical style of the letters, which trumpet the reputation of philosophy, does not match the self-critical tone of "authentic" Platonic dialogues. But this is to be expected, given the audiences of the letters: students of philosophy in hostile territory needing steady encouragement, and a tyrant not open to Socratic *elenchus* but impressed by reputation. The letters, especially the second letter, give a superficial impression of philosophy, but this is probably all that a tyrant could take.

Even if the letters were written by a gifted student of Plato and not the teacher himself, still they provide us with a narrative of a failed reconciliation between wisdom and power, a theme consistent with the Platonic corpus, here given dramatic, historical content.

I have used the Loeb Classical Library edition as my source for Plato's letters. Quotations from the letters are my translation.

2. For first-person accounts from those who lived under tyranny and resisted—from a resistance fighter in the Polish underground to a lawyer for Algerian rebels to a German officer who helped in an attempt on Hitler's life—see Eugene Meinler, ed., *Resistance against Tyranny* (London: Routledge, 1966).

3. For a contemporary version of this argument from a liberal democratic perspective, see Michael Ignatieff, *The Lesser Evil: Political Ethics in an Age of Terror* (Toronto: Penguin, 2004). Ignatieff argues that democracy and dictatorship can be complimentary, that "democracies are not self-sustaining; rather, as the Romans thought, their executives recurrently need dictatorial prerogatives to cope with crisis" (38).

4. For an example of this kind of criticism applied to the related term "totalitarianism," see Benjamin Barber and Herbert J. Spiro, "Counter-Ideological Uses of 'Totalitarianism,'" in *Politics & Society*, 1 (1970).

5. President Ronald Reagan's "Evil Empire" speech to the National Association of Evangelicals in Orlando, Florida, March 8, 1983, http://cbn.org/CBNNews/News/Reagan_NAESpeech.asp (accessed August 10, 2005).

6. President George W. Bush's State of the Union Address, January 29, 2002, http://www.whitehouse.gov/news/releases/2002/01/20020129-11.html (accessed August 10, 2005).

7. 2002 National Security Strategy of the United States of America, http://www.whitehouse.gov/nsc/nss.html (accessed August 10, 2005).

8. A Human Rights Watch report shows that the fifty failed assassination attempts on Iraqi leadership early in the Iraq war (a one-hundred-percent failure rate) were the major exception to the generally low incidence of civilian casualties from U.S. bombing raids. See Marc Garlasco, *Off Target: The Conduct of the War and Civilian Casualties in Iraq* (New York: Human Rights Watch, December 2003), http://www.hrw.org/reports/2003/usa1203/ (accessed August 10, 2005). Figures for Iraqi casualties are not officially recorded, though a number could not adequately represent the scope of human tragedy and the lasting effects on Iraqi civil society. The bomb blasts echo in the minds of the survivors and spur the ongoing insurgency.

One example, from a missed attempt on the life of Lieutenant General `Ali Hassan al-Majid, the notorious "Chemical Ali," gives some sense of the effects. In the early morning of April 5, 2003, two five-hundred-pound laser-guided bombs were dropped on a "target of opportunity" in a densely populated neighborhood. Though the General was not killed, the homes of the Hamudi and al-Tayyar families were destroyed. Those who died in the Hamudi home include the following:

Dr. Khairiyya Shakir, 68, wife, gynecologist;
Wisam `Abid Hassan, 38, son, computer engineer;
Dr. Ihab `Abid Hassan, 34, son, gynecologist;
Nura, 6 months, granddaughter (daughter of Dr. Ihab);
Zainab Akram, 19, granddaughter, pharmacist;
Zain al-`Adidin Akram, 16, grandson;
Mustafa Akram, 14, grandson;
Hassan Iyad, 11, grandson;
Zaina Akram, 12, granddaughter;
`Amr Muhammad, 19 months, grandson.

The dead from the al-Tayyar family include the following:

As'ad `Abd al-Hussain al-Tayyar, 30, son;
Qarar As'ad al-Tayyar, 12, grandson (son of As'ad);
Haidar As'ad al-Tayyar, 9, grandson (son of As'ad);
Saif As'ad al-Tayyar, 6, grandson (son of As'ad);
Intisar `Abd al-Hussain al-Tayyar, 30, daughter;
Khawla `Ali al-Tayyar, 9, granddaughter (daughter of Intisar);
Hind `Ali al-Tayyar, 5, granddaughter (daughter of Intisar).

Certainly, bombing civilians in hit-or-miss assassinations is not a good way to liberate them from a tyrant and assuage the terror that sustains tyranny. If the war in Iraq is being fought for a virtuous cause—liberating Iraqis from tyranny—then the war makers should be judged by accordingly high standards of conduct.

9. Roger Boesche has a similar reading of Plato's account of tyranny as a pathology that affects the psyches of both tyrant and demos in a mutually reinforcing way. See *Theories of Tyranny from Plato to Arendt* (University Park: Pennsylvania State University Press, 1996), 25–48.

10. I point to Larry Diamond's essay in *Foreign Affairs* (Sept/Oct 2004), "What Went Wrong in Iraq," in which he addresses the need for social reconstruction, "including the renewal (or in some cases, creation) of a civil society and political culture that foster voluntary cooperation." The successes of American rule in Iraq that Diamond trumpets loudest are not its military and counterinsurgency campaigns, but its support for local civil-society organizations.

11. For more on the conditions surrounding Dionysius I's accession to power, see Brian Caven, *Dionysius I: War-Lord of Sicily* (New Haven, CT: Yale University Press, 1990), 50–59. Also see Ludwig Marcuse's philosophical narrative, *Plato and Dionysius: A Double Biography* (New York: Alfred A. Knopf, 1947), 3–39. On the succession of the Syracusan tyranny from father to son, with emphasis on its popular support, see Diodorus' history of Sicily (bk. 15, 73–74).

12. *Republic*, 566e.

13. On the question of the authenticity of the letters, we could take this parallel passage from the *Republic* as an argument for either side: it could be taken to demonstrate consistency of authorship, or it could point to a forgery by a student copying his teacher's words—an irresolvable antinomy.

14. Quoted in Michael Gordon, "Poor Intelligence Misled Troops about Risk of Drawn-Out War," *New York Times*, October 20, 2004, http://www.nytimes.com/2004/10/20/international/20war.html?pagewanted=4&th&oref=login (accessed August 10, 2005).

SOURCES

Barber, Benjamin, and Herbert J. Spiro. 1970. "Counter-Ideological Uses of 'Totalitarianism.'" In *Politics & Society*, 1.

Boesche, Roger. 1996. *Theories of Tyranny from Plato to Arendt*. University Park: Pennsylvania State University Press.

Bush, George W. 2002. *State of the Union Address*, January 29. http://www.whitehouse.gov/news/releases/2002/01/20020129-11.html (accessed August 10, 2005).

Caven, Brian. 1990. *Dionysius I: War-Lord of Sicily*. New Haven, CT: Yale University Press.

Diamonds, Larry. 2004. "What Went Wrong in Iraq." *Foreign Affairs*, Sept./Oct.

Diodorus. 1967. *Diodorus of Sicily*. Trans. C. H. Oldfather. Cambridge, MA: Harvard University Press.

Garlasco, Marc. 2003. *Off Target: The Conduct of the War and Civilian Casualties in Iraq*. New York: Human Rights Watch, December. http://www.hrw.org/reports/2003/usa1203/ (accessed August 10, 2005).

Gordon, Michael. 2004. "Poor Intelligence Misled Troops about Risk of Drawn-Out War." *New York Times*, October 20.

Hobbes, Thomas. 1985. *Leviathan*. London: Penguin.

Ignatieff, Michael. 2004. *The Lesser Evil: Political Ethics in an Age of Terror*. Toronto: Penguin.

Machiavelli, Niccolò. 1974. *The Discourses*. Trans. Leslie J. Walker. London: Penguin.

———. 1977. *The Prince*. Trans. Robert Adams. New York: W. W. Norton.

Marcuse, Ludwig. *Plato and Dionysius: A Double Biography*. New York: Alfred A. Knopf, 1947.

Meimler, Eugene, ed. 1966. *Resistance against Tyranny*. London: Routledge.

Plato. 1991. *Republic*. Trans. Allan Bloom. New York: Basic Books.

———. 1999. *Timaeus, Critias, Cleitophon, Menexenus, Epistles*. Cambridge, MA: Harvard University Press.

Reagan, Ronald. 1983. "Evil Empire" speech to the National Association of Evangelicals, Orlando, Florida, March 8. http://cbn.org/CBNNews/News/Reagan_NAESpeech.asp (accessed August 10, 2005).

Rousseau, Jean-Jacques. 1967. *The Social Contract and Discourse on the Origin of Inequality*. Trans. Lester G. Crocker. New York: Washington Square Press.

U.S. National Security Council. 2002. *2002 National Security Strategy of the United States of America*. http://www.whitehouse.gov/nsc/nss.html (accessed August 10, 2005).

Chapter 14

The Folly of the Wise?

Thomas Smith

The Lord of the Rings is an anti-quest. The point is not for a strong knight to attain some grail of strength, but for a weak hobbit to destroy a token of power. Yet the Ring Frodo sets out to destroy is the very thing that the heroes in the book apparently need to defeat the tyranny that threatens to overwhelm them. By rejecting it, they open themselves up to a powerful objection: the high-minded abandonment of power in the name of morality is actually cruel insofar as it allows evil to triumph.[1] Perhaps the only reason the heroes' response to tyranny works lies in the author's control of the narrative. From this point of view, Tolkien's fantasy is an expression of a childish wish fulfillment: if we refuse to play the game of power, tyranny will be defeated.

What sense can we make of Tolkien's response to tyranny? The wizard Gandalf personifies it. He is clearly the wisest character in the story.[2] Further, Gandalf rejects the Ring when Frodo offers it to him, and later recommends that the hobbit walk into the tyrant's land to destroy it. Is Gandalf foolish in this? Two other characters in the books who enjoy a reputation for wisdom think so.[3] Saruman the wizard and Denethor the steward of Gondor have very different strategies for dealing with Sauron, the tyrant in *Lord of the Rings*. We must restate their alternatives in order to see whether or not Gandalf's course of action, and thus Tolkien's response to tyranny, makes sense.

Saruman has a preferred policy and a second-best option. Each is based on a hardheaded recognition of the situation Sauron's enemies face. Saruman has an accurate assessment of Sauron's vastly superior military strength due to the *palantír* of Orthanc, which allows him to see things at great distances. Saruman reasonably concludes that Sauron will win the coming war—easily if he discovers the Ring and regains his full power, less easily if he does not. Saruman's first choice is to find the Ring and use it himself. This will allow him first to defeat Sauron's tyranny. It would then enable Saruman to use the Ring to rule according to his own superior wisdom. Saruman thinks his own rule would be infinitely preferable to Sauron's because he seeks order and justice rather than mastery.[4] If all this fails, however, Saruman's second-best option is to recognize Sauron's inevitable triumph, ally himself with Mordor, and use this cooperation as an opportunity to moderate the tyrant's rule. Speaking to Gandalf, Saruman says,

> A new Power is rising. Against it the old allies and policies will not avail us at all. . . . We may join that Power. It would be wise, Gandalf. There is hope that way. Its victory is at hand; and there will be rich rewards for those that aid it. As the Power grows, its proved friends will also grow; and the Wise, such as you and I, may with patience come at last to direct its courses, to control it. We can bide our time, we can keep our thoughts in our hearts, deploring maybe the evils done by the way, but approving the high and ultimate purpose: Knowledge, Rule, Order; all the things we have so far striven in vain to accomplish, hindered rather than helped by our weak or idle friends. There need not be, there would not be, any real change in our designs, only in our means (*LotR*, 253.II.2).

These policies have much to recommend them. They are realistic about the probable outcome of the coming war and the nature of the enemy's rule if he wins it. They seek to defeat the enemy first, but failing that, to make his rule less oppressive.

Denethor's policy is different. He believes that using the Ring against Sauron would have morally disastrous consequences because the Ring corrupts those who use it (*LotR*, 795.V.4). So he recommends that it be kept hidden from the enemy, only to be used in a situation of extreme need (*LotR*, 795.V.4). Denethor has been pursuing a successful containment policy against Sauron for a long time, and at the beginning of the story he seems to think that it will keep working, provided the enemy does not get the Ring. Yet Gandalf's policy practically guarantees this. Indeed, whatever their differences, Denethor and Saruman agree on one thing: sending the Ring into the heart of the enemy's realm with two weak hobbits is idiotic. It practically guarantees that the tyrant will acquire the power he needs to triumph decisively. For these men, Gandalf's policy has nothing to recommend it. For Saruman, it wastes opportunities both to get rid of Sauron once and for all and to gain access to the kind of power that is needed to order society with wisdom. For both Saruman and Denethor, it guarantees Sauron's victory because the hobbits are almost certainty doomed to failure. These are powerful, commonsense observations. Gandalf seems foolish because he both ignores the realities of the situation and relies on weakness when strength is demanded.

Let me expand my point about Gandalf's apparent foolishness in a different way. When Frodo offers Gandalf the Ring, the wizard rejects it, saying that it tempts him by playing on his desire for mercy and justice, especially for the weak. He says, "Yet the way of the Ring to my heart is by pity, pity for weakness and the desire of strength to do good. Do not tempt me! I dare not take it, not even to keep it safe, unused. The wish to wield it would be too great for my strength. I shall have such need of it" (*LotR*, 60.I.2). Gandalf is not tempted to power for its own sake. Rather, he wants to order the world with justice and mercy, and the Ring promises him that ability. Yet if so, why reject it? Are not his desires manifestations of the virtues of a good statesman? If so, the Ring is an opportunity to be embraced. Again, why does Gandalf reject the Ring if it can be used not only to defeat tyranny, but to ensure justice?

FANTASY AS AN ESCAPE TO REALITY

Let me begin answering these objections by reflecting on contemporary fantasy, which Tolkien practically invented. The authors of this genre reject the conventions of the modern novel. Since its inception, the characteristics of the modern novel dictate that its readers will encounter only reality. That is, we will read about people more or less like us, and situations that we would expect to encounter in everyday life. Supernatural beings will not enter the story, nor will it suspend the physical laws that govern the natural world. In this sense, the birth of the modern novel signals the death of the ancient and medieval worldview. It expresses disenchantment with the notion that the fantastic can intrude into everyday life.

> *Don Quixote* is considered . . . the first—and probably the greatest—novel in the European tradition in part because it makes this claim to represent "ordinary life" a central and profound aspect of the plot. Cervantes' fiction is a sort of birth announcement—droll and yet decisive—for realism itself. It betokens a new human attitude. By showing Quixote driven mad by the involuted, highly stylized, comically implausible heroic romances of the later Middle Ages, . . . Cervantes was not just spoofing an out-of-date literary mode; he was also marking the obsolescence of the philosophical world-view it embodied. Don Quixote is far more, one soon realizes, than just a comic assault on some fanciful old stories; in its deepest aspect it is a metaphysical statement—a revolutionary affirmation of that secular and humanistic point of view we associate with modernity itself.[5]

However, if the birth of the modern novel signals a turn to realism, those who reject its conventions are expressing a different disenchantment. For many fantasy writers, modern notions of realism tilt at windmills insofar as they neglect or render opaque central dimensions of human life, categories like mystery or soul. Fantasy is a postmodern genre. In the twentieth century, modern reductions of reality bore fruit in tyranny and violence, and this led to massive disillusionment with those notions. This point has led Tom Shippey to argue that "the dominant literary mode of the twentieth century has been the fantastic."[6] Fantasy writers like Tolkien, Ursula LeGuin, William Golding, George Orwell, Aldous Huxley, J. K. Rowling, C. S. Lewis, Kurt Vonnegut, or Bill Pullman understand their work this way. Often these authors are particularly concerned with exploring the nature and reality of evil. Several lived through various horrors of the twentieth century, and

> were bone-deep convinced that they had come into contact with something irrevocably evil. They also . . . felt that the explanations for this which they were given by the official organs of their culture were hopelessly inadequate, out of date, at best irrelevant, at worst part of the evil itself.[7]

For Tolkien, a survivor of the Somme, the "realism" that the official organs of his culture promoted was revealed as at best unrealistic about the human condition and at worst disastrous.[8] As Shippey writes,

> If one considers the whole history of Tolkien's youth and middle age, from 1892 to 1954, a period marked not only by two world wars and the rise of Fascism, Nazism, and Stalinism, but also by—I give them more or less in chronological order—the routine bombardment of civilian populations, the use of famine as a political measure, the revival of judicial torture, the "liquidation" of whole classes of political opponents, extermination camps, deliberate genocide and the continuing development of "weapons of mass destruction" from chlorine gas to the hydrogen bomb, all of these absolutely unthinkable in the Victorian world of Tolkien's childhood, then it would be a strange mind which did not reflect, as so many did, that something had gone wrong, something furthermore which could not be safely pushed off and blamed on other people.[9]

In response to this view of reality and its fruits, Tolkien created an alternative world in which the experiences he had lived through could be articulated and explored. His point in doing so was not to advocate institutional or political responses to tyranny, although he was not opposed to these. Rather, like Plato, Tolkien believed that such responses can become part of the problem if we do not realize that evil arises not from unjust institutional structures or insufficient Enlightenment, but from the human heart—including the hearts of those who resist evil. So political responses are worse than useless in the absence of a realistic assessment of the attractions we have to tyranny in our own souls. Again like Plato, Tolkien believed that the recesses of our souls can be revealed by writing them large in myth.[10] The point of these stories is not to advocate political responses to tyranny. Rather, it is to dramatize the workings of the human heart in order to uncover our underlying psychic attractions to power so that our responses to tyranny will not participate in the same evil we are trying to resist.

WHAT IS THE RING OF POWER?

Thus, understanding why Gandalf rejects the Ring entails understanding the way it serves to dramatize our attraction to power and its consequences. We should begin by recalling why Sauron made the Ring in the first place: to rule all the lesser rings of power.[11] At the time Sauron made the One Ring, the elves had been making rings of power and giving them to the various races of Middle Earth. They made three for themselves; the Dwarves had seven; and nine were made for men.[12] Each type had a specific power. Dwarf rings were used for gaining wealth. The rings given to men made them "mighty in their day, kings sorcerers and warriors. . . . They obtained great glory and wealth."[13] Elf rings "could ward off the decays of time and postpone the weariness of the world."[14] Despite their different functions, however, the rings have a common element. Each kind was made to manage a different aspect of mortality. This should not be surprising, insofar as Tolkien says death is the main theme of his work.[15] It is not hard to understand why. Tolkien had been an orphan since his mother died when he was twelve, and had never really known his father, who passed away when he was four. Before he turned twenty, he had lost all of his closest friends in World War I. As Tolkien's biographer comments, Tolkien's experiences with mortality gave him "a deep sense of impending loss. Nothing was safe. Nothing would last. No battle would be won forever."[16]

Dwarves used their rings for acquiring wealth. Excessive love of money is a manifestation of the fear of death. Greed stems from a longing to protect oneself against the vagaries of life by having "money in the bank" that promises to ward off any and all misfortune.[17] In Tolkien's work, this attitude is symbolized by dragons who sit on hoards of gold, never spending their money or doing anything with their lives, greedily holding everything back, storing wealth up against their useless, inactive futures. Tolkien's clearest treatment of greed is found in *The Hobbit*. In this story, Bilbo Baggins, a smug, wealthy, bourgeois recluse is thrown out of his comfortable life by a wizard who aims to cure the hobbit's fear and greed. The wizard arranges for a group of dwarves to hire the hobbit to help them recover their gold from a dragon who has stolen it. However, Bilbo is cured of his own greed in the adventure, eventually giving away his share of the treasure to prevent a war between the dwarves and their enemies. Bilbo's journey away from his home to help greedy dwarves recover their treasure from a greedy dragon is at the same time a transformative journey into himself, undertaken in order to slay the life-denying, death-fearing greed that lies there.[18]

The rings given to men were used to gain glory, wealth, and power. Excessive love of glory, too, is a manifestation of fear of death. According to Augustine, the ancient Romans loved glory because of their desire to pursue a quasidivine immortality in a tangible form. That is, the attempt to build an empire that will last forever is a manifestation of a longing for immortality, which the Romans held to be inaccessible for individuals. Thus the desire to build something glorious that will last stems from both a longing for an eternal divine life and a horror at impending death. However, the self-conscious pursuit of this kind of earthly immortality actually heightens the fear of death that drives it on because as that work progresses it makes what is inchoate more self-aware. Thus as the imperial project expands in time and space, it will yield more and more self-assertion and self-aggrandizement. For Augustine, love of glory leads by a slippery slope to love of domination.[19]

The dwarf rings and the human rings explore the desire to manage insecurity by warding off death. However, the elf rings illuminate a different facet of mortality. In Tolkien's fiction, elves are immortal. By stretching out their lives, Tolkien explores the burden of living in time and the grief that comes with it. The fact that elves live forever highlights what might be called the burden of evanescence. As Legolas the elf says,

> For the Elves the world moves, and it moves both very swift and very slow. Swift, because they themselves change little, and all else fleets by: it is a grief to them. Slow, because they do not count the running years, not for themselves. The passing seasons are but ripples ever repeated in the long running stream. Yet beneath the Sun all things must wear to an end (*LotR*, 379.II.9).[20]

The point is that the transitory goods of this world are beautiful and attractive to us, and yet even as we enjoy them, we have an inkling that they will pass away—just as we will. Our enjoyment is mixed with grief because of our sense of impending loss.

This is why the Buddha speaks of existence as suffering. He does not mean that there is no happiness in life. Nor does he mean that sometimes painful moments follow happy ones in turn. Rather, he says that life is like honey on a razor; we are cut as we taste its sweetness. Even in our most joyful experiences, a tragic sense lurks that they shall pass. We tend to push that away, shielding ourselves through various distractions. We also tend to cling possessively to our positive experiences, unwilling to let them slip away. Clearly, the ordinary sufferings of sickness, old age, or mental pain constitute part of the pain of mortal life. Yet in addition to all this, there is often suffering in our joy because the flow of time insures that the transitory goods that cause our joy will not last. For the Buddha, at the heart of suffering is a clinging possessiveness that expects the universe to meet our all our demands, that refuses to let the world flow on through time because this flow frustrates our wish that enjoyment should last.[21]

The elves' immortality renders their experience of this kind of suffering particularly acute, for unlike human beings, their suffering is not ended by death.[22] Thus they somehow made their rings able to forestall the passing of the world to such an extent that the burden of evanescence is mitigated (*LotR*, 379.II.8). However, in this the elves manifest a kind of clinging possessiveness—a desire to stall the world from unwinding as it will. The various races that Tolkien invents are each dramatizations of different human potentials. The longevity of the elves highlights the world-weariness that comes from the constant frustration human beings experience when the people and things we love pass away.

> The Elves were sufficiently longeval to be called by Man 'immortal.' But they were not unageing or unwearying. Their own tradition was that they were confined to the limits of this world (in space and time), even if they died, and would continue in some form to exist until "the end of the world." But what "the end of the world" portended for it or themselves they did not know. . . . Neither had they of course any special information concerning what "death" portended for Men. They believed it meant "liberation from the circles of the world," and was in that respect to them enviable. And they would point out to Men who envied them that a dread of ultimate loss, though it may be indefinitely more remote, is not necessarily easier to bear if it is in the end ineluctably certain: a burden may be heavier the longer it is borne.[23]

These reflections on the different powers of the rings bring to light a set of question mortals face: How are we supposed to deal with evanescence? Do we hoard up our goods and talents because we are so afraid of our own passing that we wish to have an endless supply of wealth to ward off disaster? Do we protect ourselves from the grief of impending loss by refusing to engage passing goods, in effect living our lives by holding everything attractive at arm's length? Do we seek to possess passing goods, hoping that an increased measure of control will render our enjoyment of them more secure? Or do we love these goods, recognizing their vulnerability and our own, thus risking both grief and the anxiety that often attends our awareness of fragility?

Our mortality is a condition constituted not merely by the fact of our death, but also by the flux of being; the passing of time. The different kinds of rings symbolize different attempts to cling to evanescent goods so as to guarantee that they will last, or at least that their passing will not be as much an occasion for grief. Dwarves and men use their rings to forestall the passing away of things and people they love through a relentless pursuit of glory and wealth. Elves forestall the weariness that comes from the frustration we experience in the passing of temporal things by slowing down time itself. Sauron forged the One Ring to master all of these efforts. His Ring thus symbolizes a clinging, possessive attitude toward life that tries to force reality to act in accord with the tyrant's will. Tolkien says that Sauron particularly coveted the elven rings, for "those who had them in their keeping could ward off the decays of time and postpone the weariness of the world."[24] The Ring is an external manifestation of the tyrant's soul. For this reason, throughout the story, the Ring acts both as a touchstone that unveils the heart's desire of those it tempts, as well as a vehicle for testing whether the heroes can withstand the temptation to securely possess the goods they wish to safeguard.

The most obvious characteristic of the Ring of Power is its ability to dominate the world and its inhabitants.[25] However, Tolkien thinks that the tyrant does not first take up the ring to dominate. Rather, at the beginning he wants to secure some transitory good, eventually ordering his entire society around that possession. The difficulty with this attitude is that it is utterly unrealistic about the tyrant's ability to attain secure possession in a world where things pass away. The frustration and anxiety that attends such a security project will lead the tyrant to domination because only domination seems to yield the control that he wants but that constantly eludes him. In sum, for Tolkien the Ring stands for the psychic desire to possess the goods of the world securely; to stay their passing and to alleviate the anxiety and grief that comes from awareness of their evanescence. Tyranny arises originally not out of a love for evil, but rather out of a clinging desire to possess the good. Tolkien says, "[Sauron] had gone the way of all tyrants: beginning well, at least on the level that while desiring to order all things according to his own wisdom he still at first considered the . . . well-being of other inhabitants of the Earth."[26] This point is especially critical to remember for those resisting tyranny, for that resistance comes from a desire to secure some good against the tyrant. Somehow Tolkien thinks we must defend the goods that the tyrant threatens in a way that refuses to possess them. We must struggle against tyrants. We must also struggle against cultivating the tyrant's attitude in our soul, for adopting that attitude ruins the goods we seek to protect.

THE FRUITS OF POWER

Tolkien's consistent message is that we diminish our lives if we try to secure possession of evanescent goods through power. Another way of putting this is that we ruin the goods we seek to possess to the extent that we seek to possess them. For instance, the consequences of the elves' desire to stay the passing of the world through their rings of power is a retreat into the memory of past glory—a holding fast to past achievements and a waning desire to put forward anything creative and new. The elves practically cease to live in the present, insofar as the present passes away. Rather, they take refuge in memories that do not change. Thus Tolkien says that temptation of the elves is "towards a fainéant melancholy, burdened with memory, leading to an attempt to halt time."[27] The fruit of the Dwarvish desire for wealth is that they were mastered by greed and lost their hoards to dragons. The evanescence of the world leads some to think that it is stingy, and so one cannot risk giving too much away or else one will lose what one already possesses. The dragons who steal the dwarves' gold are outward manifestations of the way the dwarves ruined their ability to enjoy life because of their possessive greed. The consequences of the dwarves' excessive love of gold thus becomes a symbol of their refusal to live full lives, even in the face of their mortality. They pursued wealth in order to securely possess life, yet their lives were eventually diminished by it. Finally, Tolkien explores the fruits of the human wish for power through the Ringwraiths. Like the characters in Dante's *Inferno*, the Ringwraiths get what they wish for. Sauron gives them rings of power, and so they achieve the unending life they want. Yet their desire to possess life securely leads to lives that are sapped of vitality and freedom. They become ghosts and cease to inhabit the physical world (*LotR*, 216.II.1). They also lose their freedom to the domination of their master. The process of "wraithing" for Tolkien is one that highlights the addictive and ultimately vacuous consequences of the attempts to control mortality.[28] The search for control over mortality through clinging possessiveness paradoxically yields only a kind of depressing death-in-life, wherein one's human qualities are stripped away. The Wraiths seek an immortal life, but in the end have to endure an endless death-in-life. Apparently for Tolkien, the more we seek to possess securely the evanescent goods of life securely the more life slips through our fingers.

TRAGIC WISDOM AND DECENT POLITICS

All this means that for Tolkien, successful resistance to tyranny is partly a question of cultivating ordered loves in our souls. Genuine love does not seek to control, secure, or manage. It accepts the fragility and vulnerability of evanescent goods. So in effect, Tolkien holds that the only way of properly engaging the goods we want to love well is to make ourselves vulnerable to their passing. If we refuse—if we seek secure possession to such a degree that we refuse to risk losing what we seek to protect—we take on an ethos that is the same as the tyrant's. And in doing so we choke the life out of the very goods we seek to enjoy. Thus, for example, Frodo saves the Shire, his home, from evil, but the risks he takes and the wounds he endures in the process ultimately mean that he has lost it for himself (*LotR*, 1006.VI.9). Or Aragorn agrees to risk much of his army in a desperate attempt to distract Sauron in order to give Frodo a chance to destroy the Ring (*LotR*, 862.V.9). Since to love well is to love that which inevitably passes, risking loss is the only way to love appropriately. Love that accepts its dependence and vulnerability is more realistic than power precisely insofar as it refuses to control an evanescence that is ultimately beyond its control. This is why Gandalf rejects Denethor's policy. His desire to secure Gondor at all costs leads him to be unimaginative in his response to tyranny. For Tolkien, we cannot do anything about the passing of good things in the world, including ourselves. To try is to diminish our lives; it is to ruin the goods we seek to protect, and render our lives a kind of sleepy death-in-life.[29] Love that risks loss and that thus shoulders sacrifice is at the heart of Tolkien's response to tyranny.

All this may explain why Gandalf refuses to use the Ring of Power to defeat Sauron. However, isn't Gandalf foolish to reject power in order to ensure justice and wise rule, as Saruman the Wizard points out? If his desires are ordered well, won't power provide him the ability to insure justice and protect the weak?

For Tolkien, decent politics requires ordered desires. However, it also requires a lively sense of the limits of our wisdom. That is, decent politics requires the kind of wisdom Socrates practiced—knowing one does not know. Grasping this point requires a rich understanding of the meaning of politics. Much of the business of politics is an exercise in ordering complex systems; it is a problem of collective action. Some of the most important work politicians do is coordinating the various complex activities in a society in a way that makes it flourish. Our usual notion of politics comes from a tradition that views human beings as asocial and politics as instrumental. On this view, the political task is to ensure the way of our future desires through the public construction of individual freedom. Politics is an artificial system that provides utilities like security and wealth that can be put to any and all private uses. Interest-group politics determines the distribution of these utilities and the burdens of paying their costs. Competition, not conviviality, is the law of the jungle. By contrast, in the classical tradition, politics is architectonic because it aims at fostering and protecting a way of life; in Aristotle's terms, it seeks a conception of human flourishing. Thus a political regime decisively affects every aspect of human life, including the individual's formation.[30] In architecture, for example, the various subcontractors and craftsmen take their cue from the architect, who decides the shape and function of the building. The architect coordinates the work of the subcontractors responsible for lighting or plumbing in light of the end for which the building will be employed. In a similar way, a political regime manages the overall shape and direction of the constituent parts of the community because its participants are always acting on some conception of what is good for human beings to be and do when they pass laws or engage in typically respectable practices. To be sure, Aristotle takes issue with the notion of the human good most actual regimes cultivate; he does not think most actual regimes actually foster the virtue and happiness at which they aim. Yet this does not mean he denies that actual regimes always aim at some determined notion of human flourishing by loving what they love.

Human life requires division of labor, trust, partnerships, and cooperation. *Harmonious* life requires the practically wise coordination of the various activities of a society. Zoning boards help determine the shape of a community. Tax laws influence our practices of family, justice, and generosity. Laws managing the shape of our economic lives affect the way we interact with each other and the world in a host of ways. Criminal laws reflect the way we conceive of our sexuality, our mortality, and our need for moderation and responsibility. Thus every political act implies an answer to the question, "How do we become human together?"[31]

Gandalf sees his desire to claim the Ring so as to protect the weak as a temptation. His point is that genuine authority serves; it exists to coordinate the practices of a whole community in a way that fosters genuine flourishing of every part rather than the aggrandizement of the ruling part. The Ring seems to guarantee Gandalf the power to carry out this process. To take possession of the Ring is to seek to possess what it promises to secure. However, Gandalf understands that the conditions for genuine authority stem from the ordering of one's desires through right love, and the comprehensiveness of one's practical wisdom. He rejects the Ring because he trusts neither in his wisdom nor his desires. His wisdom stems from a tragic realization of his own limits. That is to say, Gandalf knows that his wisdom is partial and fragmentary. To order a political community for the sake of perfect justice, the ruling authority must have the most comprehensive wisdom possible; he or she must be able to fit all the parts of the community into a proportionate and beautiful whole in which each part plays its part well.

Yet it seems that Gandalf's tragic wisdom reaches the conclusion that he can never generate sufficient knowledge of the business of his community to order his community's business perfectly. That problem is simply too complex for a mortal mind to resolve exhaustively. This is the problem that faces the most well-intentioned people in politics. It is tremendously difficult to love rightly rather than possess. Yet even when our love is ordered rightly (which is hard enough to achieve), we can never know enough about our own business, much less about the cosmos in which our community participates, to order our community with perfect justice.[32] And the tragic sense of the disproportion between our desire to order well and the ability of our minds to order well tempts us mightily to reach out for the kind of power that seems to promise us the certainty that we can carry off that task. The love of perfect justice, married to an overestimation of our capacity for wisdom, is part of the origin of the desire for power.

Gandalf knows that his rule would create only a partial, fragmentary order of justice. But if he is not careful, his knowledge that the justice he would create is partial would drive him to want to order and then to reorder all the bits and pieces that don't quite fit with the program as he sees it. The Ring promises precisely a comprehensive capacity to possess this order—it promises to "rule them all and bind them." Yet Gandalf denies that his wisdom could yield comprehensiveness of this kind. This is why he disagrees with Saruman's policies. Gandalf's virtue is only partial, and so comprehensive power would yield injustice. In the end, if Gandalf took the Ring, he would become a different kind of tyrant than Sauron; he would be a self-righteous one. Gandalf would resemble Robespierre more than Idi Amin. He would begin wanting to foster justice, but the partiality of his wisdom and the fragmentary nature of his love would lead inexorably to domination and injustice. Alfred North Whitehead once defined evil as the brute motive force of fragmentary purpose.[33] By rejecting the ring, Gandalf agrees. In short, for Tolkien, Gandalf is wise because he is humble in this sense: he has a realistic notion of his need for wisdom and love. In turn, this intimate sense of his neediness focuses his efforts to love rather than possess because it attunes him to the fragility of passing goods.[34]

TRAGEDY AND WISDOM

Tolkien's wisdom is tragic but hopeful. As the poet says in *Antigone*, human beings are the masterpiece of creation. However, while mankind might master earth, wind, sea, beast, and disease, "death he never cures."[35] Life provides us with the longing for the fullness of life, but in the end, despite all our hopes and desires, our lives end in death. Yet, for Tolkien a catharsis lies in this realization. We are shocked into wonderment and thus appreciation for the people and things we love precisely when we realize we may lose them. This catharsis depends on a commiseration and therefore an identification with the tragic hero who risks loss in order to save what he loves. This is the heart of Tolkien's tragic wisdom—an appreciation for evanescent goods that arises precisely from an acceptance of their eventual passing. Wisdom for him stems from the acceptance of limits, from a kind of humility. Those who want the Ring of Power are tempted to a clinging possessiveness that claims to be able to protect us by managing the evanescence of the world. Wanting to possess the Ring manifests a desire to control fate. By contrast, a wise resistance to tyranny eschews the desire to control human destiny and relationships because it recognizes that such control is beyond human capacity and knowledge. Tragic wisdom issues in love.

This does not mean that Tolkien advocates passivity or even pacifism. If his fiction teaches anything, it teaches that evil must be fought with courage.[36] The point is that those who engage in this fight must do their best not to take on the attitude of the tyrant. In this fight, one must be open to one's need for wisdom and love, and accept the risk of loss and suffering that neediness implies. Indeed, Tolkien's fiction shows that to be open to one's need for wisdom and love is to risk loss and suffering. As in Greek tragedy, Tolkien offers hope that our suffering can have transformative effects that cultivates wisdom.[37] As Aristotle says, wonder is the beginning of wisdom. Tolkien believes that an incapacity to wonder at the sheer beauty and givenness of the world has psychic causes that lie at the root of the impulse to tyranny. He argues that,

> the things that are trite or (in a bad sense) familiar, are the things that we have appropriated. . . . We say we know them. They have become like the things which once attracted us by their glitter, or their color, or their shape, and we laid hands on them, and then locked them in our hoard, acquired them, and acquiring, ceased to look at them.[38]

The fruit of the unrealistic attempt to possess life securely through power is a diminished life, a life not awake to the wonder of being. We lose our capacity to be astonished by what is around us when we cling to it possessively. For Tolkien, the desire to possess renders the other less interesting, less awesome. The desire to possess is also a desire to control through power. And this desire to exercise power stands in the way of our fascination—our wonderment—at the world around us. For Tolkien, the minute we start to manipulate through power in order to securely possess another person or good, we start to lose the capacity to be astonished and fascinated. In this way we lose the capacity for wonder, the beginning of wisdom.

The heroes who try to get rid of the Ring dramatize an attitude toward life that stands opposed to the tyrant's. The hobbit's journey away from home to destroy the Ring and save his home is a symbol of the interior journey we must make in order to rid ourselves of the attitude of possessiveness that would stand in the way of fullness of life. Accepting loss is the only way of protecting the integrity of our relationship to that which we love, because in the end, it is the attitude that is most realistic about evanescence. The dialogue between Gimli and Legolas when they leave the Edenic forest of Lórien illuminates this point. Gimli begins the conversations by expressing his grief at leaving this paradise: "Tell me, Legolas, why did I come upon this Quest? Little did I know where the chief peril lay. . . . Torment in the dark was the danger that I feared, and it did not hold me back. But I would not have come, had I known the danger of light and joy. Now I have taken my worst wound in this parting, even if I were to go straight to the Dark Lord. Alas for Gimli son of Glóin!" However, Legolas reminds him that acceptance of loss is the condition for keeping trust with his friends, and thus for a decent life: "Nay!" says Legolas. "Alas for us all! And for all that walk the world in these after-days. For such is the way of it: to find and to lose, as it seems to those whose boat is on the running stream [the River Anduin, throughout the book a symbol of mortality]. But I count you blessed, Gimli son of Glóin: for your loss you suffer of your own free will, and you might have chosen otherwise. But you have not forsaken your companions." (*LotR*, 369.II.8).

Tolkien's presentation of tyranny is one with his tragic but hopeful attitude toward our mortal condition. His fiction dramatizes the effects of a clinging possessiveness toward life that refuses the burden of mortality and leads us to lose our fascination with the world and ourselves. Tolkien believes that this attitude leads to domination rather than acceptance, wisdom, and wonder. At the same time, his fiction is a therapy that offers us consolation by viewing the tragedy and grief of our mortal condition as "eucatastrophes" that can lead us out of suffering to joy if we do not push them away.[39] Tolkien's fiction gives us a catharsis if we let it. His heroes' risks and losses give us a renewed wonder and joy at the life we have been given for a time and seek to possess at the cost of our soul.

NOTES

1. "And many have imagined republics and principates that have never been seen or known to be in truth; because there is such a distance between how one lives and how one should live that he who lets go that which is done for that which ought to be done learns his ruin rather than his preservation—for a man who wishes to profess the good in everything needs must fall among so many who are not good. Hence it is nec-

essary for a prince, if he wishes to maintain himself, to learn to be able not to be good, and to use it and not use it according to necessity," Machiavelli, *The Prince*, trans. Leo Paul S. de Alvarez (Prospect Heights, IL: Waveland Press, 1980), 93.

2. Gandalf is a wizard and a Maiar, an angelic being sent to Middle Earth to help men and elves in their struggle against Sauron. In the *Silmarillion*, Tolkien writes that Gandalf was "wisest of the Maiar" (30). Gandalf learned wisdom from the Valar (an angel of a higher order) called Nienna. Tolkien writes of her, "She is acquainted with grief, and mourns for every wound. . . . But she does not weep for herself; and those who hearken to her learn pity, and endurance in hope," J. R. R. Tolkien, *The Silmarillion*, ed. Christopher Tolkien (Boston: Houghton Mifflin Company, 1977), 28. I will return to this theme later, but it is crucial here to emphasize the relationship of wisdom to suffering in Tolkien's work.

3. In fact, Gandalf himself entertains this possibility. For Gandalf's doubts about his policy, see *Lord of the Rings*, 797.V.4. All citations to Tolkien's *Lord of the Rings* (henceforth *LotR*) are taken from the one-volume edition published by Houghton Mifflin (New York, 1987). Due to the many editions with their different paginations, I will refer to the book and chapter numbers, as well as to the page numbers from that edition.

4. Saruman says, "The time of the Elves is over, but our time is at hand: the world of Men, which we must rule. But we must have power, power to order all things as we will, for that good which only the wise can see," *LotR* 252.II.2. See also 253.II.2.

5. Terry Castle, "High Plains Drifter," *The Atlantic Monthly*, January/February 2004, 186–87.

6. *J. R. R. Tolkien: Author of the Century* (New York: Houghton Mifflin, 2001), vii. As Bruno Bettelheim has pointed out, "Myths and fairy stories both answer the eternal questions: What is the world really like? How am I to live my life in it? How can I truly be myself?" *The Uses of Enchantment: The Meaning and Importance of Fairy Tales* (New York: Alfred Knopf, 1976), 45.

7. Shippey, *Author of the Century*, xxx.

8. For accounts of Tolkien's experiences during World War I and its effect on his work, see John Garth, *Tolkien and the Great War: The Threshold of Middle Earth* (New York: Houghton Mifflin, 2003).

9. Tom Shippey, *The Road to Middle Earth* (New York: Houghton Mifflin, 2003b), 324–25.

10. So, for example, in Plato's *Republic*, Socrates constructs the city in speech to show the effect of injustice on the individual soul, for the soul is difficult to see. Plato also believes that children should be raised on myth, not discursive accounts of reality (*Republic*, 376aff). And his dialogues are peppered with fables and myths aiming to explore experiences and realities that discursive rationality cannot exhaust. For a sympathetic treatment of Plato's use of myth, see Eric Voegelin, *Plato and Aristotle* (Baton Rouge: Louisiana State University Press, 1957).

11. "Now the Elves made many rings; but secretly Sauron made One Ring to rule all the others, and their power was bound up with it, to be subject wholly to it and to last so long as it too should last. . . . And while he wore the One Ring he could perceive all the things that were done by means of the lesser rings, and he could see and govern the very thoughts of those that wore them," *Silmarillion*, 287–88.

12. Thus the importance of the famous opening poem: "Three Rings for the Elven-kings under the sky, / Seven for the Dwarf-lords in their halls of stone, / Nine for Mortal Men doomed to die, / One for the Dark Lord on his dark throne / In the Land of Mordor where the Shadows lie. / One Ring to rule them all, One Ring to find them, / One Ring to bring them all, and in the darkness bind them / In the Land of Mordor where the Shadows lie."

13. *Silmarillion*, 289.

14. *Silmarillion*, 288.

15. See Humphrey Carpenter, ed., *The Letters of J. R. R. Tolkien* (Boston: Houghton Mifflin, 1981), 267.

16. Humphrey Carpenter, *J. R. R. Tolkien: A Biography* (New York: Houghton Mifflin, 2000), 39.

17. Tolkien says, "[The dwarf lords] used their rings only for the getting of wealth; but wrath and an overmastering of greed of gold were kindled in their hearts," *Silmarillion*, 288–89.

18. Thus *The Hobbit* is a paradigmatic example of a classic mythical hero narrative. For a good description of the characteristics of this genre, see Joseph Campbell, *The Hero with a Thousand Faces* (Princeton: Princeton University Press, 1972).

19. Augustine, *City of God*, V.12, V.14, XVII.2. For an elaboration of this point, see Thomas W. Smith, "The Glory and Tragedy of Politics," in *Augustine and Politics*, ed. John Doody, Kevin Hughes, and Kim Paffenroth (Lanham, MD: Rowman & Littlefield, forthcoming).

20. To this, Frodo replies, "But the wearing is slow in Lorien. The power of the Lady is on it. Rich are the hours, though short they seem . . . where Galadriel wields the Elven-Ring" (*LotR*, 379).

21. "What is it that the Buddha is telling the world here? First, that by the mere fact of being born under the conditions of finite existence every living creature is subject to the evils of sickness, old age, and death, and to the sadness that comes when his loved ones are stricken by these ills. These inevitable occasions of unhappiness (*dukha*) constitute the problem of life. But they would not make us unhappy were it not for the blind demandingness (*tanha*) in our nature which leads us to ask of the universe, for ourselves and those specially dear to us, more than it is ready or even able to give. Moreover, it is this same unrealistic and selfish craving which, frustrated as it inevitably becomes, moves us to act in ways that increase the unhappiness of others," E. A. Burtt, ed., *The Teachings of the Compassionate Buddha: Early Discourses, the Dhammapada, and Later Basic Writings* (New York: Mentor, 1982), 28.

22. The elves call death "the Gift of Men," *Letters*, 267.

23. *Letters*, 325 (letter 245). For a paradigmatic dialogue between elves and men concerning mortality, see *Silmarillion*, 265.

24. *Silmarillion*, 289.

25. For this, see Matthew T. Dickerson, *Following Gandalf: Epic Battles and Moral Victory in* The Lord of the Rings (Grand Rapids, MI: Brazos Press, 2004), 96.

26. *Letters*, 243–44 (letter 183). The nature of Sauron's attempt to cling possessively to a fragmentary good is captured in Tolkien's description of the changes he brought to Numenor after he repented his misdeeds and offered to make amends early

in his career. Note the implicit connection between the desire to secure the good and its underlying sense of insecurity that leads to a lust for domination: "At first he revealed only secrets of craft, and taught the making of many things powerful and wonderful; and they seemed good. Our ships now go without the wind, and many are made of metal that sheareth hidden rocks, and they sink not in calm or storm; but they are no longer fair to look upon. Our towers grow ever stronger and climb higher, but beauty they leave behind upon earth. We who have no foes are embattled with impregnable fortresses—and mostly on the West. Our arms are multiplied as for an agelong war, and men are ceasing to give love or care to the making of things for use or delight. But our shields are impenetrable, our swords cannot be withstood, our darts are like thunder and pass over leagues unerring," J. R. R. Tolkien, *The Lost Road and other Writings: Language and Legend before 'The Lord of the Rings,' Vol. 5, History of Middle Earth*, ed. Christopher Tolkien (Boston: Houghton Mifflin, 1987), 67.

27. *Letters*, 267.

28. For an illuminating account of the "wraithing process," see Shippey, *Author of the Century*, 121–28.

29. See Plato, *Apology of Socrates*, 30e; *Gorgias*, 505d.

30. Aristotle, *Nicomachean Ethics*, 1141b21, 1141b24–28; *Politics*, 1252a1–8, 1260a17–19. For an elaboration of this point, see Thomas W. Smith, *Revaluing Ethics: Aristotle's Dialectical Pedagogy* (Albany: State University of New York Press, 2001), chap. 1.

31. *Nicomachean Ethics*, 1093a27–1094b10.

32. This is why in Tolkien's fiction, practical wisdom is manifest in a healthy disregard for rules and laws when they stand in the way of the good. It is astonishing to note how many of the best characters in the *Lord of the Rings* break the law in order to uphold right. Faramir, second in command of Gondor, disobeys his father's orders when he decides not to bring Frodo and the Ring back to Gondor. Hama, the doorwarden of King Theoden, refuses to confiscate Gandalf's staff out of a concern with hospitality, and so betrays his king's orders. Yet Hama actually winds up saving the king because Gandalf uses his staff to heal the king. For an excellent account of the relationship between law and justice, see Edward A. Goerner, "Letter and Spirit: The Political Ethics of the Rule of Law versus the Political Ethics of the Rule of the Virtuous," *Review of Politics* 45 (1983): 553–75.

33. Cited in Gerhart Niemeyer, *Aftersight and Foresight: Selected Essays* (Lanham, MD: University Press of America/Intercollegiate Studies Institute, 1988), 231.

34. See, especially, Tolkien's comments on Gandalf in *Letters*, 202.

35. Sophocles, *The Oedipus Plays*, trans. Paul Roche (New York: Penguin Books, 1996), 207.

36. The only pacifist in the *Lord of the Rings* is Tom Bombadil. Tolkien explains the importance of the character this way: "The story is cast in terms of a good side, and a bad side, beauty against ruthless ugliness, tyranny against kingship, moderated freedom with consent against compulsion, and so on; but both sides in some degree, conservative or destructive, want a measure of control. But if you have, as it were, taken a 'vow of poverty,' renounced control, and take your delight in things for themselves without reference to yourself, watching, observing, and to some extent even

knowing, then the question of the rights and wrongs of power and control might become utterly meaningless to you, and the means of power quite valueless. It is a natural pacifist view, which always arises in the mind when there is a war." However, Tolkien continues by pointing out the limits of this attitude: "But the view of [the Wise] seems to be that it [Bombadil's attitude toward the world] is an excellent thing to have represented, but that there are in fact things with which it cannot cope, and upon whom its existence nonetheless depends. Ultimately, only the victory of the West will allow Bombadil to continue, or even to survive. Nothing would be left for him in the world of Sauron," *Letters*, 178–179.

37. For an excellent statement of the relationship of wisdom to Greek tragedy, see Joe Sachs, "Aristotle's *Poetics*," *Internet Encyclopedia of Philosophy,* http://www.utm.edu/research/iep/a/aris-poe.htm.

38. See J. R. R. Tolkien, "On Fairy Stories," in *The Monster and the Critics and Other Essays* (London: Harper Collins, 1997b), 147.

39. Tolkien, "On Fairy Stories," 155–56.

SOURCES

Aristotle. 1962. *Nicomachean Ethics*. Trans. Martin Ostwald. New York: Prentice Hall.

———. 1984. *Politics*. Trans. Carnes Lord. Chicago: University of Chicago Press.

Augustine. 1972. *City of God*. Trans. Henry Bettenson. New York: Penguin Books.

Bettelheim, Bruno. 1976. *The Uses of Enchantment: The Meaning and Importance of Fairy Tales*. New York: Alfred Knopf.

Burtt, E. A., ed. 1982. *The Teachings of the Compassionate Buddha: Early Discourses, the Dhammapada, and Later Basic Writings*. New York: Mentor.

Carpenter, Humphrey, ed. 1981. *The Letters of J. R. R. Tolkien*. Boston: Houghton Mifflin.

Carpenter, Humphrey. 2000. *J. R. R. Tolkien: A Biography*. New York: Houghton Mifflin.

Castle, Terry. 2004. "High Plains Drifter." *The Atlantic Monthly* (January/February): 186–89.

Garth, John. 2003. *Tolkien and the Great War: The Threshold of Middle Earth*. New York: Houghton Mifflin.

Goerner, Edward A. 1983. "Letter and Spirit: The Political Ethics of the Rule of Law versus the Political Ethics of the Rule of the Virtuous." *Review of Politics* 45: 553–75.

Machiavelli, Niccolò. 1980. *The Prince*. Trans. Leo Paul S. de Alvarez. Prospect Heights, IL: Waveland Press.

Niemeyer, Gerhart. 1988. *Aftersight and Foresight: Selected Essays*. Lanham, MD: University Press of America.

Plato. 1961. *Collected Dialogues*. Ed. Edith Hamilton and Huntington Cairns. Princeton, NJ: Princeton University Press.

Sachs, Joe. 2005. "Aristotle's *Poetics*." *Internet Encyclopedia of Philosophy*. http://www.utm.edu/research/iep/a/aris-poe.htm.

Shippey, Tom. 2001. *J. R. R. Tolkien: Author of the Century*. New York: Houghton Mifflin.

———. 2003. *The Road to Middle Earth*. New York: Houghton Mifflin.

Smith, Thomas W. 2001. *Revaluing Ethics: Aristotle's Dialectical Pedagogy*. Albany: State University of New York Press.

———. 2005. "The Glory and Tragedy of Politics." In *Augustine and Politics*, ed. John Doody, Kevin Hughes, and Kim Paffenroth. Lanham, MD: Rowman & Littlefield.

Sophocles. 1996. *The Oedipus Plays*. Trans. Paul Roche. New York: Penguin Books.

Tolkien, J. R. R. 1987. *The Lost Road and other Writings: Language and Legend before 'The Lord of the Rings,' Vol. 5, History of Middle Earth*. Ed. Christopher Tolkien. Boston: Houghton Mifflin.

———. 1994. *The Lord of the Rings*. Boston: Houghton Mifflin.

———. 1997a. *The Hobbit*. Boston: Houghton Mifflin.

———. 1997b. "On Fairy Stories." In *The Monster and the Critics and Other Essays*, 109–61. London: Harper Collins.

——— 1999. *The Silmarillion*. Ed. Christopher Tolkien. Boston: Houghton Mifflin.

Voegelin, Eric. 1957. *Plato and Aristotle*. Baton Rouge: Louisiana State University Press.

Chapter 15

In the Shadow of the Fortress

Barry Strauss

High on a ridge dominating the city of Syracuse in Sicily sits the fortress of Euryelus. Magnificent and fearsome, the imposing stone structure covers 15,000 square meters (54,000 square feet) with its still-standing catapult towers, its deep defensive ditches, its network of underground galleries, and its high walls. It is the most complete and important surviving ancient Greek fortification. Built between 402 and 397 B.C. by Dionysius I, tyrant of Syracuse, and refurbished by his successors, it kept all enemies out for nearly 200 years. It also kept the Syracusans in. (For an introduction, see Grady 2003, 329–30).

Euryelus is the symbol of tyranny. No other ancient Greek city had as many or as famous tyrants as did Syracuse, from Gelon to Dionysius to Agathocles to Hieron. No other ancient Greek tyranny made so much progress in the perverted art of mass killing: it was, for example, Dionysius I's engineers who invented the first catapult and Hieron II's engineer who invented antisiege machines so destructive that they terrified even the Romans (that engineer was no less a figure than Archimedes). By the same token, no regime other than a tyranny could have mustered the resources to build a fortress like Euryelus—or could have tolerated its symbolism of control.

The Syracusan tyrants were no savages. They subsidized poets and philosophers from Pindar to Plato to Theocritus, and they left behind the ruins of theater and temples. But these tyrants were not liberals either.

To contemplate the ruins of Euryelus today is to engage in an act of political theory. The splendid structure symbolizes not just the crushing power of tyranny but its allure. Tyranny offers not merely repression but grandeur. But it was grandeur at a price, and Euryelus stands witness to the cost.

We contemporaries make a mistake if we measure freedom by a regime's ability to erect monuments, to patronize the arts, or to build protective walls.

Likewise, we need to resist the temptation of letting artists, actors, or architects play a leading role in the politics of a free society. They are entitled to a voice, of course, but it must be measured skeptically against the knowledge that art and liberty do not necessarily share the same interests. Likewise, we must not let ourselves be distracted from the business of self-government by undue attention to monument building. There is something unseemly about the intense focus of the public mind in recent decades on memorials ranging from the Vietnam Wall to the Holocaust memorials in Berlin and Washington to the rebuilding of Ground Zero in New York City. A free society is too busy to have much time for monuments; freedom's greatest monument is itself. Nor does a free society place its defense in walls so much as in an aroused and active citizenry.

These points become clearer in the case study of classical Greece. Let us turn to an examination of Greek tyranny and freedom, of the relationship of each regime to the arts, and of the commentary of classical philosophers on these matters.

Today there is a common perception that artists are the strongest supporters of freedom of speech and that artists are the plainspoken truth tellers of the land. John F. Kennedy, for example, is quoted in the rotunda of the James Michener Art Museum in Doylestown, Pennsylvania, as saying, "If art is to nourish the roots of our culture, society must set the artist free to follow his vision wherever it takes him." Censorship is considered a particular disaster for artists. On its website, for example, the American Civil Liberties Union warns,

> Today, the creators, producers and distributors of popular culture are often blamed for the nation's deep social problems. Calls for censorship threaten to erode free speech (http://www.aclu.org/FreeSpeech/FreeSpeechMain.cfm).

Yet as a matter of historical record, artists have not always supported freedom of speech. Indeed, artists have not only survived in unfree societies, but have sometimes emigrated from a free republic to a tyranny in order to secure the patronage of a tyrant. But how could that be the case? Do not artists require freedom, which all tyrants oppose? In fact, artists require only *artistic* freedom, not *political* freedom. The two are not the same thing. The American Civil Liberties Union equates artistic freedom with freedom of expression (ACLU Briefing Paper Number 14, "Freedom of Expression in the Arts and Entertainment," http://archive.aclu.org/library/pbp14.html). But this is wrong. History shows that given a choice between, on the one hand, complete freedom of expression along with poverty and, on the other hand, little freedom of expression but generous funding for their art, many artists choose the latter. For example, neither the composers Richard Strauss, nor Carl Orff, nor the conductor Wilhelm Furtwängler considered it necessary to emigrate from

Hitler's Germany, and the conductor Herbert von Karajan joined the Nazi Party there. Strauss was not a supporter of the Nazis, but nonetheless he composed the Olympic Hymn for the 1936 Games, held in Berlin and turned into a showcase of the Third Reich by Hitler and his propaganda minister Josef Goebbels. Albert Speer thrived under the Nazis as an architect and a top industrial official. Expressionist poet Gottfried Benn not only declined to join other literary émigrés from Germany but staunchly defended the Third Reich. German actor Emil Jannings won an Oscar in America and then returned to Germany where he eventually starred in Nazi propaganda films. None of these artists felt the need for freedom of expression. What they wanted, instead, was to make art. Political freedom calls for as little as the ability to speak one's mind in public. Artistic freedom is frequently expensive: for example, a sculptor cannot make a fine statue without marble, nor can a conductor conduct a symphony without an orchestra and a concert hall.

Nor is the creative process the same as the process of expressing a political opinion. Artists are craftsmen, able to take satisfaction in the process of creation. Poets and painters, says Socrates in Plato's *Republic*, are more interested in beauty than in truth; more interested in emotion than in reason (602a–605b). He adds that artists have no practical wisdom, except in their ability to make things—even ugly things—look beautiful (600a, 601a–b). Art qua art is not about changing the world.

Politics, by contrast, is indeed about change and is an example of practical wisdom. Since political freedom may effect change, it is necessarily inimical to tyranny. Artistic freedom is flexible: a poet may write fine dactyls under a tyrant, but a politician is strictly limited in what he can say.

Besides, artists and tyrants share a common commitment to sensuality. An artist must explore his senses, and who better than to guide him than a tyrant, with his well-known appetite for sensual amusement. Tyrants are famous for their access to any pleasure, including sights, sounds, food, drink, and sex. For Plato's Socrates, the tyrant is the sensualist par excellence (Plato 1984, 571a–575a). Indeed, as Xenophon has the poet Simonides say to the tyrant Hiero, ordinary people envy tyrants because of their extraordinary enjoyment of pleasures (Xenophon 1997, 1.8–9).

Tyrants like artists, as Aristotle writes, because artists flatter them (Aristotle 1984, 1313b1). For instance, just as in modern times, German dictator Adolf Hitler enjoyed the services of filmmaker Leni Riefenstahl, who glorified Nazism in her documentary *Triumph of the Will*—a classic both of cinema and propaganda, so in ancient times Hiero, tyrant of Syracuse (chief city of Greek Sicily) was celebrated in the classical verse of the poet Pindar. Hiero was as patron as well of other leading Greek poets, including Aeschylus, Bacchylides, and Simonides.

Italian dictator Benito Mussolini had his praises sung by the leading Italian poet Gabriele d'Annunzio and the world-famous inventor Gugliemo Marconi, while Polycrates, tyrant of the island Samos (ca. 535–ca. 522 B.C.) basked in the flattery of the great Anacreon as a court poet and considered his prize possession to be a ring made for him by the gem cutter Theodorus. Many other poets, craftsmen, architects, and engineers graced Polycrates' court, but not the philosopher Pythagoras: a native of Samos, Pythagoras moved to Italy—it is said, because of the growing severity of Polycrates' tyranny (Laertius 1972–1979, 9).

Aristotle also mentions two less direct reasons for tyrants' affection for artists. First, art is expensive, and tyrants have an interest in raising taxes and spending the people's money because otherwise that money might be used to buy arms to support a revolt; besides, poverty deprives people of the leisure time needed plot revolution (ibid.) The height of tyrannical patronage of the arts, suggests Aristotle, is monumental construction, presumably because of its huge expense. The philosopher comments,

> Examples of this are the pyramids in Egypt, the monuments of the Cypselids [tyrants of Corinth], the construction of the temple of Olympian Zeus by the Pisistratids [tyrants of Athens], and the work done by Polycrates [tyrant of Samos] on the [temples] at Samos. All of these things have the same effect—lack of leisure and poverty on the part of the ruled. (Aristotle, *Politics*, 1313b1, trans. Lord, 1984, 174)

A second indirect reason why tyrants subsidize artists, according to Aristotle, is that art is international. Great artists can be brought in from abroad, which gives a tyrant the company of foreigners—and that is companionship that a tyrant indeed craves, knowing as he does the enmity of his own people (Aristotle 1984, 1314a1).

To sum up, ancient Greek history and philosophy demonstrate a community of interests between artists and tyrants, as well as a certain similarity of temperament. Freedom of speech does not appear necessarily to have been a matter of concern to artists in ancient Greece. This is not to say that ancient artists were unanimously indifferent to political freedom. It is hard to imagine democratic Sophocles or irreverent Aristophanes at a tyrant's court, for example. But they were exceptions to the usual relationship between artists and tyrants, which is better represented by their fellow Athenian dramatists Aeschylus (in Sicily) and Euripides (in Macedon under the tyrannical king Archelaus), each of whom ended his life as a poet in residence in a tyranny far from their native Athens.[1]

Let us return to Euryelus, that mighty symbol of tyranny. The fortress signifies not only what ancient Syracuse was, but of what it wasn't. Euryelus is no monument to freedom. Strictly speaking, freedom is incompatible with monuments unless the monument is the result only of voluntary activity. In general, the bigger the monument, the greater the taxes imposed to build it. Nor are fortresses compatible with freedom, strictly speaking, since fortresses entail a system of passive defense, while a free people engages in active defense. Free people do not wait for enemies to attack them; rather, they go out and fight trouble abroad before it threatens their homeland. No wonder the inspiration for modern freedom lies not in Syracuse but in Athens and Sparta.

Freedom is threadbare. Consider first Athens, the greatest ancient example of democracy, and a polity whose watchwords were freedom and equality. To be sure, Syracuse, too, experienced periods of democracy, for example, when Syracuse defeated Athens' invading armada in the harbor of Syracuse in 413 B.C. But no monuments to this victory survive; Euryelus comes from the next generation, when Syracuse had become a tyranny.

By the same token, democratic Athens also produced fortresses, whose imposing ruins may be seen today in the hills of Attica at sites such as Gyphtokastro (perhaps ancient Eleutherae) and Fili (ancient Phyle). But these works date not to the era of Athens' greatest power but to a period a hundred years later, in the mid-fourth century B.C., when Athenians had lost the conviction that freedom was worth fighting for abroad in expeditions in which they risked their own bodies. The orator Demosthenes constantly tried to convince his countrymen to serve as citizen soldiers and to battle Philip of Macedon in northern Greece before he attacked the Athenian homeland. But the Athenian public had no stomach for the enterprise, preferring instead to sit behind an ancient Maginot Line of border forts—until in 338 B.C. they finally fought in Central Greece, at Chaeronea. But by then it was too late (On these forts, see Ober 1985; cf. Munn 1993).

Yet some may object that except for the accident of survival, Athens' greatest ruined fortress today would consist of the remarkable Long Walls that once connected the city to its ports at Phaleron and Piraeus, about three and four miles away, respectively. The Long Walls date precisely to the era of Athenian greatness under Pericles in the fifth century B.C. So, for that matter, does one of the most famous monuments of antiquity, the Parthenon. This temple was built by the Athenian democracy, using public funds. But the Parthenon is no monument to freedom. It was paid for by tribute from the ca. 250 allied city-states in the naval confederacy of which Athens was hegemon, the so-called Delian League (478–404 B.C.) Pericles famously characterized works such as the Parthenon as "refinement without extravagance" (Thuc. 2.40.1, trans. Strassler, 1988, 113). His political opponents spoke for many Greeks, however, when they called the Parthenon an abuse of power. They said that Athens' allies would consider the beautiful temple to be "an act of bare-faced tyranny, when they see that with their own contributions, extorted from them by force for the war against the Persians, we are gilding and beautifying our city, as if it were some vain woman decking herself out with costly stones and statues and temples worth millions of money" (Plutarch *Life of Pericles*, 12.3, trans. Scott-Kilvert, 1960, 177–78).

Indeed, they could point to other Athenian examples of Athenian arrogance and of high-handedness toward the allies, such as requiring them to use Athenian weights, measures, and coins and insisting that all major court cases in the allied states be decided not locally but centrally, in Athens with Athenian juries. And the Long Walls represented Athenian determination not to give in to the pressure of invasion by other Greeks who insisted that Athens make concessions to the allies—what the invaders called "freeing the Hellenes." No wonder that Athens' detractors at the time referred to her as the "tyrant city" (Thuc. 1.122.3, 1.124.3; on the Athenian Empire, see Meiggs 1972).

Athenian freedom, therefore, went hand in hand with measures of repression. For an example of a Greek city-state that exercised hegemony without imposing taxes abroad to support public works at home, we need to turn southward, to the Peloponnese. The classic case of a free society without walls or substantial monuments is found there: it is ancient Sparta, which had its heyday between ca. 600 and ca. 350 B.C. For most of this period, Sparta was the leading land power of all the ca.1500 Greek city-states. Its people had a reputation for prowess, toughness, and public-spiritedness. The Spartan ideal was one of citizen service: every male was supposed to serve the city in war and government, while every female was supposed to bear children and to raise a new generation of heroes. Solidarity was highly esteemed. For example, Sparta dubbed its adult males "Peers" because of what made them similar: citizenship, military service, a voice in the assembly, the possession of a state-granted, inherited land allotment, and a common responsibility to educate the next generation in the duties of a Spartan. Solidarity even extended to the bedroom: adult Spartans practiced wife swapping in order to produce more children, while teenage Spartan males idealized homosexual love among soldiers.

The flip side of the coin was the presence of a common enemy to unite Spartans: the large, restive population of unfree laborers known as helots, a group far outnumbering the citizens. Repression of the helots was a shared responsibility (and preoccupation) of Spartans. Although Spartan citizens were expected to sacrifice private interests for the good of the community, they enjoyed freedom from having to earn their daily bread, thanks to the public land grants and the forced labor of helots.

By today's standards, the helots might qualify the entire Spartan state as a tyranny, but all ancient Greek city-states employed unfree labor; Athens, for example, had a big population of slaves. Yet the contrast between slavery and freedom at Sparta seemed particularly glaring to some in antiquity: Plutarch cites a saying, apparently by the late-fifth-century B.C. Athenian critic and revolutionary Critias, that "there is nothing to match either the freedom of the free man at Sparta or the slavery of the slave" (Plutarch *Lycurgus*, 28.2, trans. Talbert, 1988, 41).

Spartans prided themselves on a citizen army so good that theirs was the only great city in Greece left unfortified; all the other major cities of Greece were protected by walls. Spartan urban space was also unique. In order to promote the military virtue of toughness, Spartan citizens were required to live very austerely. The result was a city of modest public buildings adorned with little of the sculpture, wall paintings, or mosaics that were common elsewhere in Greek temples, stoas, gymnasia, and baths. With its spectacular buildings and art, Athens gave a visitor the impression of wealth and power, while the unembellished public space of Sparta did little justice to the might of Greece's greatest land power. Thucydides comments on this paradox:

> For I suppose that if Sparta were to become desolate, and only the temples and the foundations of the public buildings were left, that as time went on there would be a strong disposition with posterity to refuse to accept her fame as a true exponent of her power. And yet they occupy two-fifths of the Peloponnesus and lead the whole, not to speak of their numerous allies outside. Still, as the city is neither built in a compact form nor adorned with magnificent temples and public edifices, but composed of villages after the old fashion of Hellas, there would be an impression of inadequacy. Whereas, if Athens were to suffer the same misfortune, I suppose that any inference from the appearance presented to the eye would make her power to have been twice as great as it is. (Thuc. 1.10.2, trans. Strassler, 1996, 8)

The early modern philosopher Rousseau, a great admirer of Sparta, writes in a similar vein, "Of its inhabitants nothing is left to us except the memory of their heroic actions" (Rousseau 1964, 43).

Rousseau associated the arts and sciences with decadence, so he gloried in Sparta's know-nothing attitude toward culture. The arts did not ennoble Athens, he argues; they corrupted it. It was no accident, says Rousseau, that a tyrant, the Athenian Pisistratus (ruled ca. 560 and ca. 546–527 B.C.), sponsored the first canonical version of Homer, or so tradition has it. Rousseau writes,

> Could I forget that in the very heart of Greece rose that city as renowned for its happy ignorance as for the wisdom of its laws, that republic of demi-gods rather than men, so superior did their virtues seem to human nature? O Sparta! you

> eternally put to shame a vain doctrine! While the vices which accompany the fine arts entered Athens together with them, while a tyrant there so carefully collected the works of the prince of poets, you chased the arts and artists, the sciences and scientists away from your walls. (Rousseau 1964, 43)

The Greeks saw Sparta's polity and tyranny as ideal types at the opposite ends of a scale of regimes. A historian today might well see a great deal of truth in this. Spartans prized freedom, austerity, and citizen solidarity, while tyrants practiced repression, aimed to keep citizens divided from each other, and promoted art and public works.

Alone among the major city-states of Greece, Sparta did not experience a tyranny (until the third century B.C.) Opposition to tyrants was a guiding principle of Spartan foreign policy in the sixth and early fifth centuries B.C. Not that Sparta was always consistent on that score: its cagey and opportunistic leadership was more than capable of making alliances with tyrants such as Hippias of Athens and Polycrates of Samos when such a policy promoted Sparta's self-interest. But the antityrannical ideal always struck a chord in Sparta, and Thucydides was impressed by its practical application over time:

> But at last a time came when the tyrants of Athens and the far older tyrannies of Hellas were, with the exception of those in Sicily, once and for all put down by Sparta; for this city, though after the settlement of the Dorians, its present inhabitants, it suffered from factions from an unparalleled length of time, still at a very early period obtained good laws, and enjoyed a freedom from tyrants which was unbroken; it has possessed the same form of government for more than four hundred years, reckoning to the end of the late war, and has thus been in a position to arrange the affairs of other states. (Thuc. 1.18.1, trans. Strassler, 1996, 13–14)

Austere, militaristic, uncultured, and class-ridden: what can Sparta, which was all these things, have to offer us today? It offers us an invaluable lesson. Sparta demonstrates that the opposite of tyranny is not creativity; the opposite of tyranny is freedom. Neither charming nor artistic, freedom is fierce and frugal. Every major city-state in Greece boasted better art and better monuments than Sparta, but no Greek citizens were as free as were Spartans. In fact, the more tyrannical was a city-state, whether at home or abroad, the more likely it was to sponsor great art. Athens, Corinth, Syracuse, and Samos all had beautiful monuments, and they all were tyrannies at one time or another. Sparta had no walls to compare with Euryelus and no temples to compete with the Parthenon, but it was always free of tyrants.

Measure a country's freedom not by its creativity and even less by its monuments. Measure it, rather, by a people's public-spiritedness, by their vigilance against tyrants, and by their willingness to sacrifice luxuries in order to forge the weapons of freedom. In order to enjoy the fruits of the refinement of Athens and the science of Syracuse, we must first accept the duties of Sparta's citizens. That is the best way to step out from under the shadow of the tyrant's fortress.

NOTE

1. Aristotle even reports that Archelaus handed over a man named Decamnichus to Euripides for flogging, because the man had made an infuriating insult about Euripides' bad breath. Later, the vengeful Decamnichus stirred up a revolt against Archelaus. (Aristotle 1984, 1311b).

SOURCES

Aristotle. 1984. *The Politics*. Trans. Carnes Lord. Chicago: University of Chicago Press.

Grady, Ellen. 2003. *Blue Guide, Sicily*, 6th ed. New York: W. W. Norton.

Laertius, Diogenes. 1972–1979. "Pythagoras," 8.3, in *Lives of Eminent Philosophers*. Trans. R. D. Hicks. Cambridge, MA: Harvard University Press.

Meiggs, Russell. 1972. *The Athenian Empire*. Oxford: Clarendon Press.

Munn, Mark H. 1993. *Defense of Attica: The Dema Wall and the Boiotian War of 378–375 B.C.* Berkeley: University of California Press.

Ober, Josiah. 1985. *Fortress Attica: Defense of the Athenian Land Frontier, 404–322 B.C.* Leiden: E. J. Brill.

Plato. 1984. *The Republic*. Trans. G. M. A. Grube. Indianapolis, IN: Hackett.

Plutarch. 1960. *The Rise and Fall of Athens: Nine Greek Lives*. Trans. Ian Scott-Kilvert. Harmondsworth, UK: Penguin.

———. 1988. *Plutarch on Sparta*. Ed. and trans. Richard Talbert. London and New York: Penguin Books.

Rousseau, Jean-Jacques. 1964. *The First and Second Discourses*. Ed. Roger D. Masters. New York: St. Martin's Press.

Strassler, Robert B., ed. 1996. *The Landmark Thucydides: A Comprehensive Guide to the Peloponnesian War*. New York: Touchstone Books, Simon & Schuster.

Xenophon. 1997. *Hiero the Tyrant and Other Treatises*. Trans. Robin Waterfield, intro. and notes by Paul Cartledge. London and New York: Penguin Books.

Chapter 16

The New Age of Tyranny

Mark Lilla

In his 2002 State of the Union Address, President Bush described Iraq, Iran, and North Korea as an "Axis of Evil" and expressed his resolve to meet any threat they might pose to the United States. This phrase, obviously meant to echo Ronald Reagan's characterization of the Soviet Union as an "evil empire" two decades ago, was coolly received at home and abroad, and the president has not emphasized it since. Yet we would be unwise to forget it. While rhetorical overreach in the wake of the 2001 terrorist attacks may be understandable, the hollowness of the president's formulation betrays a strategic disorientation that merits examination.

This disorientation affects all Western governments today and not just the United States, although ours is certainly the most consequential. It arises from the fact that the political language for describing the international environment remains rooted in the distinctive experiences of the twentieth century. The birth of the fascist axis, its defeat partly through democratic mobilization and resolve, the postwar spread of the Soviet empire, the gulags and concentration camps, the genocides, the espionage, the nuclear arms race—these are the political phenomena for which the century is today remembered. Already we are beginning to see that this was not the whole story, that other developments—such as decolonization, the integration of world markets, the technological shock of digitalization—were also revolutionary. Conceptually and rhetorically, however, the twentieth-century confrontation with totalitarianism still sets our intellectual compass.

The term "totalitarianism" first entered the English language in the 1920s after Benito Mussolini popularized it in Italian, referring in his speeches to "*lo stato totalitario*" and "*la nostra feroce voluntà totalitaria*." The word then gained wide currency after the Allied victory in World War II and the onset of the Cold War, and was used as a general noun describing both fascism and communism, and distinguishing them from earlier forms of tyranny. Hannah Arendt was only the most prominent thinker to maintain that fascism and communism had given birth to a genuinely new type of political regime, for which new concepts and standards were required. Historians and political scientists alike have debated the concept ever since, as well as related terms like authoritarianism, dictatorship, absolutism, autocracy, praetorianism, sultanism, patrimonialism, and others still more arcane. But in the public mind, the concept of totalitarianism remains firmly planted.

However adequate one finds that concept for describing fascism and communism, the fact is that the phenomenon it once referred to has all but disappeared. A ghostly, emaciated version of it still exists in North Korea, and one can argue about the degree to which the term still applies to, say, China or Cuba, but elsewhere the main institutions of totalitarian rule— charismatic leadership, a mobilizing ideology, relentless surveillance—have broken down, leaving in their wake a piebald map of tyrannical regimes that harm their own people and threaten their neighbors in very different ways. But what are we to call such nations? New terms like "rogue states," "failed states," and "illiberal democracies" point to the problem of nomenclature but don't go far in resolving it. Nor do they help us to distinguish among such states morally and strategically. Our situation is extremely paradoxical: the more conscious the West has become of the evils of twentieth-century totalitarianism, the less capable it has become of understanding the phenomenon of tyranny in the twenty-first.

The ancient Greek term *tyrannos*, which may have come from Lydia, was originally neutral and interchangeable with *monarchos*, and simply meant one who rules alone. By the fifth century, however, a distinction had grown up between a king who rules with the consent of the governed through established laws and institutions (*basileus*) and a tyrant who does not. Both of these political arrangements, kingship and tyranny, were distinguished from despotism (*despoteia*), which the Greeks used to describe non-Greek regimes they considered to be unpolitical and under a kind of household rule.

In the writings of Plato and Xenophon, we discover a Socrates who makes the first sustained inquiry into the nature of political tyranny, which he associates with a spiritual disorder in which the natural hierarchy of the soul and the polity are similarly disturbed. Tyranny, on this view, is the most corrupt form of government because it serves only the base desires of the ruler and ignores the counsel of the wise. Aristotle offered an important refinement of this analysis by pointing out that a tyrannical style of rule is not limited to evil kings or princes, that extreme forms of oligarchy and even democracy can be considered tyrannical if they are lawless, arbitrary, and set against the public interest. Tyranny thus understood is a general class of extremely bad regimes that deny the basic goods political life can offer.

During the European Middle Ages, this more general understanding of the many species of tyranny was lost to view for the simple reason that monarchy became the only form of government Europeans knew at first hand, and thus the term "tyrant" referred again narrowly to an unjust king (*rex iniustus*). Scholastic thinkers developed a voluminous philosophical and theological literature on this problem, which concerned the virtues of the ideal Christian prince, how he should be educated, and when and under what circumstances tyrannicide might be justified. The concepts and terms used in this literature were rooted in the Christian tradition and later were used against the church, or at least against the popes, during the Reformation. As modern political thought began to develop, this Christian scholastic language became less compelling, and new concepts and terms entered political discourse, such as "rights" and "sovereignty." Yet the classic problem of tyranny remained paramount for all early modern thinkers—even for figures like Machiavelli and Hobbes who played with tyrannical fire. By the time of the Enlightenment, explicit reference to the Christian political tradition had all but ceased, and the campaign against the current form of tyranny, absolute monarchy allied with Church dogma, had to be waged differently. In France, for example, one attacked *despotisme*, a term that traditionally referred only to non-European regimes but now provided a convenient way of criticizing absolutist French kings by appearing to condemn the Turks.

Despite the changes in conceptual language, however, it is no exaggeration to speak of a continuous tradition of political theory, running from the Greeks down to the Enlightenment, that took the phenomenon of tyranny as its theoretical starting point, and the establishment of barriers against tyrannical rule as its practical aim. That tradition came to an effective halt with the French Revolution. This need not have been the case, but it was. Because the main focus of Western political thinking for nearly a millennium had been on tyrannical kingship, little thought had been given to the tyrannical propensities of other political arrangements, including republican democracy, which many considered a simple antidote to the evils of absolutist monarchy.[1] The Revolution was seen by its partisans and critics alike as an epochal event, after which the paternalistic claims of monarchy would have no place, and a wholly new order of things would be established, for better or worse.

They were right, at least about Europe. But did that mean that tyranny, too, was a thing of the past? The Terror and Napoleon gave alert thinkers like Benjamin Constant and Tocqueville the disturbing premonition of new forms of political tyranny, having little to do with monarchical despotism, arising in the democratic age. In the end, though, it was thinkers like Hegel in Germany and Auguste Comte in France who set the tone in Europe by offering a loftier historical vantage point from which to see the democratic age, one in which the problem of tyranny seemed to disappear. Hegel and Comte expressed themselves in different conceptual languages, but their vision was identical: the Terror and Napoleon were mere detours on the road from absolutist monarchy to rational, bureaucratic, industrial states, which all European nations were destined to become. This destiny left no room for political tyranny, as traditionally understood.

Interestingly, the concept of tyranny did not disappear in the nineteenth century, it simply migrated from the realm of politics to that of culture: political optimism and cultural pessimism went hand in hand. Tocqueville set the tone when he spoke of the "soft despotism" of public opinion and the "tyranny of the majority" that modern mass forms of democracy made possible. For John Stuart Mill, the real challenge to human liberty no longer came from wicked kings or corrupt institutions; it came from "the tyranny of the prevailing opinion and feeling," while for Marx industrial capitalism maintained its tyranny over the working classes through the subtle workings of bourgeois ideology, which was more successful than political force in maintaining the modern system of production. As the great nineteenth-century intellectual system builders probed ever deeper into the shadows of human experience, they found tyranny everywhere—everywhere, that is, except on the surface of political life.

Freud and Max Weber were the last representatives of this tradition. Freud wanted to help modern individuals cast off the tyranny of a past that enslaved them unconsciously. Weber wanted to reconcile them to living in the "iron cage" of a rationalized, bureaucratic world that had been thoroughly "disenchanted." Both would die at a loss to explain the rebirth of political tyranny in the twentieth century. It is telling that in the two hefty volumes of Weber's posthumously published summa of modern sociology, *Economy and Society*, we find only two pages devoted to the problem of the tyrant, and these treat it as an exclusively ancient form of "illegitimate rule."

As one looks back on nineteenth-century Europe, it is hard to avoid the impression that advances in so many domains of intellectual inquiry went hand in hand with the atrophy of one of the most important, political science. A work like Montesquieu's *The Spirit of the Laws*—whose analysis of the nature of different political regimes in rapport with national customs and habits shaped the political thinking of the entire eighteenth century—was unthinkable in the nineteenth century. Montesquieu was not unaware of the psychological dimension of tyranny, as we know from his *Persian Letters*; but he was convinced that the psychological harm arose from a political source, not a merely cultural one. No such conviction was evident in the nineteenth century. Under the influence of

Hegel and Comte, Europe gave birth to new philosophies of history, of law, and of religion, as well as the new "social sciences" of sociology, psychology, and economics. But there was to be no new political science devoted exclusively to the problem of political form and its abuse, because the problem that originally inspired that science seemed destined to disappear.

This is the intellectual background to the post–World War II debate over totalitarianism. The degree to which the Communist and fascist regimes of the twentieth century were novel, what characteristics they shared, and how they should be distinguished analytically and morally—these historical questions are still with us, as they should be. But we need to remember that much of the shock Europe felt when these regimes arose derived from the fact that for a century and a half, serious thought about political tyranny had ceased in Europe. The continent was dripping with cultural pessimism in the decades before and after World War I, but somehow it never occurred to anyone that the coming catastrophe would take distinctly political form. When it did, destroying so much and so many with the aid of modern technology and ideas, the temptation was great to see communism and fascism as entirely new phenomena and not appeal to the long European tradition of understanding and guarding against tyranny.

Had communism been defeated along with fascism in the Second World War, it is likely that the term "totalitarianism" would have been forgotten or remained a strictly historical concept. But in view of the cold war of attrition against Soviet communism, and the fact that the Soviet empire was indeed an extreme tyranny, the term seemed appropriate and useful, at least rhetorically. Its limitations, however, were soon felt when it was applied to political developments outside the Communist bloc. As large swaths of Africa and Asia were rapidly decolonized following the war, nations around the globe found themselves part of a struggle for power waged in terms—democracy and totalitarianism—that were foreign to their experience. The architects of Western foreign policy in the Cold War found themselves trapped by the rhetoric of totalitarianism, but their critics were no less prisoners to it. It became easy for the critics to argue that, since most third-world regimes and revolutionary movements resisted by the West were not in the strict sense totalitarian, the Cold War was nothing more than a cynical cover for expanding Western economic and military dominance. What such critics failed to see, or did not permit themselves to see, was that such regimes and movements were nonetheless tyrannical, often classically so, and that they promised nothing but misery to their peoples.[2]

This is the paradox of Western political discourse ever since the Second World War: the more sensitive we became to the horrors brought on by the totalitarian tyrannies, the less sensitive we became to tyranny in its more moderate forms. Take, for example, the tortured debate within Europe over how to respond to the recent war in the Balkans. Europeans today still find themselves locked into the rhetoric of antifascism, understood primarily as resistance to all forms of militarism and racism. The problem in the Balkans was that these two elements of antifascism pointed in opposing directions: antifascism could be used to justify intervention, on the grounds that the Serbs were committing genocide, but it could also justify neutrality, on the grounds that the European military should never again be mobilized except in case of direct attack (if then). Very few Europeans were able to make the more moderate case that while Milosevic was not Hitler, he was a dangerous tyrant who had to be combated with means commensurate to the threat he posed. American policymakers find themselves in a similar bind today when building their case against Saddam Hussein's Iraq.

Sooner or later the language of antitotalitarianism will have to be abandoned and the classic problem of tyranny revisited. This is not to say that ancient concepts of tyranny can be imported wholesale into the present—though it is striking how many bad regimes today display pathologies that political thinkers from antiquity to early modern Europe were totally familiar with: political assassination, torture, demagoguery, contrived states of emergency, bribery, nepotism, and the like. Mario Vargas Llosa's recent realistic novel about the Trujillo years in the Dominican Republic, *The Feast of the Goat*, reads as if it were copied from Suetonius; the democratic demagogue Hugo Chavez of Venezuela, recently removed in a oligarchic coup and then returned to power in a popular military countercoup, could be the subject of a new chapter in Plutarch's *Lives*.

Still, much has changed, and not simply because we live with new forms of technology, or economic power, or ideology. The most significant difference between our situation and that of older students of tyranny is that we are in need of political concepts that apply universally around the globe. The Greek analysis of tyranny was limited to areas where Greek was spoken, and "barbarians" were thought to live in an undifferentiated area of despotism. Medieval and early modern political thinkers in the West focused on the perversion of European monarchy and, on occasion, of republics, but there was little felt need to develop political categories that would apply to "savages" and "infidels" as well. Racism played a large role in this, but so did plain ignorance and the fact that, while the existence of other peoples posed anthropological puzzles, they did not pose a political challenge to Europe until the age of modern colonialism. Colonialism took the problems of Western politics to far-flung corners of the globe, and then through a reflux action brought those problems back home to the West in the form of colonial wars, immigration, and economic and military integration. Greeks and medieval Europeans could afford to be indifferent to the intellectual problem of tyranny outside their home region; modern Western governments, and especially the United States, cannot.

But where to begin? Academic political science, which once considered the categorization and study of different regime types one of its main tasks, no longer does. Daunted by the variety of types and their rapid transformations, and perhaps also worried about appearing judgmental or racist, political scientists today have retreated to formal "models" or statistical studies of the phantom "processes" of democratization and economic modernization. Tyranny as such is simply not an issue or a recognized term of analysis. For the human rights movement it is, and if one consults the publications of Amnesty International or Freedom House, for example, one will find helpful documentation regarding the human rights records of every tyranny on earth. But these organizations are not interested in investigating the *nature* of modern tyranny; they are interested in combating particular human rights abuses such as torture, arbitrary arrest, suppression of dissent, censorship, and the like. As noble as their work is, it does not take us very far in understanding how different kinds of modern tyranny operate or in finding feasible alternatives to them in particular cases.

And so we find ourselves at an impasse today. For as long as anyone living can remember, the fundamental political problem of our time has been captured, well or not, by the slogan "totalitarianism or democracy," a distinction thought useful for the purposes of serious political analysis and public rhetoric alike. That age is definitely past. As the threat of totalitarianism has receded, we find in its wake few functioning democracies, only a variety of mixed regimes and tyrannies that pose new challenges to our understanding and our policies. From Zimbabwe to Libya, from Algeria to Iraq, from the Central Asian republics to Burma, from Pakistan to Venezuela, we discover nations that are neither totalitarian nor democratic, nations where the prospects of building durable democracies in the near future are limited or nil. The democratic West does not face an "Axis of Evil" today; it faces the geography of a new age of tyranny. That means we live in a world where we will be forced to distinguish, strategically and rhetorically, among different species of tyranny, and among different sorts of minimally decent political regimes that might not be modern or democratic, but would be a definite improvement over tyranny. As yet, we have no geographers of this new terrain. It will take more than a generation, apparently, before two centuries of forgetfulness about tyranny can themselves be forgotten.

This chapter is reprinted from the *New York Times Review of Books* with kind permission.

NOTES

1. The exceptions were those, like the American founders, whose reflections on the experience of early-modern Italian republics made them aware of how even republican government could decay into tyranny.

2. Even good-faith attempts to break out of this box failed. For example, when Jeane Kirkpatrick tried to distinguish among tyrannies in *Dictatorships and Double Standards* (1982), a fierce polemical struggle broke out over her views on Latin America, and her more general argument—which cut many ways—was ignored.

Index

About the Contributors

Ronald Beiner is a Professor of Political Science at the University of Toronto. His academic interests include contemporary political philosophy and the history of political thought. His current research focuses on nationalism, liberalism, and citizenship—exploring liberal, illiberal, and "post-liberal" approaches. He has published numerous scholarly articles and books, including *Liberalism, Nationalism, Citizenship: Essays on the Problem of Political Community*.

Mark Blitz (A.B and Ph.D. from Harvard University) is Fletcher Jones Professor of Political Philosophy at Claremont McKenna College. He served during the Reagan administration as Associate Director of the U.S. Information Agency. He has been Vice President of the Hudson Institute and has taught political theory at Harvard University and at the University of Pennsylvania. He is the author of *Duty Bound: Responsibility and American Public Life*; *Heidegger's "Being and Time" and the Possibility of Political Philosophy*; and is coeditor (with William Kristol) of *Educating the Prince*.

Roger Boesche is Professor of Politics and The Arthur G. Coons Professor of the History of Ideas at Occidental College in Los Angeles. His most recent two books are *Theories of Tyranny: From Plato to Arendt* and *The First Great Political Theorist: Kautilya and His Arthashastra*.

Leah Bradshaw is an Associate Professor of Political Science at Brock University. Her primary area of research is classical and contemporary understandings of tyranny, an interest developed from scholarship on Hannah Arendt's interpretation of totalitarianism in the twentieth century. She has published numerous articles on political theory. Her book *Acting and Thinking: The Political Thought of Hannah Arendt* was selected by *Choice* as one of the outstanding scholarly books in its year of publication.

Daniel Chirot is a Professor at the University of Washington in Seattle. He is the author of *Modern Tyrants* as well as other scholarly works. His newest book is *Why Not Kill All of Them? The Logic of Mass Political Murder and Finding Ways of Avoiding It*, coauthored with Clark McCauley.

Toivo Koivukoski teaches political philosophy and international relations at the University of Ottawa and Carleton University. He received his Ph.D. from Carleton University in 2003. His Ph.D. dissertation on mythical thinking and specifically the myths of Homer and the *Kalevala* was nominated for a Senate Medal. His previous publications include the collection *Globalization, Technology, and Philosophy*, coedited with David Tabachnick, and a series of fact sheets on Canadian democratic institutions for the Privy Council of Canada. He is presently completing a book project on the topic of technological empire, titled *After the Last Man.*

Mark Lilla is a Professor of Social Thought at the University of Chicago. He received his Ph.D. from Harvard University in 1990; his dissertation on Giambattista Vico was awarded the Leo Strauss Award by the American Political Science Association for the best dissertation in political philosophy in the United States. He has published numerous scholarly articles and books, including *TheReckless Mind: Intellectuals in Politics* and *G. B. Vico: The Making of an Anti-Modern.*

Douglas Moggach is a Professor of Political Science and Philosophy at the University of Ottawa. He has held visiting appointments in Cambridge, Toronto, and Pisa, and has published extensively on German philosophy and aesthetics. Publications include *The Philosophy and Politics of Bruno Bauer*; and *The New Hegelians: Politics and Philosophy in the Hegelian School.*

Waller R. Newell is Professor of Political Science and Philosophy at Carleton University in Ottawa, Canada. His books include *The Code of Man: Love, Courage, Pride, Family, Country*, *What Is A Man? 3,000 Years of Wisdom on the Art of Manly Virtue* and *Ruling Passion: The Erotics of Statecraft in Platonic Political Philosophy.*

Thomas W. Smith is Chair of the Humanities Department at Villanova University and Associate Professor of Political Science. He is the recipient of the Martin Manley Distinguished Teaching Award and the Lindback Award for Teaching Excellence. Author of *Revaluing Ethics: Aristotle's Dialectical Pedagogy*, his scholarly articles have appeared in journals such as *American Political Science Review*, *Review of Politics*, *Polis*, *Polity*, and the *Journal of Politics*.

Barry Strauss is author of *The Battle of Salamis: The Naval Encounter that Saved Greece — and Western Civilization*, which the *Washington Post* named as one of the best books of 2004. He is professor of History and Classics at Cornell.

Tracy B. Strong is Distinguished Professor of Political Science at the University of California, San Diego. He is the author of several books, including *Friedrich Nietzsche and the Politics of Transfiguration*, *Jean Jacques Rousseau and the Politics of the Ordinary*, and, most recently of *Public Space and Democracy* (with Marcel Henaff) and *The Many and the One Ethical Pluralism in a Comparative Perspective* (with Richard Madsen). From 1990 until 2000 he was editor of *Political Theory*.

David Edward Tabachnick is an Assistant Professor of Political Science at Nipissing University in North Bay, Ontario, Canada. A former Fulbright Scholar and University Chair, his publications include the coedited collection *Globalization, Technology, and Philosophy* and various articles in the areas of "History of Political Thought" and "Philosophy of Technology."

Nathan Tarcov is Professor in the Committee on Social Thought, the Department of Political Science, and the College at the University of Chicago, where he has served several times as chair of the Committee on Social Thought, for many years directed the John M. Olin Center for Inquiry into the Theory and Practice of Democracy, and received the Quantrell Award for Excellence in Undergraduate Teaching. He also taught at Harvard University, served on the Policy Planning Staff of the Department of State, as a Secretary of the Navy Senior Research Fellow at the Naval War College, and a Carl Friedrich von Siemens Fellow at the Siemens Stiftung. He is the author of *Locke's Education for Liberty* and articles on Machiavelli, Locke, Leo Strauss, Quentin Skinner, and American political thought and foreign policy, and is editor and translator with Harvey C. Mansfield of Machiavelli's *Discourses on Livy*, editor with Ruth Grant of Locke's *Some Thoughts Concerning Education* and *Of the Conduct of the Understanding*, and editor with Clifford Orwin of *The Legacy of Rousseau*.

Simon Tormey is Professor of Politics and Critical Theory at the University of Nottingham, UK. His recent publications include *Key Thinkers from Critical Theory to Post-Marxism*; *Anti-Capitalism*; and *Agnes Heller: Socialism, Autonomy and the Postmodern*. He is an editor of the journal *Contemporary Political Theory*.

Catherine H. Zuckert is Nancy Reeves Dreux Professor of Political Science at the University of Notre Dame where she also serves as editor-in-chief of *The Review of Politics*. Her publications include *Natural Right and the American Imagination: Political Philosophy in Novel Form, Postmodern Platos: Nietzsche, Heidegger, Gadamer, Strauss, Derrida* and *Strauss: Political Philosophy and American Democracy*, coauthored with Michael Zuckert. She is currently working on a three-volume study of *Plato's Philosophers*.